Manage Your Time, Manage Your Work, Manage Yourself

MERRILL E. DOUGLASS and
DONNA N. DOUGLASS

AMERICAN MANAGEMENT ASSOCIATION

This book is available at a special
discount when ordered in bulk quantities.
For information, contact Special Sales Department,
AMACOM, a division of American Management Association,
135 West 50th Street, New York, NY 10020.

Library of Congress Cataloging in Publication Data

Douglass, Merrill E.
    Manage your time, manage your work, manage yourself.

    Includes index.
    1. Time allocation.   2. Management.   3. Success.
I. Douglass, Donna N., joint author. II. Title.
HD38.D64   650.1   79-55062
ISBN 0-8144-5597-2
ISBN 0-8144-7632-5 pbk

8-85

First AMACOM paperback edition 1985.

Printing number
10 9 8 7 6 5 4 3 2 1

To STEVE, who says he's already old enough
to take over the business.

To SUSAN, who likes play time more than work time.

To JENNIFER, who was our first successful joint effort.

Preface

IN THIS BOOK we have shared our insights into successful time management—those techniques that seem to work. In doing so, we hope to help others live more fulfilling lives by accomplishing more in areas important to them.

We take full responsibility for the ideas expressed here. These thoughts have been nurtured over the years by friends, colleagues, writers, and critics and have been enhanced by personal experiences, observations, and extensive discussions between us. Some of the ideas are new and some are old thoughts expressed in a new way. Our deepest wish is that the combination of these ideas and insights will help unlock the secrets of success for the reader.

Time management, we have found, is really self-management. Self-management grows uniquely with each individual, as we have continually pointed out in this book. The techniques and methods, however, are similar for everyone. Each person must clean the rubbish out of his or her own life and must develop some systematic approach to managing that portion of time which is controllable while learning to accept that portion which cannot be controlled. We hope our efforts will help accomplish this goal.

Our thanks to Bonnie Baird, Anita Hozeski, and Cathy Thompson, who stayed with us through the various ups and downs, drafts and redrafts, tears and smiles, of developing the manuscript. Without their dedication, skills, and effort, this work would never have been published.

Portions of the book have been adapted from previously published articles by Merrill Douglass. We specifically thank the publishers for their permission to utilize material from the following articles:

"How to Conquer Procrastination," *Advanced Management Journal* (Summer 1978).

"Managing Time Effectively," *Business* (formerly Atlanta Economic Review) (May–June 1978).

"Creative Use of Time," *Personnel Administrator* (October 1975).

"Organizing Your Desk and Your Paperwork," *Personnel Administrator* (January 1976).

"Test Your Assumptions About Time Management," *Personnel Administrator* (November 1976).

"Stress and Personal Performance," *Personnel Administrator* (August 1977).

Thanks, too, to our children for understanding that, for a while, much of the time that their parents usually spent with them had to be given to "the book." We are especially thankful that, when the writing was finally over, we could still smile and share a laugh over a glass of champagne.

Merrill E. Douglass
Donna N. Douglass

Contents

1
Characteristics of Time

VOLTAIRE, THE GREAT French writer and philosopher, posed an interesting question in his book *Zadig: A Mystery of Fate*. The Grand Magi asked Zadig, "What, of all things in the world, is the longest and the shortest, the swiftest and the slowest, the most divisible and the most extended, the most neglected and the most regretted, without which nothing can be done, which devours all that is little and enlivens all that is great?"

Without hesitation, Zadig answered, "Time." He added:

> Nothing is longer, since it is the measure of eternity.
> Nothing is shorter, since it is insufficient for the accomplishment of our projects.
> Nothing is more slow to him that expects; nothing more rapid to him that enjoys.
> In greatness, it extends to infinity; in smallness, it is infinitely divisible.
> All men neglect it; all regret the loss of it; nothing can be done without it.
> It consigns to oblivion whatever is unworthy of being transmitted to posterity, and it immortalizes such actions as are truly great.

Few of us today still read Voltaire. We would, however, agree with Voltaire's assertion that nothing is shorter than time. Most of us never seem to have enough of it.

Time is an elusive sunbeam, an evaporating raindrop, a wilted dandelion on a windy day. We cannot, physically, catch it; nor can we harness it and make it our own. Time management is an illusion,

1

because no one can really manage time. Time, simply, is a constant. Time is a measurement of intervals. It moves at the same rate regardless of who we are or what we are trying to accomplish. Time respects no one. No one can convert, change, or otherwise mitigate time. Despite this, we continue to use the phrase "managing time" to identify our efforts to use our allotted moments meaningfully. Managing time really refers to managing ourselves in such a way as to optimize the time we have. It means conducting our affairs within the time available so that we achieve gratifying results.

Many people operate under the mistaken belief that they really do have enough time for everything, if only they could organize their hours more efficiently. The result is often an attempt to work faster at their tasks. They try to "hurry up." They reason that if they can just go fast enough, they can get ahead of all their activities and actually have time left over.

Of course, this never works. As a strategy for using time, it offers very little. To be sure, there are occasions when working faster makes sense. This is especially true if people have approached their daily, routine tasks slowly or at a lazy pace. In this case, when people are actually taking more time than necessary, working faster can be valuable.

But, most often, working faster produces problems. Under "hurry up" conditions, people make more mistakes. They have even less time to think, plan, and reflect before taking action on problems. The days begin to appear frenzied.

When acceleration doesn't work, a second strategy is often adopted: working longer hours. Everyone does this from time to time, but if working longer hours becomes a regular occurrence, more problems develop. Workweeks stretch into 50, 60, 70, 80, or even more hours. Personal time disappears as work time increases. Fatigue becomes a factor—both physical fatigue and mental fatigue. Judgment is less clear. Hours may be spent trying to solve problems that a fresh mind could solve in minutes.

If both "work faster" and "work longer" are poor strategies for managing time, why do people use them so often? The best answer seems to be that people believe these approaches will enable them to accomplish all the things that seem to need doing. They fail to realize that, no matter how much they do, there is always more to be done. They doom themselves to a life of frustration, disillusionment, and disappointment. They simply cannot do everything. They must make choices. They must make those tough priority decisions and have the courage to follow the decisions with action. They must learn to ignore the low priorities.

Time is a paradox. We never seem to have enough time, yet we have all the time there is. No matter how much we do, there are always endless alternatives for spending time. The solution to the paradox of time, then, is to focus on the most important things first, realizing that there is always enough time for the really essential matters.

CHARACTERISTICS OF TIME

Once you have accepted the fact that you cannot do everything and have stopped living as though you can, you have taken a big step toward becoming an effective time manager. Identifying priorities will become second nature. Acting on the basis of priorities will become easier. In your efforts to control time, your understanding of time and attitude toward time are crucial to your success.

Many people refer to time as a resource. A resource is something that lies ready for use, or something that can be drawn upon for aid. Time fits this definition. Begin to accept time as your most important resource. Time is a tool that can be drawn upon to help you accomplish results, an aid that can take care of a need, an assistant in solving problems. However, time is not like other resources, because you can't buy it, sell it, rent it, steal it, borrow it, lend it, store it, save it, multiply it, manufacture it, or change it. All you can do is spend it.

As a resource, time poses another paradox: If you don't use it, it disappears anyway. Thus the quality of your resource depends on how well you use it. The knowledge that you are wasting this very personal resource when you do not spend it properly should be enough to keep you on track, resolving to spend your time better.

Your attitude toward time is also affected by the fact that time is free—you do not have to buy it. You receive 24 hours simply by waking up each morning. Many people do not place much value on things that cost nothing or on things obtained with little effort. If you had to "buy" your time, you'd probably spend it much differently than you do now.

Not only is time free; it is equitable. Everyone receives exactly the same amount each day. But this is a deceptive equality, since some people always manage to get more out of their 24 hours than others. Still, time is one of the truly democratic aspects of our lives.

Even if we use our time well, we do not receive an extra amount. We still receive the same daily allotment as the person who squanders time.

QUALITY TIME

Since you cannot increase the quantity of time you receive, the quality of time is the only variable. Your time is *your* time. It belongs to no one else. No one else can spend it for you. Other people may make demands on how you spend your time, but it is still you who must do the spending. Only you can improve the quality of your time. Ultimately, you spend your time as you will.

No one can force you to spend your time effectively; no one can prevent you from wasting your time. Many people maintain that others control their time, but this is not totally true. In the last analysis, no one has any more control over your time than you are willing to allow. Most people have far more potential for managing their own time than they realize. Much of the control they impute to others is really lack of self-control. They are intimidated by the demands of others and thus allow themselves to be controlled.

The way you spend your time defines who you are. More than what you say, what you wear, what friends you choose, or what you think, the way you spend your time describes you. Many people say one thing, but their actions relay another message. For example, many people identify family as the most important aspect of life. Yet they spend relatively little time playing with their children, relating to their spouse, or visiting with their parents—participating in the myriad activities that define family relationships. It is what a person does—not what a person says—that is important.

To discover where people's values lie, look at how they spend their time. The person who claims to value family above all other things yet spends little or no time with the family has some serious questions to consider. Is the family truly as important as claimed? Or is family only supposed to be important? If the family is actually a high-priority item, quality as well as quantity of time should be placed on this aspect of a person's life. Excuses for why this is not possible won't do. Remember, time is life. The way you spend your time defines your life—who you are. Your time is your own and your commitment to time management is really a commitment to yourself—and what is important to your life.

PEOPLE ARE ADAPTABLE

Time is not adaptable, but people are. Managing time means adapting ourselves to its passage in some appropriate, satisfying manner. It means managing ourselves. If time seems to be out of control, it means that we are out of control. To bring ourselves back under control, we must learn to adopt new, more appropriate habits. We have to change. Change is difficult because most of our habits are deeply ingrained. We have to declare war on ourselves if we ever hope to change the way we spend our time. None of us can change major habits casually, but we can change—if we plan carefully. And, remember, a change in one activity will cause a change in all other activities.

How do you change—really change—your habits? First of all, you must have a sincere commitment. How much do you really want to change? Are you willing to make the necessary sacrifices to ensure that you will get what you say you want? Do you have a list of "justifications" ready to appease your conscience when things don't work out as planned? Be honest with yourself at the beginning.

Second, put your goals in writing. Divide them into subparts. Set specific, measurable objectives for each subgoal and define the activities necessary to meet these objectives. Schedule your time, daily, to include activities that you have determined are important for satisfying your goals.

We will discuss goal setting more in Chapter 16. It's really as simple as knowing you *can* take control of your time and your life. It's really as simple as doing the required actions now—instead of next week or next month. It's really as simple as achieving a small success and building larger successes from it.

PERSONALITY AS A TIME FACTOR

Personality has a great effect on time orientation. In order to manage time, you must believe that you do, in fact, have some control over your environment. Yet large numbers of people do not believe this.

Psychologists in recent years have analyzed people's attitudes toward controlling their environment. At the one extreme are the "internals," people who believe strongly in their ability to influence the world around them. Although they may not be able to control everything, they believe they can at least have an impact on the

significant things that happen to them. At the other extreme are the
"externals," people who believe that they are at the mercy of their
environment, that they have no control or influence over the significant things that happen to them. These people tend to feel pushed
around and simply react to their environment.

Everyone falls somewhere along this external–internal continuum.
The closer you are to the internal side, the more likely you are to
gain control of your time. The closer you are to the external side, the
more difficult it will be for you to gain control of your time, because
you feel it is not possible to do so.

What is your attitude toward control? Take a moment for an honest self-analysis. Where would you place yourself on the external–
internal continuum?

EXTERNAL ＿＿/＿＿＿/＿＿＿＿/＿＿＿＿/＿＿＿＿/＿＿ INTERNAL

| I can control nothing in my life. | I can control a few things in my environment. | I have control over a lot of things, but there are many things I have no control over. | I can control most of my environment. | I can control everything in my life. |

The more you believe you can control, the more you will control.
Of course, there are certain calamities that none of us can control,
but letting the possibility of such disasters govern our daily behavior
is self-defeating. Most of us operate in a circle somewhat smaller
than cosmic events, and it is this circle, this area of relevant operation, that concerns us most.

Some people claim that time management is "too regimented" for
them. Generally such people know very little about the subject and
are reacting to thoughts of canceled freedoms. The truth is these
people are regimented, not by time but by their personal habits—the
repetitive patterns that govern their lives. Instead of thinking about
time, these people should focus on their habit patterns. They should
ask themselves, "Which set of habits would enable me to live the
way I prefer to live and accomplish what I want to accomplish?"

If you take control of your own life through proper planning and
proper time techniques, you are not regimented at all. You are freeing yourself to soar toward your desired goals. People who form the
habit of using time well actually gain more freedom and autonomy in

their work and in their lives. They have more time to take advantage of serendipitous opportunities to enrich their lives.

The people who seem to be most concerned with time are those who are trying to accomplish more in their personal and professional lives. They become concerned with time because they realize there is a great deal they wish to accomplish and very little time to do it all. If you are unconcerned with accomplishments, time tends to be of little consequence. If you have more than enough time to accomplish your objectives, time is also of very little importance. It is when you have more to accomplish than you can easily do in the time available that you become concerned about using time in better ways.

When you have many things to do, you hate wasted time. You develop the uneasy feeling that there is something better, but you're not always sure what it is. You suffer from remorse as you look back and think, "If only I had used my time more wisely."

This book cannot change your personality. The best it can do is help you change your behavior. Your personality will determine your ability to make the kinds of changes we recommend. The good news, however, is that time and personality are compatible. Proper utilization of time will help you to reach the heights that your personality and talents allow.

AGE AND CAREER DEVELOPMENT

Personality is not the only factor affecting your time orientation. Your age and the developmental stage of your career also influence your priorities and attitudes toward time.

Time seldom means a great deal to people in their twenties. The twenties are a time for beginning. Most people get married in their twenties and reshape their life as part of a twosome. Within two or three years, they often become parents.

Most careers also start in the twenties. This is a time for discovering what it is you want to do, a time for making mistakes and for starting over again. Organizations expect less from people in their twenties than from more experienced employees. As a result, many poor work habits get started here. As a rule, people in their twenties do not see time as oppressive.

In the thirties time becomes somewhat more demanding. You and your spouse have established some comfortable means of living together. Your children are engaged in numerous activities that require your involvement—and make you more time-conscious.

The thirties are also a time for building your career. Companies expect you to give all you have in the thirties, and then some. "Potential" is no longer enough. Responsibility is growing. The push is on. You have about ten years to demonstrate that you can handle things, that you have what it takes to progress up the ladder. It's now a matter of being in the right spot at the right time, and making the right decisions. During the thirties you begin to realize how much there is to be done, and how little time there is available. Time becomes demanding and unfriendly. Bad habits that weren't so serious in the twenties now become crucial obstacles. You need something better.

Then, before you realize it, you're in the forties. Your children begin moving out on their own. The ones that remain at home are fairly independent and need you less and less. They ask for advice less and less—at a time when you want to give it more and more. You see them leaving and, regretting that you didn't give them more time earlier, attempt to draw them closer before they establish households of their own.

The forties are a time for solidifying your career. If you managed to come through the thirties in good shape, you're now a veteran. You've learned how to survive. Younger managers look up to you. You're on target with your own career objectives. You've learned to adapt and use time well. The oppressive edge is gone. You can enjoy the fruits of your effort and relax a bit. But you must be careful not to relax too much; if you spend too many days relaxing in the sun, a horde of people in their twenties and thirties will run right over you.

The forties also mark the passage to middle age. Your body catches up with you. You don't have the energy you used to have. You don't recover as fast. You've got aches and pains you never had before. Neurologists and cardiologists are getting rich at your expense. You're finally realizing that your body won't last forever.

Then, you're fifty. Interesting changes begin to happen in the fifties. Your children are grown and you have more time to develop your own interests. Most careers peak in the midfifties. A few people will go on to make significant career advancements beyond the fifties, but the majority have gone about as far as they will go.

The realization of peaked careers causes a number of reactions. Some people change careers. The rationale seems to be, "If I've gone about as far as I'm going here, I'd rather be somewhere else, doing other things." Vice-presidents of manufacturing become high school history teachers. Marketing executives move south and rent bicycles on the beach. Advertising executives go off to Vermont and open flower shops.

Most people in their fifties, however, stay right where they are and continue to make a positive contribution. Others, realizing that their career has peaked, retire mentally and emotionally. They continue in a holding pattern, waiting for their pension.

Careers wind down in the sixties. Most of us will be forced to retire somewhere between age 62 and age 70. Life insurance companies report a grim statistic for the sixties. Half of all people who die beyond the age of 62, die within 18 months of retiring from their jobs. Career is one of the most important determinants of a person's self-concept. For many people, when career is gone, there's nothing left. Many other people, though, seem to come alive with retirement. Retired executives start their own businesses. Active octogenarians claim that they are so busy now they can't understand how they ever had time to hold down a full-time job.

Time means different things all along this age–work continuum. Perceptions and values change. Job-related values gradually give way to personal values. One thing, however, remains true throughout your life: If you wish to be successful at whatever you're doing, you must spend your time wisely. Quality in time relates to who you are, where you are, what results you seek, what you spend time doing, and whom you spend time with.

THE CURRENT CONCERN ABOUT TIME

Although time management has always been important, it is only in recent years that large numbers of people have devoted much attention to how their time is spent. Twenty years ago there were no books on this subject and very few articles. Within the last two decades, dozens of books and hundreds of articles have appeared—all with time management as their focus. Several things have occurred during this period that account for the increased attention to time management.

First of all, expectations of what people should accomplish in their work have been going up each year. Every year, your organization expects more from you than it did the year before. Very seldom do people report that this year their organization expects *less* of them than last year!

Second, the business environment has become more complex. Each new legislature seems committed to writing more legislation, and more complex legislation, than the legislature that preceded it. Today OSHA, ERISA, affirmative action plans, equal opportunity commissions, anti-pollution programs, environmental protection agencies, and literally hundreds of similar government controls affect the way in which jobs are performed.

Third, the rate of change has been increasing each year. Alvin Toffler described this phenomenon in *Future Shock*. Everyone has an ability to absorb change within some range. When the rate of change becomes greater than an individual's ability to cope with it, problems develop. Most of these problems seem to revolve around time.

Fourth, there has been an increasing emphasis on individualism. As organizations and governments become larger and broaden their influence, the amount of personal autonomy decreases. People have begun to seek more control over their own lives. Individual freedom involves control of time.

All these events—increasing expectations, increasing business complexity, increasing rate of change, and increasing individualism—have enhanced people's awareness of time. We have no more time now to accomplish results than we did 20 years ago, yet the difficulty involved in accomplishing results has increased dramatically. The increasing pressures in all aspects of our lives have forced us to rethink what time means and how we can use our time best.

In many ways, time management is simply common sense, but that doesn't make it simple. As Will Rogers frequently observed, "Just because it's common sense, doesn't mean it's common practice." There is a huge difference between knowing what to do and actually doing it. Knowing is not enough. It takes a knowledge of procedure—and desire—to turn common sense into common practice for you.

Our primary objective in this book is to help you be successful. We will share with you many of our ideas about time. We will help you develop an action plan for solving some of your biggest time problems. We will discuss several principles of time management, examine your assumptions, and discuss solutions to your specific time problems. By the end of the book, you should have a better understanding of your time problems and a clear plan of action for immediate implementation. In addition, we will talk about ways to help you gain the motivation and commitment necessary to implement your plan.

Most of this book will focus on time problems on the job. But the ideas that help solve work time problems also solve personal time problems. Sometimes, too, there are conflicts between work time and personal time. Therefore, part of this book will be devoted to personal time concerns. We'll show you how to make best use of time in all parts of your life.

If you make an effort to carefully identify your purpose, this book will be more meaningful to you. Therefore, before you go any further, take a few minutes to answer this question: "What do I really want from this book?" Be as specific as possible. The statement "What I'd like to have from this book is a way to manage my time" is too vague. Specifically what aspect of your time would you like to control? What is not happening in your life that you really wish were happening? What is currently missing from your schedule that you wish you had time for?

As another beginning step toward solving your time problems, take the time management survey on the following pages. The few minutes you invest in this exercise will help you develop a personal time profile and point out your strengths and weaknesses.

As you proceed through the book, attempt to merge the time management concepts you learn into meaningful actions in your own life. Adapt our suggestions to your own personality and lifestyle. Learn to question your present behavior and open your mind to useful change. Delight in the knowledge that you cannot do everything. Set your priorities carefully, because what you pursue you will probably find.

Voltaire suggested that time enlivens all that is great. Let the greatness of your potential run free. Let the time of your life be all it can be. Take control, and live like a winner!

2
Assumptions About Time

TIME IS A uniquely personal concept. Learning to manage time is a personal undertaking. How we spend our time defines our life. To be effective in managing time is to be effective in living. For many of us, this is easier said than done. Part of the difficulty lies in the way we approach our various activities. Our approach is governed by the assumptions we hold about the nature of our jobs, the nature of events around us. Often, we are not even aware of our assumptions. But these assumptions, conscious or unconscious, guide our behavior.

In discussing time management problems with a variety of executives, we have discovered a number of key assumptions that shape their efforts to gain more control of time. Following is a list of two dozen assumptions. Read over the list and decide whether you believe they are generally true or false.

Test Your Assumptions

	True	False
1. Most people are overworked because of the nature of their job.	_____	_____
2. Your job is unique and not subject to repetitive time patterns.	_____	_____
3. No one ever has enough time.	_____	_____
4. Higher-level people with more authority usually make better decisions.	_____	_____
5. Further delay will probably enable you to improve the quality of your decisions.	_____	_____

True   *False*

6. Most people can find many ways to save time. _____ _____
7. Managing time better is essentially a matter of reducing the time spent in various activities. _____ _____
8. Your job deals with people, and since all people are important, you can't establish priorities. _____ _____
9. Delegating will probably free a great deal of your time and relieve you of some responsibility. _____ _____
10. Finding a "quiet hour" is usually impossible, especially in small offices. _____ _____
11. Most people can solve their time problems by working harder. _____ _____
12. People who concentrate on working efficiently are the most effective performers. _____ _____
13. If you do it yourself, you can get more done in less time. In other words, "If you want it done right, you'd better do it yourself" is still the best advice. _____ _____
14. Most of the ordinary day-to-day activities don't need to be planned, and most people couldn't plan for them anyway. _____ _____
15. It isn't always possible to work on the basis of priorities. _____ _____
16. Finding the problem is easy; it's finding the solution that is difficult. _____ _____
17. A good way to reduce wasted time is to look for shortcuts in managerial functions. _____ _____
18. Most people know how they spend their time and can easily identify their biggest time wasters. _____ _____
19. If you really managed your time well, you'd be working and living like a robot. _____ _____
20. The busy and active people who work the hardest are the ones who get the best results. _____ _____
21. If you really tried to control or manage your time, you would miss out on many unexpected opportunities. _____ _____
22. The problem with time management is that it doesn't allow for spontaneous behavior; it's dull and mechanical rather than dynamic. _____ _____
23. It isn't necessary to write out your objectives. _____ _____
24. Most of the results you achieve are produced by a few critical activities. _____ _____

As with many things, there is no absolute "right" or "wrong" response to these statements. However, some responses are generally better than others for managing time effectively. As you read through the discussion of each assumption below, remember that the recommended responses are based on observations of many managers. In each case, you can probably find an exception to the rule. This only underscores the point that there are no absolutes.

1. *Most people are overworked because of the nature of their job.* FALSE. It isn't the nature of the job, it's the nature of the person. From time to time everyone is overworked. However, if this is a normal occurrence, something is wrong. The something wrong is usually you. Overwork is often the result of failing to delegate, being unable to say no, failing to establish proper priorities, spending too much time on details and trivia, or having sloppy work habits. The job seldom overworks the person, but people often overwork themselves.

SUGGESTION: Take an arm's-length look at your job. What are you doing that doesn't need to be done or could be done by someone else? Do you have trouble saying no to people? How important are each of your activities? Do you need additional staff, or do you need new ways to work? Finding answers to these questions will get you moving in the right direction. (See Chapter 5.)

2. *Your job is unique and not subject to repetitive time patterns.* FALSE. All jobs have patterns. If your job appears to be nonpatterned, you don't know the nature of the pattern. To discover the pattern, you need data—and you need to think about cause-and-effect relationships. An example will help clarify this concept. Many people consider the telephone a major time waster. Yet they seldom know what pattern is involved in their use of the phone. For instance, how many calls do they handle each day—at what times, from whom, about what? How many problems or questions are resolved on the initial call? How many require one or more callbacks? Do particular people call about certain things or call at specific times each week or month? With enough data you can identify the pattern. Once you know the pattern you can predict events, and with prediction you can gain more control. Once you can anticipate, you can schedule.

SUGGESTION: Realize that every job is patterned. Discover the major patterns in your job and you will take a big step toward managing your time more effectively. (Chapters 4 and 5 will help here.)

3. *No one ever has enough time.* FALSE. Time is a paradox. No one ever has enough, yet everyone has all the time there is. There simply isn't any more time to go around. The problem is not the amount of time you have but how you spend your time.

The dilemma goes deeper than an apparent shortage of time. It is basically a matter of priorities and values. There isn't enough time to do everything that seems to need doing. The way out of the dilemma is to manage your time. Otherwise, you will continue to settle for a vague, random existence—responding to outside pressures and demands and letting other people determine how you spend your time.

To manage time is to control time. The secret to controlling time is to remember that there is always enough time to do what is really important. The difficulty is knowing what is really important. The answer requires some thoughtful analysis of who you are, where you are going, and how you plan to get there. Most people are too action-oriented to spend much time in thoughtful analysis. They prefer to be doing rather than thinking. Consequently, they seldom discover the right answers.

SUGGESTION: Think about who you are and what you're trying to accomplish. Write out your objectives and set priorities. Rearrange your schedule so you spend more time on high-priority items and less time on low-priority items. You will be amazed at how much time you really do have. (See Chapters 4, 6, and 16.)

4. *Higher-level people with more authority usually make better decisions*. FALSE. Lower-level people are perfectly capable of making good decisions, and their decisions are often better because they are closer to the situation. The assumption that decisions made at higher levels are better can lead to two problems. First, people may refer too many decisions upward to superiors. Some decisions should be routed upward, but most need not be. Often the person who refers decisions upward lacks confidence in his or her ability to make good decisions. Or the person believes that people with more authority should make decisions, and that such decisions are automatically better.

Second, people may fail to delegate authority to subordinates. This is often accompanied by the belief that subordinates simply can't make decisions as good as the manager can. Most often, the real problem is inadequate training and development of subordinates. Well-trained subordinates do make good decisions.

SUGGESTION: For the first problem, begin building your confidence. Start making decisions in minor areas. Work your way up to bigger decisions. Succeeding with larger and larger decisions will provide a tremendous boost for your confidence. For the second problem, make sure that your subordinates are adequately trained. Wean yourself from too much decision making by delegating smaller decisions first, and gradually move up to larger decisions. You will probably be pleasantly surprised at the capabilities of your subordinates. (Delegation is discussed in Chapter 11.)

5. *Further delay will probably enable you to improve the quality of your decisions.* FALSE. Unnecessary delay seldom improves the quality of decisions. It is simply procrastination. You are probably fearful of making a mistake or have a very strong desire to be right. Younger people seem to have greater difficulty here than more experienced managers. It is always nice to have complete information before deciding, but in practice that is seldom the case. You should make the decision when you reach the point where additional information is not likely to make a significant improvement in your decision. This point is not always easy to identify. But if you habitually delay decisions until you have every bit of information, you are undoubtedly going too far. Occasionally you can benefit from "sleeping on" a decision, but if you overdo it you will only have nightmares.

SUGGESTION: For every decision, there is a deciding point. Try shortening the time for some of your decisions. Don't become a hasty decision maker, but don't drag decisions out too long either. A little experimentation will help you learn the proper timing for various decisions. (Techniques for overcoming procrastination are discussed in Chapter 14.)

6. *Most people can find many ways to save time.* FALSE. There is no way to save time. All you can do is spend time. When you say you're saving time, you usually mean that you will spend less time on a particular task. But this "saved" time can't be banked for future spending. All time is current time. It must all be spent now. Too often people will reduce time in one area only to have other things expand to fill the gap. Parkinson's Law ("Work expands to fill the time available for its accomplishment") is very real, and hoped-for benefits from saving time are often never realized.

SUGGESTION: Stop concentrating on how to save time. Instead, focus on how to spend time. The only way to manage your time better is to spend your time better. (Chapters 7 and 8 discuss several concepts about spending time.)

7. *Managing time better is essentially a matter of reducing the time spent in various activities.* FALSE. Managing time better involves spending the appropriate amount of time on every activity. For some tasks, this means cutting down on the time involved. For other tasks, it means increasing your time commitment. You will probably try to cut down on the time you spend in meetings and casual conversations, in handling reports and correspondence, and similar activities.

You will probably try to increase the time you spend in planning, thinking, developing subordinates, and other important activities. The key is that you must subtract before you can add. Remember, you're spending all your time now.

SUGGESTION: Look at all your activities. How important is each one in terms of what you're trying to accomplish? Where could you reduce your time commitment? Where should you increase your time commitment? Are there things you're not doing at all that should be added? Your activities should always be consistent with your objectives. (See Chapter 6.)

8. *Your job deals with people, and since all people are important, you can't establish priorities.* FALSE. All people may be important, but all the events people wish to involve you in are not equally important. In fact, in terms of your job, not all people are equally important. Are there some people within your organization that have more influence than others? Do you really treat everyone equally? This is not to dismiss the value of individuals or to deny human dignity. People who hide behind this assumption are usually the ones who don't want to make the hard decisions. All people are important as human beings; however, the activities, demands, pressures, and problems presented by various people are not equally important.

SUGGESTION: Learn to separate the person from the issue. Be patient but persistent, polite but tactful, diplomatic but firm. Managing your time to accomplish important objectives sometimes requires making hard decisions about how to respond to particular people. (See Chapter 9.)

9. *Delegating will probably free a great deal of your time and relieve you of some responsibility.* FALSE. In the long run, delegation may provide you with more time, but delegation never relieves you of any responsibility. In fact, delegation creates more total responsibility. After delegating a task, you are still responsible, or accountable, to your superior; but now your subordinate is also responsible to you. If you are not delegating adequately now, learning to do so will take some time. You will have to train subordinates to properly accomplish the delegated tasks. In the short run, this may be more time-consuming than doing the tasks yourself. Failing to delegate, however, is disastrous. Not only do you cheat your subordinates but you wind up buried under a mountain of detail.

There are almost as many reasons for not delegating as there are people not delegating as much as they should. The most frequently mentioned reasons are untrained subordinates, lack of confidence in subordinates, fear of mistakes, occupational paranoia (fear that a subordinate will take over one's job), and lack of time. But consider the consequences of not delegating. You become overburdened. Subordinates are not trained and do not develop as they should. Morale declines. In short, the entire organization suffers.

SUGGESTION: Look at all your activities. Eliminate those that simply don't have to be done. Of the remainder, decide which ones really must be done by you. Then make plans to delegate the balance. This may mean taking the time to train and develop staff people. It may mean learning to think about yourself and your job in new ways. But, ultimately, everyone will benefit—you, your staff, and your organization. Delegation is a case of investing time now to gain time later. Take the time to train subordinates and begin to systematically delegate greater authority to them. (Read the discussion on delegation in Chapter 11.)

10. *Finding a "quiet hour" is usually impossible, especially in small offices.* FALSE. Almost anyone can find a quiet hour—an uninterrupted block of time for concentrating on major projects. Why don't more people utilize the quiet hour concept? Many people simply don't believe it will work in their situation. They believe that they should always be available to their staff or that staff members will resent their quiet hour.

Consider the consequences of not finding a quiet time for yourself. Jobs that might be done quickly take much longer with all the interruptions. Your train of thought is broken and your creativity is decreased. Staff members seldom resent quiet hours. On the contrary, they will help you eagerly, especially if you help them find their own quiet hour.

SUGGESTION: If your job could benefit from a quiet hour now and then, think about how to make it happen. Pick the most appropriate time of day. Discuss with your staff what you are doing and why. Enlist their cooperation and help them find a quiet hour when needed. (The concept of quiet hours is discussed in Chapter 8.)

11. *Most people can solve their time problems by working harder.* FALSE. Working smarter always beats working harder. This assumption starts early in life. From childhood you are admonished to keep trying, to try just a little bit harder, to remember that working hard leads to pleasant rewards. "If at first you don't succeed, try, try again." The problem, of course, is not so simple. Sometimes working harder is the best way. However, many people never respond any other way. They do not consider that there might be a way to shorten the task, eliminate some steps, combine some parts, and actually work easier while getting more done. Doing the wrong thing

harder doesn't help. The people who believe that the way to get more done is simply to work harder are the ones who work extra-long hours, take work home every night, suffer from stress and tension, punish their bodies needlessly, and still don't obtain results.

SUGGESTION: Work smarter, not harder. Try finding ways to reduce the number of tasks. Make the job easier or quicker. Analyze the work flow periodically to keep things running smoothly.

12. *People who concentrate on working efficiently are the most effective performers.* FALSE. Efficiency does not necessarily lead to effectiveness. People often equate efficiency with effectiveness, but the two are very different.

Efficiency concerns the cost of doing something, or the resource utilization involved. This is commonly measured in such terms as money, materials consumed, and number of people required. To be efficient is to use the fewest resources for a given task. Effectiveness, on the other hand, refers to goal accomplishment. You either reach your objective or you don't.

Efficiency is sometimes referred to as "cost-effectiveness," which only adds to the confusion. Cost-effectiveness is usually expressed as a ratio of costs to results, or inputs to outputs. If your goal is efficiency, then becoming effective is an appropriate term.

Many people set out to become more efficient in the belief that doing so will make them more effective. The result is that they become quite efficient at doing things that don't need to be done at all or that contribute very little to their main objective. As Peter Drucker observed, "Doing the right thing seems to be more important than doing things right."

SUGGESTION: Focus first on effectiveness, then on efficiency. Determine first what you should be doing. Then determine how to do it most efficiently. Do the right things right.

13. *If you do it yourself, you can get more done in less time. In other words, "If you want it done right, you'd better do it yourself" is still the best advice.* FALSE. Doing it yourself may seem faster and better in the short run, but it is never faster and better in the long run. As long as you believe that only you can do it right, or better, or faster, you will delegate very little. This can be a formidable block. You may end up neglecting the training and development of subordinates, taking on more than you can reasonably handle, getting involved with too much routine detail, and generally winding up with the job on top of you rather than vice versa.

When you begin your career, you are totally involved with your own task performance. The better you perform, the faster you are promoted. As promotions lead to managerial jobs, the delegation problem begins. Before, promotion and other rewards depended on your performance. Now, more and more, rewards depend on the performance of others. Yet you may continue to rely on personal performance, especially in critical areas, at the expense of training and developing your subordinates.

SUGGESTION: Recognize that your ability to achieve results is closely tied to the performance of your subordinates. It isn't just your efforts that count, but the collective efforts of your staff. Your talents and time are limited now. If you fail to develop subordinates, your time and talents will be even more limited in the future. Don't be fooled by the apparent truth of this assumption in the short run. The more you are inclined to "do it yourself," the more likely your time is not being well used. You are probably spending too much time on relatively unimportant things and not enough time on the important things that only you can do. (Chapter 11 offers several suggestions for improving delegation skills.)

14. *Most of the ordinary day-to-day activities don't need to be planned, and most people couldn't plan for them anyway.* FALSE. The ordinary day-to-day activities are the ones that need planning the most if you want to control your time. Too many people maintain that their situation is unique. ("Others can plan their day, but it won't work with me.") Too many people accept crises and confusion as part of their job description. Nonsense. Anything can be planned. Those random, hectic days follow some kind of pattern. Some patterns may be harder to discover than others, but they do exist. Discover the pattern and you have the key for anticipating future events—and for scheduling and planning your time. Failing to plan day-to-day activities means settling for random direction. Failing to plan is planning to fail. Whatever happens takes control of your time. To break the haphazard approach, you must plan.

SUGGESTION: Keep a daily time record to help identify the patterns involved in your job. (Chapter 5 discusses how to do this.) Then use the information in planning and scheduling every day. Remember, though, to leave room in your schedule for the unexpected. In your planning, emphasize early actions. As the morning goes, so goes the day. (Scheduling techniques are described in Chapter 8.)

15. *It isn't always possible to work on the basis of priorities.* FALSE. Not only is it possible, it is essential. You will never gain control of your time unless you approach various tasks on the basis of priorities. Managing your time means spending it in the best way possible.

Not everything is equally important. When you fail to establish and follow priorities, you literally guarantee that you will be spending some part of your time on less important activities at the expense of important ones. Learning to work on a priority basis requires planning. It also requires constant attention and comparison. When you are tempted to deviate from your plan, stop and ask yourself, "Is what I'm about to do more or less important than what I had planned to do?" If it's more important, go right ahead and deviate from your plan. You'll still be on the right track. If it's less important—and this is usually the case—look for ways to avoid it, postpone it, reschedule it, or delegate it.

SUGGESTION: Make priorities a work habit. Continually ask yourself, "What is the best use of my time? What's most important?" Importance is always based on the objectives you are trying to achieve. (See the discussion of priorities in Chapter 3.)

16. *Finding the problem is easy; it's finding the solution that is difficult.* FALSE. Failing to identify the problem properly is perhaps the greatest obstacle to solving it. The temptation to jump in with a remedy is very strong. The result is that you are busy treating symptoms while the problem remains untouched. To understand the nature of the problem, you will probably have to obtain data. For instance, don't just say that interruptions are a problem. Find out what kinds of interruptions they are—how often they occur, with whom, and for what purposes. With this approach you will find that many problems carry with them the seeds of their own solution.

SUGGESTION: Don't confuse symptoms and problems. Collect data to understand the exact nature of the problem. Solutions then become much easier and are more likely to work well. (A system for solving time-wasting problems is outlined in Chapter 9.)

17. *A good way to reduce wasted time is to look for shortcuts in managerial functions.* FALSE. Many managerial shortcuts ultimately cost a great deal of time. When constantly pressed for time, many managers try to shortcut some part of the job. Unfortunately, the things that get shorted most often are the important things that only the manager can do—things like planning and developing subordinates. These important managerial functions are often neglected in favor of less important tasks that appear to be urgent.

Whenever important tasks wait while urgent ones are attended to, problems arise. Urgent things must be done, of course, but not everything that appears to be urgent really is urgent. Nor must urgent things necessarily be done by the manager. Urgent tasks tend to have short-range consequences. Important tasks tend to have long-range consequences. Managers who try to shortcut important activities often wind up with horrendous time problems.

SUGGESTION: Look over all your activities. Which ones are most important in relation to your objectives? Which ones are least important? Look for shortcuts in the routine, trivial activities. Be sure to make sufficient time available for the really important tasks. (The analytical techniques described in Chapter 5 will help you get started.)

18. *Most people know how they spend their time and can easily identify their biggest time wasters.* FALSE. Few people really know how they spend their time. You don't believe this? Try reconstructing last week accurately. Like most people, you will probably be unable to remember many of the things you did. Why? Simply because so much of your behavior is habitual. Habits are automatic behaviors. When you act out of habit, you are not concentrating on your activities. You follow set routines and patterns. Even if your job consists of unique tasks, you probably approach them in routine ways. When you do not really know your time habits, you can easily spend time poorly. Your time patterns may become inconsistent with what you're trying to accomplish. And, of course, you wind up wasting time. Most people waste at least two hours every day.

SUGGESTION: Keep a time log on yourself. Record your time use for a week or two. Discover your time habits and patterns. Verify where your time is really being wasted. You will be surprised at what you find. (Time logs are discussed in Chapter 5.)

19. *If you really managed your time well, you'd be working and living like a robot.* FALSE. It's only when you really manage your time well—doing what is important in all areas of your life—that you achieve the kind of freedom you seek. Psychologists tell us that very few people feel successful, regardless of how success is defined. The reason is that people have no objectives. It's hard to feel successful without specific accomplishments. Most people shift from one activity to another without any directed purpose, naively assuming that things will take care of themselves or will be taken care of by others.

To manage your time is to control your time rather than having your time control you. To control time, you must plan. Things don't happen by accident. Things happen because people make them happen. Planning requires objectives. Without objectives, there would be nothing to plan. This is not the dull, routine working of a robot. This is the free, dynamic, exciting operation of a person who has begun to take responsibility for his or her own life. People who plan their time are people who are alive, accomplishing things they value and achieving satisfaction and fulfillment.

SUGGESTION: Clarify your objectives. What do you really want to accomplish with your life? What are your goals at home, at work, at play? Then match your activities, your use of time, to these objectives. Plan your time better. Your time is your life. Waste your time and you waste your life. Instead, why not live your life? (See Chapters 16 and 17.)

20. *The busy and active people who work the hardest are the ones who get the best results.* FALSE: Being busy and active doesn't necessarily mean achieving results. This notion is instilled in us early in life by parents and teachers who continually admonish us to "keep busy." It is reinforced at work by supervisors who are constantly looking for ways to keep subordinates engaged. Few of us escape this "busyness" trap. Few of us are encouraged to spend more time thinking about what we're doing. Physical activity seems to be far more valued than mental activity. As a consequence, many of us jump right in and start "doing something" without taking the time to think and plan. This kind of activity leads nowhere. It consumes time but returns little in the way of significant accomplishments. Too much time is spent on low-value activities that contribute little or nothing to high-priority objectives.

SUGGESTION: Spend some time each day thinking about your activities. How much does each activity contribute to your objectives? What activities should you be doing that you are not presently doing? Thinking before you act usually leads to better results.

21. *If you really tried to control or manage your time, you would miss out on many unexpected opportunities.* FALSE. You are far more likely to miss out on opportunities because you haven't managed your time well and thus "don't have the time" to pursue them. Good time management assures that time is spent on the most important activities and that wasted time is minimized. Good time management means decreasing time commitments to marginal activities and increasing time commitments to more important activities. Those people who can effectively control time are in the best position to take advantage of unexpected opportunities.

SUGGESTION: Take a look at your objectives and the way you use your time. Are your activities consistent with your objectives? How many opportunities have you missed because your time was mismanaged? Get control of your time and you'll find more ways to take advantage of your opportunities.

22. *The problem with time management is that it doesn't allow for spontaneous behavior; it's dull and mechanical rather than dynamic.* FALSE. People who manage their time well actually have more time available for pursuing new opportunities and for engaging in spontaneous behavior. Furthermore, they do so without feeling guilty about it. The reason is simple. Manage your time well and you're almost certain to get at least the same results in less time. Hence, you will have more time for other things you'd like to do.

SUGGESTION: Schedule some fun into your life. A strong motivation for learning to manage your time better is that you get more time to do the things you enjoy. Start on a program of "planned spontaneity." If you are on top of things, schedule time off for yourself. For example, you might take Wednesday morning off. You need not make specific plans for Wednesday morning. Do whatever you feel like, or whatever strikes your fancy.

23. *It isn't necessary to write out your objectives.* FALSE: Writing out your objectives is important for three reasons. First, it enables you to clarify them. If you only make a mental note of your objectives, they will probably be vague and poorly defined. You may not remember them exactly the same way each time you think about them. Second, putting your goals in writing ensures that you won't forget them. You can keep the goal statement in front of you as a reminder of what you're trying to accomplish. In this way, no matter how hectic your days become, you can keep yourself on track. Third, and perhaps most important, writing out your goals increases your commitment to them. The greater your commitment, the more likely you are to begin accomplishing them. Writing your goals is a valuable motivational technique.

SUGGESTION: Put your goals in writing, and keep the list in front of you. As you write down your goals, keep the following criteria for good goal statements in mind: Goals should be (1) measurable, (2) specific, (3) realistic, (4) compatible, and (5) time-scheduled. (See the discussion of these criteria in Chapter 6.)

24. *Most of the results you achieve are produced by a few critical activities.* TRUE. This truth was first expounded by Vilfredo Pareto, a nineteenth-century Italian economist. It is more commonly called the 80–20 rule: "80 percent of the value lies in 20 percent of the elements, while the remaining 20 percent of the value lies in the remaining 80 percent of the elements." This means that only a few activities are critical to your success. Can you identify your few high-value activities?

SUGGESTION: Recognize that some things are far more valuable than others in terms of accomplishing your objectives. Examine all your activities to discover which ones really are most important. Then begin to focus on these high-value activities.

How did you score? Were all your answers in agreement with the general rule, or did you have some disagreements? Score yourself as follows:

22 to 24 correct answers	Excellent—you are undoubtedly making good use of your time.
19 to 21 correct answers	Good—you're on your way to becoming a first-class time manager.
16 to 18 correct answers	Fair—you're still in pretty good shape, but you'd better review your assumptions.
Fewer than 16 correct answers	Poor—your assumptions are probably getting the best of your attempts to manage time better.

If most of your answers agreed with the general rule, you should have very little difficulty improving your time management skills. If several of your responses disagreed with the general rule, you should objectively and honestly examine your assumptions. It may well be that you're suffering from "assumption allergy." You have some basic blocks to overcome in implementing better time management techniques. You may have to change some of your assumptions before you can manage your time well.

Time is personal. Learning to manage your time better is a personal affair. Only you can do it. Furthermore, you can do it only if you are willing to do it, and if you believe you can. Examine all your assumptions. Are they accurate? Are they reasonable? Your behavior patterns are closely tied to the assumptions you make. Change your assumptions and you will find it much easier to change your behavior. When your behavior is consistent with your objectives, you're managing your time effectively.

3
Time and Personality

IT IS COMFORTING to talk about time in units—seconds, minutes, hours, days, years, and centuries. They are so beautifully exact. We have contrived these measurements to establish a quantitative control over that elusive element called time. The exact units we use serve as a convenient shorthand. We work from 8 to 5, with one hour for lunch. We know that one typist can type 90 words per minute while another can type only 45 words per minute. It's easier to decide which person to hire—if your job requires a fast typist. It's easy, too, to project a quarter million dollars of additional business by one year from today. When we talk about dollars and cents coupled with a convenient unit of time, we can be certain that everyone knows what we are talking about.

Unfortunately, "true time" is not so neatly defined. Time is hopelessly wrapped up in the lives of the people who live it. It is precisely for this reason that time is so difficult to manage, yet filled with unimaginable possibilities.

As managers, we all want subordinates who will perform their assigned work perfectly. We want them to be on time, not waste time; work fast, not miss a day, and get everything done at least three days before the deadline. When we remember, however, that our superiors want the same thing from us we realize that people mix themselves with their skills and their time when they work. These "selves" are not perfect; they get sick, are hampered by memories of their fathers scolding them, get irritated because the toast burned at breakfast, and go through some sort of trauma in middle age.

How a person allocates time is a very complex undertaking that depends on many factors. But one of the most important factors is how a person habitually behaves. Most people are not aware of their habits. A habit by definition is an activity that is done at a semiconscious, automatic level. In order to use time better, people must change some of their basic habits. Specific techniques for changing habits will be discussed in the next chapter. At this point, though, we might consider what some of these habits are.

TIME ALLOCATION

Why do we do what we do when we do it? What criteria do we use for allocating our time? Each of us has many different ways of deciding what we are going to do at any given point during a day. Following is a list of some of the more common criteria that govern the way we allocate our time:

1. We do what we like to do before we do what we don't like to do.
2. We do the things we know how to do faster than the things we do not know how to do.
3. We do the things that are easiest before doing things that are difficult.
4. We do things that require a little time before we do things that require a lot of time.
5. We do things for which the resources are available.
6. We do things that are scheduled (for example, meetings) before we do nonscheduled things.
7. We sometimes do things that are planned before we do things that are unplanned.
8. We respond to demands from others before we respond to demands from ourselves.
9. We do things that are urgent before we do things that are important.
10. We readily respond to crises and emergencies.
11. We do interesting things before we do uninteresting things.
12. We do things that advance our personal objectives or that are politically expedient.
13. We wait until a deadline approaches before we really get moving.
14. We do things that provide the most immediate closure.
15. We respond on the basis of who wants it.

16. We respond on the basis of the consequences to us of doing or not doing something.
17. We tackle small jobs before we tackle large jobs.
18. We work on things in the order of their arrival.
19. We work on the basis of the squeaky-wheel principle (the squeaky wheel gets the grease).
20. We work on the basis of consequences to the group.

Some of these criteria represent long-standing habit patterns. Consider the matter of deadlines (item 13 above). The closer we are to a deadline, the more likely we are to do whatever activities are necessary in order to meet it. This pattern has been going on since grade school. Look back. When did you do your assigned homework? The night before (sometimes the hour before) it was due, right? This same pattern is usually continued into adult life and therefore into the workplace.

The matter of closure (item 14 above) is of special concern. Most of us need at least some closure in our lives. Some of us, however, need far more closure than others. Many people can live with ambiguous situations comfortably; others can tolerate very little ambiguity. Consider the symbols in Figure 1. These symbols are a simple way of indicating the need for closure. If you have a high need for closure, these incomplete symbols will probably annoy or trouble you. You may even feel compelled to take up a pen and close them. If you have a low need for closure in your life, these symbols will not trouble you.

If you have a high need for closure, you will react to many of the things throughout your day in the same way you reacted to these symbols. You will do things that provide immediate closure before doing things that may never provide closure. For example, it may be weeks, months, or even years before you get closure on certain types of planning. On the other hand, straightening your desk provides immediate closure.

Figure 1. The need for closure.

Try this exercise to help determine which patterns you use to allocate your time. First, list all your job activities, everything you did during the day or week. Then ask yourself, "Why did I do that specific activity at that particular time?" Think about the list of criteria given earlier. Do you tend to do the things you like before you do the things you dislike? Do you tend to do the things you do well before you take on unfamiliar tasks? Do you tackle easy things before complex things? Do you "finish off" trivial chores that can be completed quickly before digging into the important tasks that take more time? This exercise can be very valuable in helping you gain some insights into your priorities.

When you seriously think about it, it is not too difficult to determine the best use of your time. You know that you ought to do the things that are most important, those valuable activities that contribute to your objectives. However, you don't always do it that way. Often, you prefer to work at tasks that you like or find interesting, even though these activities contribute much less to your objectives than the more difficult, complex activities. As you really begin to examine yourself, you may discover why you are a rather poor allocator of time.

Despite what you say is important to you on the job, what you do reflects your true choices and priorities. The several dozen incidents that engage you during a normal day all involve priority decisions. Many of these decisions are made unconsciously. Yet they are made. Whenever you decide, for whatever reason, to engage in one action, you decide against engaging in another action at that point.

A clear understanding of priorities is very important. Most people think of priorities as an arrangement of items in their order of value or importance. The dictionary defines a priority as "something that comes before something else." This definition is a little closer to the way we actually live. The way we should live is to make sure that the things we do first are the most important things. We should strive to do the most important things now and the less important things later. Personality, emotions, feelings, and attitudes, however, "get in the way." Our rational, logically determined priorities take second place to our gut reactions, preferences, and prejudices.

THE PERFECT FIT

At some point in our lives, most of us have had the experience of wearing clothes that were too large. We felt as though we were draped in a horse blanket. Our body was somewhere in there, but there was just too much room. If we wore these clothes for any length of time, we found them cumbersome and inadequate. We anxiously looked around for a "better fit."

Most of us have also had the experience of wearing clothes that were too small. Perhaps we felt the pull across our back as the material stretched to accommodate our reach. Perhaps our sleeves fell two inches above our wrists, or maybe our shoes were so tight that our toes flashed irritated pain warnings.

So it is with our work. We are more comfortable on the job as we spend our time in activities that suit our personal style, tempo, and ambitions. If the job is too easy or "too loose" or fails to present us with adequate challenge, we feel uncomfortable. We are restless and unable to give the job the level of commitment it requires.

On the other hand, if our position requires far more than an acceptable challenge, if it stretches us to the point of despair and mental exhaustion, we find that we have "too tight a fit." We have a great deal of serious thinking to do. Of course, many of us have days when our jobs are particularly hectic; but if this frantic state is a daily occurrence and we find ourselves constantly frenzied and exhausted, it may be that we "just don't fit" where we are.

It is important to remember, however, that most people have too much to do and not enough time to do it in. Over and over we hear people say that what they would most like to have is more hours in their day. Yet even if they could add more hours to their day, they would have the same problem—too many things to do and not enough time to do them in.

No two managerial jobs are alike, but most share one important characteristic: They involve tasks of relatively brief duration. This means that the manager does not spend a great deal of time on any one thing, but instead engages in a variety of different activities throughout a normal day. The average manager is interrupted approximately every nine minutes all day long. In other words, every nine minutes someone or something is pushing the manager in a direction he or she is not already moving. Every nine minutes someone or something is demanding that the manager engage in an activity he or she is not already engaging in.

If you consider that the average management workweek is approximately 55 hours, being interrupted every nine minutes means that the average manager engages in approximately 73 items in the course of a day. Furthermore, these items are not necessarily connected to one another. There is a great deal of discontinuity in the normal managerial day. Some of the items relate to objectives that the manager is trying to accomplish; others do not. In short, a normal day seems to be fragmented, haphazard. It comes in a lot of bits and pieces. It's as though someone dumped all the pieces to a puzzle on your desk early in the morning and asked you to complete the puzzle by the end of the day. Of course, most of us cynically believe that someone has stolen at least a few of the pieces so we can never complete our puzzle.

Through effective time management, the constant interruptions in our day can be minimized and controlled, but they can never be completely eliminated. Different people will react to the situation in different ways. People who have a high need for closure will find an average of 73 different and often uncompleted items each day continually frustrating. Other people will be able to handle an even higher level of ambiguity and uncertainty.

Most managers are action-oriented. They don't like to sit and think; they prefer to be doing things. In addition, they abhor paperwork. Most would gladly replace all paperwork with verbal reports if possible. They would rather talk than read or write. Given this action orientation, and the fact that the job comes in many bits and pieces, most managers will react throughout the day to items presented to them—instead of anticipating problems and goals, which requires prior thought, planning, and action. In a normal day, there is precious little time for thinking and planning.

It is easy to see how managers can become "superficial" in approaching their daily tasks. There simply is never enough time to do all the things that seem to need doing. There is never enough time to engage in activities to the extent that we might like or to the extent that the activities demand. All of us face this problem every day of our lives.

TIME ORIENTATION

If we truly hope to make headway with time, we must understand our orientation to it. Time orientation refers to how we view the past, present, and future.

Some people prefer the tried and true. They are comfortable with the past, for it is completed, can be documented, and lacks the ambiguities of the present and the unknowns of the future. Any new ideas presented to such people will be carefully measured against past practices. How does this new idea compare with a similar idea tried a couple of years ago? Has anything like it ever been successful before? What are the precedents for this approach?

Some past-oriented people will openly acknowledge their conservatism. They will refuse to accept any new ideas and say simply, "I can't do that because it's never been done." Others will not be so bold. They will resist the label "reactionary" and resent the accusation that they are overly cautious. Instead of refusing, they will continue to "check on it," "gather information," or "give it some further thought." Like an old historian friend of ours, their attitude is truly "I am not an agent of change."

The problem, of course, is that a manager in a growing enterprise must be an agent of change to some degree. Failure to make creative, thoughtful moves leads to change anyway. Lack of action will not stop change in the company, but it may cause developments in the wrong direction.

Another group of people believe only in the "here and now." For them, the past is gone and the future is no more than an uncertain dream that they can't control. The current moment is the only one that can, and must, be handled. These people are often a frenzy of activity. They enjoy any meeting that gives them a chance to chat about ideas or problems. They're great at handling the immediate crisis, for fast resolution is their trump card.

Of course, these present-oriented people can get a little irritated with a co-worker who has a past orientation. "That Sally just won't try anything!" they exclaim. "She always has to think about it—and nothing ever gets done!" The past-oriented personality, on the other hand, is not always pleased with the attitude of a present-oriented peer. "Doggone that George! Does he always have to run around like a chicken with its head cut off? He should know that doesn't work!"

A third group of people put their stock in the future. They believe they are the true progressives, with the new ideas that can save the company. Many of these ideas have no basis in reality; they are completely unfounded. Of course, this type of person has trouble standing still for the "lack of cooperation" he or she receives from the past-oriented person. "His ideas were good once," the futurist may report, "about the year 1850!" And predictably the past-oriented person has negative opinions of the futurist. "Why'd we have to hire that wide-eyed radical?"

The future-oriented person also has few kind words for present-oriented associates, accusing them of "running around doing busy work, but never going anywhere." The present-oriented person may justifiably retort that "the dreamer has holes in her head!"

These three types of people with different time orientations speak different languages. Misunderstandings are inevitable. How, we must ask, can we hope to have them work together? The following suggestions can help solve the time problems caused by various personality clashes.

Begin with yourself. Try to identify which of the three descriptions most accurately defines your perspective. Of course, you will say to yourself, "I'm not totally any one of these. I'm a little of each one." True enough, but try again. Be honest with yourself. Do you enjoy remembering all the good times you've had in the past more than you enjoy making plans for the future? Would you rather not think about either because you're too busy today? Do you listen to stories of the year 2000 with eager interest, or fear? Do you wish life would be the same for your grandchildren as it was for you, or are you excited about the difference?

Take an objective look at your co-workers. Through their actions, reactions, and comments, try to identify their time orientation. Consider why your use of time together has been fruitful—or disastrous. Try not to pass judgment. If you do, you will only be exacerbating the problem. Encourage your co-workers to make the same analysis. Suggest that they begin by identifying their own time reference point and then move on to other people in their work group. Be straightforward in your approach with co-workers, since misunderstandings can lead to additional communication problems.

Discuss personality differences with your associates. Point out that there is no "right" or "wrong" time orientation. There are advantages and disadvantages to each perspective. Each person is a product of his or her own background, environment, and experiences. Stress that the purpose of the discussion is to help provide greater service to one another and to the organization.

Discuss your strengths as a group. You are much better off if you can operate as a unified force. Through combination and integration there is strength. The past-oriented person will temper the future-oriented person by presenting some realistic concerns. The future-oriented person will help pull the past-oriented person out of the Middle Ages and bring about useful change. The present-oriented person will work out the details of the compromise—but without the perspectives of the others, he or she will be no more than a busybody.

Miscommunication, misperception, antagonism, hurt feelings, and disappointment are time wasters in any group. A move toward understanding is a step in the right direction. Ideally, each member of the group should integrate all three time perspectives into his or her perceptions. People's lives will be more satisfying if they can see themselves as part of a past, a present, and a future. Time management involves a realistic knowledge of where you've been, where you are now, and where you hope to go in the future.

A time orientation analysis can serve an additional function. It can help you determine if your job is right for you. If you delight in long-range planning and developing ideas but your job involves a great deal of tactical work or recordkeeping, you might give serious consideration to changing jobs. Similarly, if you like recordkeeping, detail work, and a minimum number of surprises in your day, you may decide that you do not fit in your present capacity as a planner-developer. You can't believe that you could have gotten that far off base? Think again. Many of us are doing what we do today more by accident than by design. We are doomed to continual frustration if we fail to give our primary time orientation careful consideration.

ASSERTIVENESS

Assertiveness is another personality dimension that has direct application to time management. This dimension is a cousin of the past-present-future orientation. With all the recent press on "assertiveness," a great deal of confusion has arisen over the meaning of the term. What exactly do we mean by assertiveness?

Dr. Richard P. Walters, a clinical psychologist, says that being assertive means:

1. Accepting that it is OK to pursue what you want out of life. This attitude affirms that you are worthwhile.
2. Recognizing that you usually do not have a right to interfere with other people as they pursue what they want out of life. This attitude affirms that other people are capable and worthwhile.
3. Knowing how to carry it out—being able to translate your attitudes into practice in "real life." This requires various personal skills, especially communication skills.
4. Having a system for control that helps you stay in the midrange of behavior without swinging to the extreme of nonassertion, which first hurts those who depend on you, or aggression, which hurts you later.

Assertiveness is the ability to realistically look the world in the eye and say, "That's all right with me!" People with this ability can comfortably give to others and find pleasure in the giving. These same people can also take from others and graciously ask for assistance when required. Assertive people can use a variety of techniques with others, depending on the situation. They can be either gentle or strong.

Some people lack all these qualities and are appropriately described as nonassertive. The nonassertive person takes action slowly and often hesitates in timid indecision. This person often misses much of the action, living life as an observer.

Lack of assertiveness can lead to many time management problems. Nonassertive people are often procrastinators. They are afraid to approach someone with a problem or a request. Their self-consciousness makes it difficult for them to deal with other people. They are easily intimidated and have a hard time saying no. Nonassertive people often have difficulty with authority figures; they are unwillingly cooperative and frequently unhappy.

A large number of nonassertive people have a past time orientation. They tend to resist change, finding security in maintaining the status quo. With this backward orientation, nonassertive people experience anxieties about the future. The unfortunate result: an immobilized present. The nonassertive person spends time regretting the past, dreading the future, and experiencing the present with a great deal of pain.

Nonassertive people tend to be less effective as leaders than more assertive individuals, and they often have morale problems in their work groups. Nonassertive managers should seek help in raising their level of assertiveness. A manager simply cannot function adequately without the ability to be assertive in making decisions.

At the other end of the assertiveness continuum is the overly assertive person, better known as the abrasive personality. An abrasive personality in the office is definitely a time waster for everyone. Judging from the number of questions we receive about abrasive personalities, there are many such people in management circles.

Abrasive people are often intelligent and innovative. They are also insistent about having their own way. They have a knack for irritating others and causing pain. They criticize and attack, often under the guise of "telling it like it is," but they rarely know what another person is feeling.

They are often impatient with those who cannot think as rapidly as they can. At times they act as though they are privileged people, far better than everyone else. They expect others to accept their logic because it is obviously the only correct opinion. Actually many of these people don't have "opinions"; they only "see the facts clearly." They rarely consider compromise, because they are certain compromise means giving in to lower standards. Any time compromise occurs, you can be certain the issue wasn't truly important.

Dr. Harry Levinson, a clinical psychologist who heads the Levinson Institute in Cambridge, Massachusetts, indicates that "the parameters of the abrasive personality are thus: self-centeredness, isolation, perfectionism, condescending contempt, and attack."* He also suggests reasons for this behavior. He contends that the more extreme a person's behavior is in one direction, the more likely it is that the person is seeking to escape from a set of opposite feelings. The intense striving for perfection really reflects an underlying sense of inadequacy and helplessness. The perfectionist has a low self-image. He or she strives for a level of perfection that will bring invulnerability. Control becomes all-important.

If you must deal with an abrasive person in your office, there are several things you can do to make the situation more tolerable. To begin with, you can try to change the abrasive person. Tactfully explain the negative effect his (or her) behavior is having on the rest of the people in the office. State your observations uncritically. Ask him how he thinks others feel when they are the target of criticism and abuse. Ask him if he obtained the reaction he desired. Approach the abrasive person from his selfish side; point out that it is difficult for him to achieve what he really wants from his job when he is always offending other people. Be careful not to attack him directly or he will become defensive.

Although you might have some success with this approach, it is unlikely that you will really be able to change an abrasive personality. A far better approach is simply to forget about the abrasive person and get your own act together. You can live with him in several ways:

1. Learn from him. The abrasive person frequently possesses a keenly analytical mind which is capable of cutting to the core of a problem. He is often imaginative in his pursuit of broader achievements. These traits can be beneficially adapted into your own personality—and improved upon. Be as objective as possible in distinguishing positive from negative qualities.

2. Be secure in yourself. Take derogatory, condescending comments with a grain of salt. Note carefully the source of the comments

* "The Abrasive Personality at the Office," *Psychology Today* (May 1978).

and remember that there is good evidence that this behavior results from insecurities. The attacks have little to do with your self-worth. It is not *your* problem.

3. Learn to identify the situations that will set off offensive comments and behavior. Walk away. If walking away is inappropriate at the time, think "Nuts to you" while wearing a Cheshire-cat smile.

4. If you are unable to do any of the above, avoid the abrasive person altogether. You cannot enjoy him or learn from him. The psychological abuse you will suffer is not worth it. No matter how interesting or stimulating the abrasive person may be, you are wasting your time dealing with him. Make the only acceptable decision possible and act on it swiftly: Move on to a more pleasant environment.

TIME MANAGEMENT AND LEADERSHIP STYLE

Leadership style has a direct bearing on the nature of the time problems a manager faces. All leadership styles involve time problems of some sort, but some are more demanding than others. Three styles of leadership are particularly relevant to time management:

1. Autocratic.
2. Permissive.
3. Participative.

The autocrat, the manager who makes a decision and simply announces it, saves some time by making most decisions himself. He doesn't have to confer with anyone and is saved the effort of "appearing" democratic. On the other hand, he must live with the resentment and discontent that often develop among his staff. He may miss out on many important pieces of information. This manager, therefore, must expect many interruptions from staff members as things predictably go wrong. He is in a double bind because, as an authoritarian leader, he has failed to delegate problem-solving authority to any of his subordinates.

The permissive leader often has a different set of time problems. She permits her subordinates to function within limits defined by her and thus has fewer time problems on a day-to-day basis. Still, when time problems do arise, they can be extremely demanding. If the leader has failed to carefully define the parameters of the job to her subordinates, their misjudgments could involve lengthy untangling.

Since she, as the manager, is ultimately responsible, solving the problem may involve a great deal of time.

The participative leader, the manager who shares responsibility and authority with subordinates, is in the best position to implement the many time management principles suggested in this book. Because the manager works with his staff instead of above or apart from them, he is able to express his time problems and time needs. He has the best possible working relationship with everyone and thus is in a position to analyze group needs and individual strengths in order to help his people make the maximum use of their time.

CHANGING VALUES AND ATTITUDES

Personal values play an important part in our attitudes on the job. As noted earlier in the chapter, we are likely to be more dedicated to our job responsibilities if we are involved in a task that suits our temperament and attitudes. Age too has a great deal to do with the attitudes people develop toward their job.

For example, if you grew up during the Depression, your family may have experienced some difficulty in obtaining the bare necessities of life. You probably learned to take nothing for granted. Getting a job during those years was extremely important and often impossible. Food, gasoline, and other commodities were carefully rationed and waste was unforgivable. The most important goal was to get a secure job and do your best to maintain it.

If you grew up during the 1950s, you had a totally different experience and quite likely developed different habits. After World War II the United States emerged as a new world leader. The country underwent a period of prosperity. Parents were eager to give their children all the advantages they did not have. Children were encouraged to express their opinions; they were heard as well as seen in their homes. They were encouraged to "find themselves" through pursuing their own interests.

Today, as these young people enter the workforce, they are not always motivated by a top salary or position. Many of them have developed an identity away from the work situation. They value autonomy and greater discretion over how and when they perform certain tasks. They are also deeply aware that there must be something in it for them—something more on a day-to-day basis. The promise of an advancement, a longer vacation, and a gold watch at retirement is no longer enough.

In increasing numbers, people want psychological satisfaction.

They want the opportunity to grow and learn, to develop their talents and skills. They want more say in planning their own time and more meaningful responsibility on the job. Leisure time has become important, for it allows people the opportunity to develop that other self which has nothing to do with the "shop."

Helping employees in their personal development now appears to be the best means of motivating them toward effective performance on the job. Flexible work schedules are a direct response to the "human liberation" movement and are a welcome relief to a growing number of Americans. "Flextime" scheduling requires that everyone be on the job between set hours—say, 10 and 4. Some workers come in at 8 and leave at 4, while others arrive at 10 and leave at 6. More and more organizations are experimenting with flextime, and this system appears to have a bright future in certain situations. Flextime cuts down on the rush-hour hassle in large cities. It costs nothing and is easy to implement. Workers seem to like it and it has proved to be a morale booster.

Permanent part-time work is another choice available to a growing number of Americans. Under this arrangement, a person regularly works something less than a full 40-hour week. Through this time scheduling an employer can cover peak hours without having to carry extra people when slack periods develop. Job sharing, in which two workers hold one job (in some cases a husband–wife team who also share household chores at home), is another alternative.

While the hours required from part-time work and job sharing are desirable from an employee's point of view (and often from an employer's point of view), some unions are concerned that workers will not receive full benefits for their efforts. Also, some people view part-time workers as less desirable employees because they "lack dedication."

Compressed workweeks—ten hours a day for four days, for example—appear to have a limited future. Currently, labor laws and unions present large obstacles. There is evidence, however, that a compressed workweek would suit some people's lifestyles and values better than the traditional five-day week. Some people seem to perform better when they work in intensive, prolonged periods followed by an extended rest.

The success of these changes in work structuring will depend on our ability to integrate all aspects of our lives. Most of us compartmentalize our lives: We "go to school," we "work," we "raise a family." We favor whatever activity we are currently pursuing. Thus students are thought "irresponsible" by blue collar and white collar workers. Workers are "part of the establishment" to students. Housewives are "unfulfilled" to many career women, while many homemakers pass severe judgment on the "women's lib types" who work.

Once people discover the true advantages of a more integrated lifestyle many of these harsh judgments will fade away. If people feel free to pursue their goals—on or off the job—they will perform more effectively. At this point, different work schedules will become a reasonable alternative to the current 8-to-5 routine.

The challenge of the 1980s will be to rethink incentives, duties, time structuring, and work motivation to better reflect the new attitudes toward work and living. If a company can demonstrate a concern for the total person, the total person will display more concern for the company and the time spent in the company's service.

TIME OUT FOR "THE SLUMP"

Each of us has experienced times when we're just not up to the job. We say we're having an "off day" or we "got up on the wrong side of the bed." We plan to work on a major report first thing in the morning, but when the time comes we just don't have what it takes. Our energy is swallowed by a yawn. We begin feeling a little sorry for ourselves, for no apparent reason. We daydream and almost enjoy the fact that we are accomplishing nothing. To use the vernacular, we have gone into a "slump."

It is sometimes difficult to identify a bonafide slump. This malady is given credit for far more than it really deserves. We often say we're in a slump when we're really just afraid to do something, don't want to do something, or find a task distasteful. We readily admit to a slump when the truth is that we are just procrastinating. Sometimes procrastination itself throws us into a slump—and a vicious circle develops.

Many people have designed Monday as a weekly "slump day." Mondays, it seems, have a bad reputation. Many of us agree it's a reputation justly deserved. Unfortunately, Mondays comprise 20 percent of a normal workweek, and if we use our time poorly on Mondays we have gotten the week off to a bad start. This has a negative effect on Tuesday through Friday. Other people have regular slump days when they return to the office after a trip or a vacation. To make Mondays and other first days back at work a little easier, consider the following ideas.

Use your days off for a change of pace. If your normal work routine involves hectic hustling, take it easy on Saturday and Sunday or the day before your "first day back." Relax. Read a book. Set no timetables. If you've been having trouble reaching your goals at the office lately, be certain to accomplish something tangible on your days off. Clean out the garage, paint the kitchen, work in the yard.

Wear your favorite clothes on your first day back. We all have an outfit that makes us feel a little better about ourselves. Make certain you look good and you'll feel challenged to match your attitude to your appearance. Also, plan one enjoyable activity during your first day back. Ask a favorite friend to meet you at a new restaurant for lunch. Make active plans for the evening and reap the benefits all day as you anticipate your evening's activity.

The state of people's health also contributes to the number of slump periods they experience. A person who enjoys proper weight, a controlled diet, and regular exercise will experience fewer slumps than less-disciplined co-workers.

Coffee, for all its value as a fellowship drink, is a quick stimulant but an eventual depressant. Most people realize this, but they refuse to give it up. There is little doubt that, in addition to causing a slump, coffee will: (1) increase your trips to the restroom, (2) make your hands quiver, (3) spill and make a mess, (4) keep you from getting back to work as you ask for "just half a cup more." A simple answer to this problem is to use a coffee substitute. Decaffeinated coffee and herb teas are also warm social drinks, but they do not have the negative side effects of coffee or the time-consuming rituals associated with it. Once you develop the "substitute" habit, you will find that you not only enjoy the freedom of being an ex-coffee drinker but also enjoy the new taste.

Sugar is another cause of severe slumps in people's workday. The worst possible way to start the day is to have a sweet roll and coffee for breakfast. People who do this are putting their daily goals in serious jeopardy. They try desperately to adhere to their time plan for the day, warding off interruptions and mistakes, only to be "done in" by their poor diet. How much more they could have accomplished if they had only put protein into their bodies instead of sugar! They would have started the day at a special advantage instead of at a self-inflicted disadvantage.

Protein is the magic ingredient for stamina and accomplishment. You don't have to love eggs to obtain the protein you need. Cheese, milk, nuts, and cold meats are delicious at breakfast and easy to prepare. If you want even less hassle, try one of the prepared high-protein foods on the market or high-protein drinks and tablets.

Exercise is important for those who hope to minimize their slump periods. Many people who walk to work happily report the benefits of their morning and evening exercise. Others have taken to riding a bike to the office or at least using the stairs at work instead of waiting for crowded elevators. Some companies have established in-house gyms for their employees. People who recharge their batteries with a little exercise during the day will find effective time management much easier. A properly kept body will be ready and eager to perform all the timewise activities the mind has declared mandatory.

MENTAL ENERGY AND PERFORMANCE

Dr. Dorothy Tennov, a behavioral consultant and professor of psychology at the University of Bridgeport, Connecticut, suggests that people have different mental energy levels at different times of the day. Dr. Tennov identifies five capability levels relating to physiological and psychological fluctuations:

1. *Peak level.* You're at your best in mental energy, in your ability to learn new things and to have new ideas. This is your most creative level.
2. *Good level.* You're better than average but not at your best. You can do most things at this level.
3. *Average level.* You can carry out complex activities, providing you aren't trying to learn them. Most people are here most of the day.
4. *Relaxed, pleasant level.* You can function well if you stick to easy things.
5. *Low level.* You don't want to have to think or make decisions.

If you want to perform more effectively, define your energy levels and become aware of your basic pattern. Begin by listing your activities in a notebook. Try to cover a variety of tasks. Do not be concerned if you miss some activities; try to capture the things you do most often.

Alongside each activity you've listed note the level of mental energy (peak, good, and so on) that you feel you need to perform the task well. Activities are usually accomplished faster and better during high-level periods. Also indicate the minimum level you'd find acceptable to handle a certain activity. Try to engage in each activity at the lowest capability level possible, thus saving your higher levels for more demanding tasks. You are definitely wasting time if you are having a cup of coffee and a danish at peak level when you have an important unfinished report sitting on your desk!

It isn't necessary to completely reschedule your day to put your capability levels to better use. Being aware of your pattern can keep you from misusing your energy. Just remember that while low-level tasks can be accomplished at high energy levels, the reverse is seldom true. If you try an activity requiring your peak level when you're at your lowest level, you are unlikely to get good results. Try to minimize your "down times" and put them to better use.

We do not tick with the predictability of a clock—yet we measure accomplishment with precise evaluating tools. When we feel despondent over human frailties (our own and others'), we may find it comforting to remember the following thought: Of all the creatures on this earth, only human beings are capable of infinite progress. We alone can continually improve ourselves. Even on our "off days," this thought can be our saving grace.

4
Changing Habits Successfully

EVERYTHING IS RELATED to everything else. Events do not stand as isolated instances in our lives; they are inextricably related to other times, places, and things. A change in one part of our life, therefore, has a direct impact on other parts of our life as well.

Habits are difficult to change because they too are interconnected. A single action becomes a cue for some other action, which in turn may be a cue for still another behavior. In this way, we develop habit sequences that form a vigorous mode of patterned behavior.

An important example of patterned behavior is the early morning ritual at the office. What activities take place during the first 60 minutes, and how valuable are they? Consider Fred's typical morning. He drives down Center Street and turns right at the light. He parks in the third row of the parking lot, fourth space in—almost as though his name were engraved on the location. He enters his office at 8:00 A.M. The first thing he does is get a cup of coffee; then he visits with his colleagues. As he finishes the coffee, he picks up the morning newspaper and browses through it for ten or fifteen minutes. It is now 8:45 A.M. Fred has been in the office for nearly an hour, but he hasn't yet started to work.

This pattern is probably repeated in half the offices in the country every morning. "But wait a minute!" you may say. "There's nothing wrong with coffee, is there? Besides, talking with colleagues develops good interpersonal relations." This may be true, but let's examine the above scenario in more detail.

People do not drink coffee for its nutritive value. Coffee drinking is habitual behavior, often cued by morning entrance to the office.

Coffee is also a social drink and generally cues people, especially in the early morning, to "shoot the breeze" with one another. What do they talk about? Early morning conversations usually center on sports, weather, family activities, television, and current events. These coffee conversations seldom concern work.

If coffee doesn't signal conversation, it signals the newspaper. In Fred's case, it signaled both. People read the sports page, comics, classified ads, and perhaps the front page. Very few businesses truly profit from employees' daily review of the morning paper, although people justify this habit as "keeping up with what's happening in the world."

There is an old proverb that says, "As the first hour of the day goes, so goes the day." This is vitally important to everyone concerned with time management. Many people waste their first hour, accomplishing little or nothing and establishing a poor pattern for the balance of the day. Furthermore, they don't even realize what they're doing to themselves.

HABITUAL BEHAVIOR

It has been said that people control habits, but habits control destinies. Clearly, a good part of our lives is spent in habitual fashion. Much of our daily behavior is patterned and routine. Habits by definition are behaviors that have been performed so often that they have become automatic. This means that habitual behavior operates just below our consciousness threshold. When we are preoccupied, or acting habitually, we are not free to manage our time. We are simply not as alert as when we are acting nonhabitually. Managing time requires accurate observation of what is taking place.

People tend to assume that habits are always bad. This is not true. Many habits are quite beneficial. If we had to consciously decide on everything we did during the day, life would become quite unbearable. Once we learn to do something well, automatic habit control is a blessing.

For example, you bathe, dress, eat, and do dozens of similar routines every day. The advantage, of course, is that you can devote your attention to other things while you carry out the task at hand. Your body continues on in the same routine fashion as long as nothing unexpected happens. If an unexpected event does occur, your mind instantly focuses on what you are doing and you are no longer behaving habitually. Driving an automobile illustrates this point well. As long as the roads, traffic, and your car function predictably, you often drive "on automatic"—with your mind a million miles away. However, if a child darts across your path, you must summon all your skills as a driver to save the child's life, and often your own as well.

In general, you will want to reduce some of your habitual behavior in order to use time more effectively. If you spend a large percentage of your day in habitual routines, you are probably not using time as well as you could. The best way to begin reducing habitual behavior is to discover your present habit patterns. As you uncover these patterns, the need for change will become obvious and you will become more motivated to make the change. You will begin to discover which of your habit patterns are beneficial and which ones are detrimental.

No one can force you to change, of course. But if you wish to improve the way you spend your time, if you wish to gain more control of your time, if you wish to achieve better results from your time, unquestionably you will have to change some habits. No one can change your behavior for you. You must do it yourself. This doesn't mean that other people will be totally out of the picture. Certain associates may play a crucial role in your efforts. Practice, however, will be up to you. Others may help to reinforce your new behaviors, but it is you who must, voluntarily, undertake them.

LAUNCHING NEW BEHAVIORS

Years ago the famous psychologist William James suggested an approach to changing habits which remains valid today. He recommended that you:

1. Launch the new behavior as strongly as possible.
2. Seize the first opportunity to act on the new behavior.
3. Never let an exception occur until the new behavior is firmly rooted.

Before you can launch a new behavior strongly, you must define what the new behavior is to be. How would your proposed behavior improve upon your present habits? What would you do and how would you do it?

Think of ways to practice the new behavior with gusto. Many people find that publicly announcing their new behavior is a strong beginning. Posting signs to remind yourself of the new habit can also be beneficial. In the beginning, your new behavior will not feel comfortable. It will not reflect what you would "naturally" do in a given situation. To keep yourself going, you may need to remind yourself daily of the benefits you will derive from the new behavior.

It is important not to deviate from your new behavior until it is firmly rooted. Many a new office routine works rather well until the next crisis develops. Then, all of a sudden, people lapse into the same bad habits that hindered them previously. The reason for the relapse is easy to identify. When a crisis hits, people swing into action automatically, reacting in the way they know best. That is, they fall back on established patterns. If you want your new behavior to take root, therefore, you will have to exercise a great deal of self-discipline.

Some people are too casual in their approach to changing habits. They mistakenly think that change is easy and that it's "all in your head." It's true that it's all in your head, but that's also the problem! You have to change your head. You need to uncover things that cue your behavior. Psychologists recognized many years ago that behavior is a response to a stimulus. We get hungry at the sight of delicious food. We desire a cigarette along with our drink. We open a newspaper as soon as we sit down in our chair at the office. We want a snack when we watch television in the evening. Cues are trigger events. When a cue occurs, we respond habitually.

Once you recognize the trigger event, you have three ways to approach habit change. You can change the trigger event, change the response to the trigger event, or change both. For instance, you could cut down on fattening snacks if you stopped watching television. Or you could learn to munch on celery sticks. You could also learn to munch on celery sticks while doing something other than watching television.

Your efforts at self-discipline can be improved if you seek ways to manipulate your environment to reinforce the new behavior. For instance, suppose you are a heavy smoker and want to stop smoking. One way to put yourself in a supportive environment would be to take a wilderness vacation for two weeks with nonsmokers. Take no cigarettes with you and make sure your vacation site is miles from the nearest store. Under those conditions it will be much easier for you to stop smoking. By the time you return from your trip, you should be well launched into your new pattern of not smoking. You must still safeguard your smoke-free status, however, because the old cues in your environment will continue to have power over you. But with a strong start you're more likely to continue.

WORK SEGMENTATION

How can you build better habits on the job? One good approach is work segmentation. Examine the different kinds of work you do in the office. If you arrange to do particular jobs in specific spots, you will concentrate better and avoid distractions. For example, you might sit at your credenza for all telephone calls and write all your financial reports at your desk. Use another work table for handling general correspondence. Do all your reading in one of the chairs at the side of your desk. Segment your job in as many ways as possible so that you have a particular place to do each kind of work. Then, whenever you approach a particular work area, you will automatically start thinking about the kinds of tasks you normally perform there.

If you can do each task at a specific time, the arrangement will be even better. For example, set aside a time for making phone calls; then go to the credenza and work off it for your calls. If you are interrupted and must do something else, switch to the appropriate location. If you begin to think about other things, get up and move for a few moments, then come back. Think of yourself as a television series: same time, same place, same content.

Of course, there are some disadvantages to this approach. When you have developed the habit of working on an activity in a specific location, it will be more difficult to perform the task in another location—for instance, to do your financial reports at some location other than your desk. If conditions change sufficiently, though, you can always recondition yourself to work at a different location.

Another way to segment your work is to use airplanes, waiting rooms, and other travel locations as extensions of your office. For example, if you fly a great deal, you might set aside certain kinds of work to be done only on plane trips. If possible, sit in the same seat on each trip and do similar kinds of work when in the air. Before long, the minute you sit down you will begin thinking about the kinds of work you generally do in that location. The trip will be less boring and you will have extended the time available for accomplishing important results.

Any change in your environment will facilitate a change in behavior. Try rearranging your office. Move the furniture around. Put desk items in different drawers. Reorganize the file drawer. Use different routes for traveling within the office building. Come in and out of different doors than usual. Do anything that is different and you will raise your general awareness of what is taking place around you. As your awareness level goes up, you will be in a better position to recognize and change your habit patterns.

Beginning a new behavior requires an emphasis on action. When William James said, "Seize the first opportunity to act," he meant do it now. Don't talk about doing it later; do it immediately! Practice the new behavior even when you don't need to practice it. Suppose that your new behavior pattern involves learning to remember people's names. You might try using a person's name frequently in conversation. If you don't meet new people regularly on your job, you can practice this polite form of "name calling" on your friends and colleagues. If you develop the habit of using names frequently when you talk to people, you will be more comfortable using a stranger's name in conversation. Through this practice, you will begin to shape your behavior and become a master of new names.

STEPS IN BEHAVIOR CHANGE

Five steps are involved in successful behavior change:

1. Desire.
2. Knowledge.
3. Visualization.
4. Planning.
5. Action.

No change will take place without the desire to make a change. How much do you really want to change your work habits so you will function more effectively? Desire is the key to success or failure. If you have a strong desire, you will probably initiate the change. If you really don't want to make the change, you will probably never do so.

One part of us likes things as they are even if they are bothersome and we complain a great deal. We're unworried and unconcerned about change. Another part of us is demanding more. It wants greater accomplishment. At any time, most of us experience some conflict between these two parts of ourselves: the one part not wanting change and the other part demanding change. The winning half says a great deal about whether or not we actually change.

The desire to change is an important first step, but it is not sufficient. Once you desire change, you must understand what needs to be changed and how to go about changing it. Knowledge is an essential next step. Knowledge means that you have to analyze some things, discover some habits, work on some routines, think about how to increase your awareness, and discover exactly what your habits are.

Once you understand what needs to be changed and how to go about changing it, you must be able to visualize yourself under the new condition. You must be able to see yourself living and performing in the new manner before you will be able to change. This was driven home vividly to us two years ago as we were teaching our son to play golf. Before he learned to swing a golf club properly, he had a very negative picture of himself as a golfer. As he began to play, he still made more mistakes than right moves. He grumbled and complained a lot, saying that he would never be able to learn to swing properly. His mental image was unsuccessful. In his mind, he could only see himself making mistakes. It was not until he was able to visualize himself as a good golfer that he began to make progress.

It works the same way with you. For instance, if you see your lack of assertiveness as a major problem in controlling your time, you will never change until you can visualize yourself acting in a more assertive fashion.

The next step is to develop a plan for accomplishing change. Most people would be reasonably good at planning if they set aside the time for it. Unfortunately, many people barge ahead without a plan, assuming that planning is necessary for others but not for them. They soon discover how untrue this is. With a good, well-thought-out plan, the final step—taking action—is much easier. No change can be accomplished unless you act on those things necessary to make the change a reality.

Believe it or not, you can develop a habit of changing. The more new habits you create, the easier it is for you to develop still more new habits. Make changes even when changes are not necessary. Pick insignificant things and develop a new habit around them. Tackle something that you fear regularly. Do things that you wouldn't normally do just for the sake of doing them. Learn to raise your general awareness level and take more control over your daily actions.

Some habits are particularly resistant to change. The tendency to put things off until a deadline approaches is a prime example. The closer we get to the deadline, the more likely we are to do whatever is necessary to accomplish the project. This habit is formed in early childhood. It is so firmly rooted in our lives that many of us will never be able to change it.

Fortunately, we can make this type of habit work for us rather than against us. In other words, if we can't change the habit, we can change the situation so that it becomes a good habit. How? Simply by rearranging the deadlines. By moving deadlines closer.

For example, you have been assigned a new project at work. The project is due in 60 days. Sixty days is a long time, and you probably won't start on it until 45 or 50 days from now. However, if you were to break that project down into a dozen or so subparts, with deadlines for each of the subparts, you would be more likely to begin working on the project immediately. You might set the first deadline for only three days from now with subsequent deadlines at four- or five-day intervals. Thus, even if you put off each subpart until the deadline approaches, you will not be able to put each piece off very long. You can still work on the basis of approaching deadlines and simultaneously allow more lead time. You will probably finish the project sooner and do a better job.

Habits play an extremely important role in time management. In the next few chapters we will be talking about the basic components of the Douglass Time Mastery System. To utilize this system, you may have to develop several new habits. If you understand habits, and if you understand how to change them, you will find it much easier to implement the system. Peter Drucker once said that people are more concerned with doing things right than with doing right things. We believe this applies to habits as well. Many people do the right things some of the time. A few do the right things most of the time. Almost none do the right things all the time. Part-time application doesn't develop good habits. Consistency and persistence are the only way to develop habits that lead to good results.

The Douglass Time Mastery System includes six steps.

1. *Analyzing time use.* Discover what's happening now and what should be changed.
2. *Clarifying objectives.* Establish a basis for evaluating the best use of your time.
3. *Setting priorities.* Focus on the most valuable items.
4. *Planning time.* Make sure that activities lead to the stated objectives.
5. *Scheduling time.* Determine when and how to do various activities.
6. *Evaluating progress.* Determine if things are working out well. Chart alternatives.

THE DESIRE FOR CHANGE

In order to change long-established habits, you must *want* to change. Note that desire was the first step in our change model. What we suggest is not simple, and change is not for everyone. All the suggestions in the world are worthless if you do not want to change. And changing the way you use your time is largely a voluntary effort. You cannot force others to use their time well and they cannot force you to use your time well. The "want to" must come from within.

Habit change is extremely difficult, but it is crucial for all serious-minded people who wish to use time well. To improve your efforts to eliminate self-defeating habits and replace them with self-reinforcing habits try the following approach:

1. *Identify the habit you want to change.* In order to pinpoint the precise behaviors that you wish to change, you will have to analyze many of your behaviors and the situations where they occur. Carefully examine your closely held assumptions to see if any of them are holding you back from achieving the change you desire. The more you know about what you do, when you do it, and why you do it, the easier it will be for you to identify habits that are detrimental.

2. *Carefully define the new habit you wish to develop.* Draw a line down a sheet of paper from top to bottom. On the left-hand side, describe the habit you wish to change. On the right-hand side, describe the new behavior you plan to adopt and the situations where it will be most appropriate. Be honest with yourself about your desire for change. Gather the information you need to implement the change and visualize yourself in your new role. Plan for action and be ready to act on your plan.

3. *Begin the new behavior as strongly as possible.* Tell everyone you can about the new habit you want to develop. Set up a routine to go with your habit. Put signs in your office reminding you of the new behavior. Remember the importance of cues and the interrelatedness of all habits. If possible, change your environment to give your new habit some "fresh air" to grow in. In short, do everything you can to develop the strongest motivation possible for engaging in the new behavior.

4. *Never deviate from the behavior until the new habit is firmly established.* You will be tempted many times to do things in the old way. Resist these temptations. Some people rationalize deviations by saying, "Just this once won't matter." The truth is that each deviation matters a great deal. Every time you deviate you must

start over again. The more you attempt to start over, the harder it is to change.

5. *Use every opportunity to practice the new behavior.* No matter how strongly you are committed to a new habit, it will not become yours until you actually use the new behavior. Seek out opportunities to use it. Arrange your schedule so you adopt the new behavior more frequently than normal. Do everything you can to practice the new behavior until it becomes a habit.

How long does it take to replace one habit with another? This, of course, depends on your personality and the nature of the habit to be changed. Many of your work-related habits can be successfully changed in three to seven weeks. In other words, if you consistently practice the new behavior for three to seven weeks, it will become your predominant response pattern. At that point, you have replaced the old habit with a new one.

Habits are the backbone of daily time use. Each action is cued by some previous action and is, in turn, the genesis of other actions. As William James observed, "The great thing, then, is to make our nervous system our ally instead of our enemy."

5
Analyzing Time

ONE RESULT OF people's failure to analyze time is that they misperceive the nature of their time problems. Things simply are not the way most people think they are. We have often asked people to describe their job as they think it is—to make a list of what they believe they do and how much time they spend doing it. When they compare the list with an actual record of what they do, large differences appear. In *The Sign of the Four,* Sherlock Holmes chides Dr. Watson by saying, "Watson, you see, but you do not observe." A similar admonition could easily be applied to most of us. We are so accustomed to doing the things we do, day in and day out, that we act without thinking.

As noted in the previous chapter, our habitual behavior consumes a great deal of our time. This behavior is often unconscious. Although we may claim to remember where our time goes, countless studies have demonstrated that we often have no idea of what is happening. Furthermore, because we misperceive time, we frequently think of it as beyond our control. No doubt some of it is beyond our control, but much of it is within our control. Before we can control time, though, we must understand how our time is actually being used. We must accept the fact that we are the cause of most of our time problems—and that solutions must also come from us, not from others.

Because all of us have so many time problems, it is important to analyze time. No problem can be solved until it is well defined. Quite often, if we try to solve the problem as we think it is, we end up solving the wrong problem, or we make the existing problem worse.

Good information about time use leads to good problem definition, which leads to good solutions. Sometimes a careful time analysis will reveal that the problem is not nearly as serious as we believed.

In order to analyze how we currently use our time, we must collect data. This chapter will describe several approaches to collecting data that can be used to gain insight into present time habits.

WHAT IS YOUR TIME WORTH?

One useful analytical approach involves determining the economic value of your time. In other words, how much are you worth? What is the monetary cost of your time to your organization? Many people have never considered the true cost of their time. For those who want to manage their time more effectively, an understanding of what their time is worth will be valuable.

The following exercise will enable you to calculate your actual cost to your organization. Your cost is based on your salary plus all the other costs to your organization of keeping you employed. This exercise assumes that you are neither underpaid nor overpaid but are being paid in direct proportion to what you contribute to your organization.

Before you do the exercise, think for a moment about what you cost your organization. If you had to guess, what would you say it costs your employer for one minute of your time? Make a note of your estimated worth. Now calculate it exactly.

		You	*Example*
1.	Annual salary.	1. _____	$ 25,000
2.	Fringe benefits. Fringes vary from 15 to 40 percent of your salary. Unless you know the exact percentage for your organization, use 30 percent of your salary.	2. _____	7,500
3.	Total salary plus fringe benefits.	3. _____	32,500
4.	Overhead—office space, furniture, telephone, electricity, heat, air conditioning, office machines, cafeterias, building maintenance, office supplies, and so on. For larger organizations overhead will vary from 75 to 100 percent of payroll and fringes. For smaller organizations overhead may		

	You	*Example*

vary from 50 to 75 percent of payroll plus fringes. Unless you know the exact percentage for your organization, use 100 percent of the figure in line 3.

4. _____   32,500

5. Secretarial support—your secretary's annual salary. If you share a secretary, use a percentage of the secretary's annual salary based on the proportion of time spent working for you.

5. _____   12,000

6. Secretary's fringe benefits. Use 30 percent of the secretary's salary unless you know the actual figure.

6. _____   3,600

7. Total secretary's salary plus fringe benefits.

7. _____   15,600

8. Secretary's overhead. Unless you know the exact percentage, use 100 percent of the figure in line 7.

8. _____   15,600

9. Other expenses—conferences, meetings, company-related travel, educational reimbursement, professional development, entertainment, or other activities reimbursed by your organization.

9. _____   2,000

10. Subtotal. Add lines 3, 4, 7, 8, and 9. This is your cost to the organization at breakeven.

10. _____   98,200

11. Profit and taxes. If your organization expects to make a profit, you need to add in your proportion of the profit. Use a figure equal to twice the profit percentage to allow for taxes. For instance, if your firm expects a 10 percent profit, use 20 percent of the figure shown in line 10.

11. _____   19,640

12. Total. Add lines 10 and 11. This is what you are worth to your organization annually.

12. _____   117,840

13. Cost per day. Divide the figure in line 12 by the number of days you work per year. Most people work 230 days a year. This assumes 52 weekends, 10

	You	*Example*

holidays, 10 vacation days, and 10 sick days or personal leave days. If you take a three-week vacation, then you have 225 working days. A four-week vacation would give you 220 working days. On the other hand, a one-week vacation would leave you 235 working days.

13.	_____	512.35

14. Cost per hour. Divide the figure in line 13 by the number of hours you normally work in a day. This will give you your hourly cost to the organization. Place that figure in line 14a. (Eight hours are used in the example.) Many people prefer to divide, not by the number of total hours on the job but by the number of productive hours on the job. To arrive at productive hours, you need to deduct time for coffee, socializing, waiting, and other nonproductive activities that you engage in each day. Most office personnel report that their productive hours range between two and five hours per day. Find the cost of productive time by dividing the figure in line 13 by the number of productive hours in your normal day. Place that amount in line 14b. (Four hours are used in the example.)

14a.	_____	64.04
14b.	_____	128.09

15. Cost per minute. Divide the hourly figure from line 14a or 14b by 60 to find the cost for each minute of your time.

15a.	_____	1.07
15b.	_____	2.13

Does your cost surprise you? Is it higher than you thought it would be? Most of us underestimate our true cost.

Now that you know how much your time is worth, you can use this information in several ways. For instance, you could calculate the total cost of a meeting to decide if it's really worth holding. You could use the money value of time to evaluate alternative uses for your time.

Many of us do not consider that wasting a few minutes here and there is really serious. But think a moment. If you saw a $5 bill on the floor, would you pick it up or ignore it? Wasting five minutes could be worth several times as much, yet you would probably feel worse about the loss of the $5 bill.

DAILY TIME RECORD LOG

What, exactly, do you do that makes you worth so much? Your time is obviously important not only to you but to your organization as well. Keeping a daily time log can help you discover how your time is used. Many people resist the suggestion that they keep a time log. They believe it involves too much work and time at a point where they are already overloaded. Besides, they think they really *do* know where their time goes, and a time log would be a useless exercise.

We disagree. From talking to thousands of managers about how they use their time, we know that people's memories are not that accurate. We also know that almost everyone who has kept a time log has been rewarded for the effort. People gain valuable insights into their hour expenditures, and they always uncover surprises.

The most common format for a time log is an abbreviated diary, as shown in Figure 2. Use the form to record everything you do, when you do it, and how long it takes. Begin your record in the morning. Enter your name, the day, and date in the top of the time log form. Place the time log on a clip board and carry it with you as you go about the day. Keeping the log in front of you will remind you to keep recording.

Record your time in 15-minute segments. During some segments you will be doing only one thing—for instance, attending a meeting. During other segments, you may be doing several things. For instance, you may receive two telephone calls, open your mail, and instruct your secretary within 15 minutes. Do not be concerned about capturing every event. Concentrate on the most important ones or the ones that take the longest. You will get enough detail to provide an accurate profile.

Record your activities as you do them. Do not wait until the end of the day. No one's memory is that good. Resist the tendency to generalize or to make yourself look good. You will be fooling only yourself, and the time invested in the analysis will be wasted. Be as detailed as possible in your recording. Use abbreviations or codes if it is convenient and make a note of what the codes mean. For instance:

> 9:45 TG dropped in to socialize
> 1:20 FM called about cost report
> 2:30 Dictated letters to BS, LR, and RT
> 3:15 Coffee

As you report each activity, circle the number indicating its importance. Importance always depends on what you are trying to accomplish. The "importance" column should provide an overall picture of your effectiveness in using your time. You may also want to make a note of how urgent the event is and why you are doing it at that particular time.

Record interruptions in the columns provided. Indicate whether they were interruptions from incoming telephone calls or from some other source. Make a brief note of the nature of the interruption and who was involved. Record outgoing telephone calls as an activity.

TIME LOG SUMMARY

When you have completed your daily time log, summarize your record. Figure 3 is a summary form. The following questions will help you analyze the results of your time log:

1. What went right today? Why?
2. What went wrong today? Why?
3. What time did you start on your top-priority task? Why? Could you have started earlier in the day?
4. What patterns and habits are apparent from your time log? What tendencies?
5. Did you spend the first hour of your day well, doing important things?
6. What was the most productive period of your day? Why?
7. What was the least productive period of your day? Why?
8. Who or what accounted for most of your interruptions?
9. What were the reasons for the interruptions?
10. How could the interruptions be controlled, minimized, or eliminated?
11. What were your three biggest time wasters today?
12. How might you eliminate your three biggest time wasters?

Figure 2. Daily time log.

TIME	ACTIVITY	IMPORTANCE	Tele.	Other	Nature
				INTERRUPTIONS	
7:00		1 2 3 4 5			
		1 2 3 4 5			
7:30		1 2 3 4 5			
		1 2 3 4 5			
8:00		1 2 3 4 5			
		1 2 3 4 5			
8:30		1 2 3 4 5			
		1 2 3 4 5			
9:00		1 2 3 4 5			
		1 2 3 4 5			
9:30		1 2 3 4 5			
		1 2 3 4 5			
10:00		1 2 3 4 5			
		1 2 3 4 5			
10:30		1 2 3 4 5			
		1 2 3 4 5			
11:00		1 2 3 4 5			
		1 2 3 4 5			
11:30		1 2 3 4 5			
		1 2 3 4 5			
12:00		1 2 3 4 5			
		1 2 3 4 5			
12:30		1 2 3 4 5			
		1 2 3 4 5			

Name _____ Day _____ Date _____

13. How much of your time was spent on high-value activity?
14. How much of your time was spent on low-value activity?
15. What did you do today that could have been eliminated?
16. What activities could you spend less time on and still obtain acceptable results?
17. What activities needed more time today?
18. What activities could be delegated? To whom?

TIME	ACTIVITY	IMPORTANCE	INTERRUPTIONS		
			Tele.	Other	Nature
1:00		1 2 3 4 5			
		1 2 3 4 5			
1:30		1 2 3 4 5			
		1 2 3 4 5			
2:00		1 2 3 4 5			
		1 2 3 4 5			
2:30		1 2 3 4 5			
		1 2 3 4 5			
3:00		1 2 3 4 5			
		1 2 3 4 5			
3:30		1 2 3 4 5			
		1 2 3 4 5			
4:00		1 2 3 4 5			
		1 2 3 4 5			
4:30		1 2 3 4 5			
		1 2 3 4 5			
5:00		1 2 3 4 5			
		1 2 3 4 5			
5:30		1 2 3 4 5			
		1 2 3 4 5			
6:00		1 2 3 4 5			
		1 2 3 4 5			
		1 2 3 4 5			
		1 2 3 4 5			
		1 2 3 4 5			
		1 2 3 4 5			

19. Beginning tomorrow, what will you do to make better use of your time?

How long should you record your time? There is no standard answer for this question. You should record your time until you believe you have covered a representative period. For some, this may be two or three days. For others, it may be several weeks or months. Most people record one or two weeks.

Figure 3. Time record summary.

ACTIVITY	TOTAL TIME	PERCENT OF TIME	COMMENTS

You should record a time log at least once each year. Furthermore, whenever significant changes occur in your job, you should record a new time log. New conditions may require changes in job habits. A time log is the single best technique for gaining information necessary to make intelligent changes. In general, you should record a time log whenever you want more information about your job.

Instead of recording the log yourself, you might have an observer follow you around during the day and record what you do. You could use a business student or a trainee at your company. The advantage of having someone else do your time log is that the other person is much more likely to be objective and accurate in recording your activities and the time spent on them. An impartial observer won't forget to record things even though your day gets hectic.

The disadvantages, of course, are that the observer may not be around often enough to capture the variety of activities that fill your days. Also, at times the need for privacy may prevent the outside observer from being present to record what is happening. Further, outside observers cost more than doing it yourself. Unquestionably, there are tradeoffs to be considered in deciding whether to record time yourself or have an observer record it for you. By carefully balancing the advantages and disadvantages, you will be able to arrive at a solution appropriate for you.

Another alternative—a variation of the observer approach just described—is to have someone check on your activities at random intervals throughout the day. If you use the random-sampling technique, it will take approximately 30 observations per day for four to six weeks to provide an accurate profile of your weekly time use patterns.

Most people, of course, do their own time log, using a form similar to the one shown earlier or a form provided by their own organization. Remember when you record your time to consider cycles and seasonal changes in your job. Your time record should cover a representative period so you can rely on the data. If your job is highly seasonal you may need two time logs—one for high season and another for low season. This may be true for cyclical swings throughout the year too.

As you analyze your time log, look for patterns and trends in the way you spend your time. Be sure to consider the question of quality time versus quantity time. Quantity is easily measured by the passing of time. Quality is much more difficult. It is normally a function not only of the amount of time you spend but of whom you spend it with and what you spend it doing.

As you uncover your time problems, some solutions will be obvious and can be implemented immediately. Other time problems may point out related difficulties. For example, you may discover that your problem is being unable to say no to people when you ought to. As you think through the problem, you may realize that your low level of assertiveness is one of the things that prevents you from saying no. Before you can solve your time problem you must first solve your assertiveness problem.

SPECIAL TIME LOGS

In addition to a regular time log, there are several special logs that may prove useful. These include a telephone log, a visitor and interruption log, and a meeting log. Examples are shown in Figures 4, 5, and 6. These specialized logs provide more detailed information than is possible with a regular time log.

Remember that the purpose of a time log is to help you define important activities. Important activities are those that will help you accomplish your objectives. A time log is ideally suited to uncovering activities that simply do not lead to objectives. As you record your activities, try to match each activity to an objective. If you discover activities that do not relate to your objectives, think about how you can modify them or eliminate them and replace them with activities that will help you achieve the results you desire.

You can also use your time log to answer the question "Who controls my time?" Go through each activity listed and ask yourself whether it represents discretionary time or time controlled by someone else. Caution must be exercised here. It is often easy to assert that someone else is in control of your time when actually you have wide discretion in performing an activity.

As you analyze your time log, you are certain to receive some surprises. You may discover that you are quite different from what you thought you were. You may be better in some ways and not so good in other ways. You may discover that you are wasting time in ways that you never realized. You will probably be amazed at how much time you spend in some areas and how little time you spend in other areas. All this information will help you verify exactly how you spend your time so you can make decisions about how to use it better.

Figure 4. Telephone record.

TIME		IN	OUT	WHO	WHAT DISCUSSED
BEG.	END				

Figure 5. Visitor and interruption record.

TIME		WHO	PURPOSE
BEG.	END		

Figure 6. Meeting record.

| TIME | | WHERE | | WHO | EFFECTIVE | | |
BEG.	END	HELD	PURPOSE	ATTENDED	YES	NO	WHY

THE TIMELOGGER

Our discussion of time records has focused on their value as analytical tools. However, they also have other uses. Many people must keep track of their time in order to bill clients or allocate costs to different projects. Examples include accountants, attorneys, and engineers. Until now, keeping track of time for these purposes has not always been easy.

The problem comes at the end of the day when you're trying to reconstruct your time. Where did the time go? How many interruptions did you account for? How much of your day is caught up in "unbillable" time? How much time did you spend with each individual client or account? It's hard to remember, isn't it?

One of the most exacting and demanding tasks faced by today's

Figure 7. The Timelogger 201 (manufactured by Dantronics, Inc., of St. Paul, Minnesota).

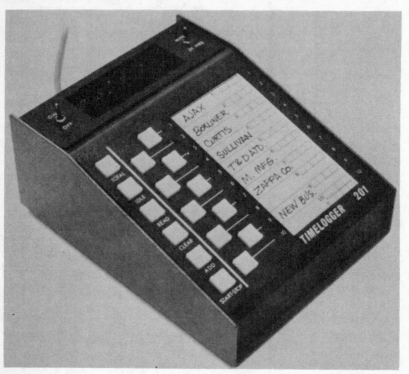

professionals is keeping accurate records of time spent working on different tasks. Many put off this chore and then find it impossible to reconstruct accurate time reports. We all have days when the hours we worked are not reflected in our billable time. The Timelogger, an electronic device that recently appeared on the market, is uniquely suited to solving this problem. (See Figure 7.) We recently obtained a Timelogger, tried it, and instantly liked it. Here's how it works.

On Tuesday morning when you arrive at the office, you know you will be spending some time with the Ajax Pontoon Company, Boxliners Inc., and Curtis Cutlery Cartel. You insert a fresh card into the Timelogger and write the above accounts in lines 1, 2, and 3 respectively. You turn on Timelogger and press Account No. 1, since you will be working on Ajax first. You can be assured that time is being logged into Account No. 1 because the verification light adjacent to Account No. 1 is on. Also, the elapsed time will be shown in the display.

You now have a phone call that you realize will not be billable time. You press Start/Stop. Time is no longer being logged to Account No. 1 and the display light and verification light go out. However, this time is being logged automatically to the internal Idle account. When the phone call is completed, you press the Start/Stop button again. The Timelogger automatically returns to logging time in Account No. 1. You continue working on Account No. 1 until you realize you must go on to Boxliners, Account No. 2.

When you press Account No. 2, the verification light on No. 1 goes out and No. 2 goes on. The display will now begin to accumulate time in Account No. 2. Each subsequent account follows the same procedure.

The Add button allows time to be added to any account. Suppose, for example, that you worked at home the previous evening for Curtis Cutlery Cartel and want to make sure that time will be included in the bill. Press the Add button and time begins to run off on the display. When the desired time shows on the display, you can add it to the Curtis account by pushing the appropriate account number.

When your day comes to an end, you can determine the total time spent on any account. Simply press the Read button and the desired account number. The time for that account will be displayed so you can make a note of it. Time can be displayed in Hrs./Min. or Hrs./.01 Hr. simply by flicking the switch. In fact, any time recorded throughout the day can be displayed in either mode. Your total for the day is displayed by pressing the Total button. The "unbillable" time is displayed by pressing the Idle button. Once you have taken the information from the Timelogger, press the Clear button to clear the accounts. The Timelogger is now ready for another full round of work. You may total at the end of each day or week, or whatever the length of your billing period.

If time logs can be done in easier, more interesting ways, perhaps more people will do them. If you're billing a client, a device like the Timelogger is almost indispensable. Even if you're not, it's extremely valuable. We anticipate many different uses for machines like the Timelogger in the future.

JOB FUNCTION ANALYSIS

Another way to collect data on your time utilization is by performing a job function analysis. You can view your job from three different perspectives: (1) what you think you are doing, (2) what you ought to be doing, and (3) what you are actually doing. Examining all three perspectives will give you valuable insight into your job and time problems. With this insight you will be able to make decisions about how you need to change your allocation of time. In order to bring the three views of your job closer together, you should complete the job function worksheet illustrated in Figure 8.

Begin the analysis by writing a brief description of what your job includes—what functions you perform in a typical week. Use the "Priority Value" column to indicate how much each function contributes to the objectives you are trying to achieve in your job. The more important the functions, the higher the priority value. Then, estimate what percentage of your time is spent in each functional area during the week. If you capture all your job functions, this column should total 100 percent.

Next, consider what isn't happening in your job. There are probably some things you ought to be doing that you are not doing at all. If so, enter those functional items and show their appropriate priority value. Then record a zero in the "estimated time" column to indicate that you aren't spending any time on those items at present.

Now look over all the things you have listed. Consider what percentage of your time you should spend on each item during the week. If you could really organize your job the way it ought to be, what would it look like? What would be the best way to allocate your time across the various functions so that each function received an appropriate amount? Record these ideal times in the third column. This column should also total 100 percent. The last column can be com-

Figure 8. Job function worksheet.

JOB FUNCTION	PRIORITY VALUE	ESTIMATED TIME (%)	IDEAL TIME (%)	ACTUAL TIME (%)
Totals		100%	100%	100%

pleted only by doing the time log mentioned earlier. The tallied results of the time log should be inserted in this column.

You are now ready to analyze the differences, or variances, between what you think you are doing, what you ought to be doing, and what you are actually doing. When you do, you will be in a better position to make the decisions necessary to take charge of your time and your job. You will know what you must do to make your time investment yield a better return.

In order to analyze your job properly, you will have to break it down into meaningful parts. For instance, should you list all your meetings together, regardless of their content, or should you divide them by type? Whatever you are doing on your job, you should break things into as many categories as necessary for the analysis to make sense to you. Don't become overly concerned with classification or other details, however. Even an imperfect analysis will be valuable. Many people find that this technique pinpoints their time problems better than any other approach they have tried.

One other point needs to be considered. Since you are spending all your time now, you must subtract before you can add. If you want to spend more time in one area, you will have to reduce the time in some other area. The adding and subtracting sometimes cross the boundary between work and personal time. All too often hours are subtracted from personal time so they can be added to work time. When this happens, you may pay a greater price than you intended.

Figure 9 illustrates a completed job function analysis. Notice the discrepancies. You can spend too much time as well as too little time on important things. It's the longer view that you should focus on. You must balance your time so you spend an appropriate amount in each area.

Many people question the value of a job function analysis. Why is it necessary? Any time analysis is done for only one reason: to discover the discrepancy between objectives and activities. Although establishing objectives is probably the single most important aspect of good time management, you cannot *do* objectives. An objective is an end result, something that is accomplished. You must do activities. If you do the right activities, you have a good chance of reaching your objectives. If you do the wrong activities, you may never reach your objectives. Activities bridge the gap between where you are now and where you want to be.

Many analyses have revealed that people engage in activities that do not relate to their objectives. Without some form of analysis, discrepancies between activities and objectives may never come to

Figure 9. Job function analysis.

JOB FUNCTION	PRIORITY VALUE	ESTIMATED TIME (%)	IDEAL TIME (%)	ACTUAL TIME (%)
Guidance and direction to subordinates to ensure that sound management practices are carried out	1	10%	20%	30%
Policy development and recommendations	6	10	10	5
Communication and coordination among primary managers	5	25	15	5
Problem identification and problem solving	3	25	15	10
Involvement with outside agencies	4	20	10	30
Basic support to subordinates to facilitate performance of their activities	8	5	10	10
Staff support and coordination with board of trustee activities	7	5	10	10
Long-range planning and development	2	0	10	0
Totals		100%	100%	100%

light. These discrepancies are not intentional. They are simply the way things develop.

URGENT VERSUS IMPORTANT

General Eisenhower used to discuss activities and priorities with his staff. He told his officers that there was an inverse relationship between things that are important and things that are merely urgent. The more important an item, the less likely that it is urgent; the more urgent an item, the less likely that it is important.

Important things are those that contribute significantly to our ob-

jectives; as such, they have high value. The more direct the contribution, the more important the activity. Important things also tend
to have long-term consequences. They make a difference for a long
time. Urgent things have short-term consequences. They must be
done now; they won't wait. They may or may not relate to our
objectives. They may or may not make significant contributions.
They frequently do not. But urgent things are far more demanding
than important things.

We live in constant tension between the urgent and the important.
Our problem is that important things seldom must be done today, or
even this week. Important things are seldom urgent. Urgent things,
however, call for our attention—making endless demands of us, applying pressure every hour, every day.

We seldom question urgent things, never knowing for sure
whether they are really urgent or only masquerading as urgent. And
sometimes we develop the habit of responding as if they were urgent
when they're not. Many apparently urgent things are indeed mas-
queraders. What we need is the wisdom, the courage, and the discipline to do the important things first. If we can break the tyranny of
the urgent, we can solve our time dilemma. The following matrix
may help:

	Important	Not Important
Urgent	1	3
Not Urgent	2	4

This matrix can be a valuable way to analyze your activities and
help discover your tendencies. To begin your analysis, think about
one cell at a time and consider which parts of your job belong in that
cell. Keep a record of your activities throughout a day; then examine
each activity and ask where in the matrix it should be placed.

Cell 1 includes those things that are both important and urgent. We
tend to call these crises. Most of us would prefer to have a limited
number of these activities on a regular basis. Examples include a
work strike, a problem with a major customer, a rapidly approaching
deadline for submitting next year's budget, and three key people
being out sick on the same day. Items that fall in cell 1 tend to be
worked on very quickly. The irony is that we frequently attend to
these items, but we do so for the wrong reason. We should be doing

them because they're important, but we often do them because they are urgent.

Cell 2 includes items that are important but not urgent. This cell is characterized by what isn't happening—or isn't happening often enough. Examples include planning and training and developing subordinates. Few of us spend as much time in these areas as we ought to. Why not? Because they're not urgent. They can be postponed.

Items in cell 3 consume a large portion of our day. These are items that are urgent but that contribute relatively little to our objectives. Telephone calls are a prime example. If we kept a record of all the phone calls we received for a period of time, most of us would find that only a small proportion of the calls are really important. Yet all of them take up time. Drop-in visitors are another example. Most drop-in visitors bring relatively unimportant news; only a few bring really important items. Still, it is not unusual for items in cell 3 to account for 50 to 70 percent of our day.

We like to believe that cell 4 does not exist. Items in this block are neither urgent nor important. Yet observation indicates that anywhere from 10 to 40 percent of our day is consistently spent on items in cell 4. Trips to the coffee machine, socializing, long lunch hours, arriving late or leaving early, putting together football pools, and dozens of similar activities are included in cell 4.

Taking the time and effort to sort out your daily activities into this important/urgent matrix is a worthwhile undertaking. It will, no doubt, show you what percentage of your time is spent on important affairs and what percentage is spent on relatively unimportant affairs. It will also indicate to you where you can find additional time to spend on important affairs. As you do this exercise, be as honest with yourself as you can. Most of us believe that virtually everything we do is important. This is simply not true. Some things are far more important than others. Even though it may be painful to admit it, we spend much of our day engaged in relatively unimportant activities.

While attempting to reallocate activities to gain more value from your time, it will be helpful to remember Pareto's Principle. Vilfredo Pareto, a nineteenth-century scholar, discovered that in any set of elements the critical elements usually constitute a minority of the set. Over the years this concept has evolved into the so-called 80–20 rule: "80 percent of the value comes from 20 percent of the items, while the remaining 20 percent of the value comes from 80 percent of the items."

For example, 80 percent of your sales may be made to 20 percent of your customers; 80 percent of your profit may come from 20 percent of your product line; 80 percent of your problems may come from 20 percent of your employees. You might even say that 80 percent of the results you achieve are accounted for by 20 percent of the things you do. What are your critical 20 percent activities?

This 80–20 rule can be related to the important/urgent matrix. Items that fall into cell 2 (important but not urgent) are probably part of the 20 percent that contribute 80 percent to your results. This was illustrated for us recently when a friend of ours suffered a heart attack and was forced to stay home for six months. At first, he was able to return to work only for three or four hours a day. Yet he discovered that he could achieve virtually the same results in three or four hours that he previously achieved in eight or nine hours. How was he able to do this? Realizing that he would have only a few hours to accomplish anything, he decided to spend those hours on only the most important activities.

The secret is simply to stop doing some of the unimportant things and begin doing more of the important things. A group of stockbrokers learned this lesson and raised their income in the process. After examining their client records carefully, they discovered that 79 percent of their total income was derived from 13 percent of their clientele. At the same time, they realized that they spent very little time with that 13 percent. By rearranging events so that they spent more time with the high-value group, they rapidly increased their total volume of business. It seems that the 13 percent were also utilizing other brokers. As the stockbrokers spent more time with these high-value clients, they began to receive an even greater percentage of their total business.

If you analyze things in terms of the 80–20 rule, you will soon discover that virtually 80 percent of everything you do is low value. If you are spending 80 percent of your time on these activities, you are not managing your time wisely. Learn to focus your time on the things that really count.

RETURN ON TIME INVESTED

Throughout this chapter, we have emphasized the return on your time investment. From the dollar-value analysis to the 80–20 rule, we have discussed various ways to help you determine the value of your present return. The following chapters will focus on how to increase that return.

As the analysis proceeds, the value of a single minute will become more and more apparent. A minute is a most revealing time unit. It is so often ignored or dismissed as unimportant. We ask others, unthinkingly, to "give us a minute." We eagerly engage in even the most useless activity because "it only takes a minute." We give little thought to being "a few minutes late." Yet minutes are all we have. A new respect for this small time unit might help us become more successful. The way we put our minutes together determines whether we achieve positive or negative results. It is by putting minutes together that our lifetime is made—or lost.

6
Clarifying Objectives

It was a regular occurrence around this busy office. The general manager was hustling to get his notes together, shouting last-minute instructions to his secretary. His staff looked a little less ambitious but moved steadily toward the conference room. After all, planning meetings were important.

The trainees were coming too. They were equipped with shiny new folders, with the company's new insignia stamped in gold on the front. Even their pens displayed the company's novel emblem.

"What do we do at this meeting?" asked the newest recruit.

"We plan," answered another with three weeks' seniority. "I'm not sure what we're planning for, but I think the others know."

THE YOUNG TRAINEE may be surprised to learn that he isn't the only one in the dark at the meeting. In fact, several of the regular planners have only a vague idea of the company's purpose—although they're very reluctant to admit their ignorance after being with the company for one, five, or even ten years. It's amazing how many people not only advocate more planning but spend hours in meetings attempting to plan without knowing their objective. Of course, most people have some vague impressions to work with, but the real objective eludes them. The result is a great deal of wasted time for all concerned. It is impossible to plan well without knowing your objective.

Most people think very little about objectives. They respond, react, or sometimes overreact, to pressures from other people or things. If you want to control your time and increase your effectiveness, you must determine exactly what your objectives are and keep them up to date. Objectives protect you from aimless wandering and point you in a positive direction. Without objectives, you are likely to find yourself being swayed by all kinds of outside pressures, first in one direction, then in another. The question you must ask is this: "What is the best use of my time?" The answer requires that you know what your objectives are—exactly what results you are trying to achieve.

THE VALUE OF OBJECTIVES

Objectives are the building blocks of better time utilization. In fact, it is impossible to make good use of your time without a set of well-clarified objectives. How can you evaluate whether one activity represents a better use of your time than another activity if you do not know what the end result of all your activities should be? How can you set priorities if you do not understand your objective? In the words of Lewis Carroll, "When you don't know where you're going, any road may take you there." And as many people have discovered, when you don't know where you're going, you'll probably wind up somewhere else.

Objectives are also an important element in maintaining personal stability. A poignant reminder of this occurred when Buzz Aldrin, one of the first astronauts to reach the moon, suffered an emotional breakdown shortly after his return to earth. To many people, this was a mystery. "Why," they asked, "should this happen to Aldrin, of all people?"

To the outside observer it appeared that Aldrin had everything going his way. And in many ways, he certainly did. He wrote a book about his experiences in which he answered the questions of puzzled observers. He said the reason for his collapse was simple. He forgot there was still life after the moon. He had no other objectives. He found it virtually impossible to function in such a personal vacuum.

Many executives dedicate all their energies to their work, live through the ups and downs of their corporation, and finally retire at 65 after accomplishing a great deal. Within 18 months, they are dead. Why? Studies strongly suggest that these executives have much in common with Buzz Aldrin: They have no further goals to live for once they reach the end of their careers. Without objectives, they lose their purpose and direction and decide, often unconsciously, that life is no longer worth living.

Maxwell Maltz, author of the bestseller *Psycho-Cybernetics,* put it this way:

> We are engineered as goal-seeking mechanisms. We are built that way. When we have no personal goal which we are interested in and means something to us, we have to go around in circles, feel lost, and find life itself aimless and purposeless. We are built to conquer environment, solve problems, achieve goals, and we find no real satisfaction or happiness in life without obstacles to conquer and goals to achieve. People who say that life is not worthwhile are really saying that they themselves have no personal goals that are worthwhile. Get yourself a goal worth working for. Better still, get yourself a project. Decide what you want out of a situation. Always have something ahead to look forward to.*

Whether you are concerned with personal time management or on-the-job time management, "objectives" is the key word—the bull's-eye word, the word you should underline in red. Without objectives, your efforts lead to nothing. With objectives, time management becomes a possibility because now you are living life and working for specific purposes. Time management becomes a tool that allows you to obtain your goals.

MANAGEMENT BY OBJECTIVES

In recent years many organizations have adopted management-by-objectives (MBO) programs. Although MBO is not our major concern here, one point about these programs should be emphasized. Many management experts have reported that a large number of MBO systems are not as successful as intended. One problem that seems to occur frequently is that people fail to share their objectives with others. They work together, but never tell anyone what they are trying to accomplish. Consequently, they can't really help each other.

One bank went through an elaborate goal-setting process every year. Each year the bank updated its five-year objectives, dropping those for the past year and adding new ones for the next year. But the chairman of the board and the president were the only ones who were allowed to see the goals each year. The objectives were kept

* Maxwell Maltz, *Psycho-Cybernetics and Self-Fulfillment* (New York: Grosset & Dunlap, 1970).

under lock and key, as if the bank feared something terrible would happen if other managers learned what the objectives were. In this atmosphere, it was very difficult for people to pull in the same direction to achieve common goals.

Another problem that often arises with MBO programs is that people fail to evaluate achievement. If we never check to see whether our objectives were accomplished, we have wasted our time writing them in the first place. Frequent evaluation is necessary to know when to adjust our plans and activities to bring them more in line with our objectives. Also, if we've written an objective we don't really mean, we have not written an objective. We frequently state an objective that is acceptable to other people, but our real objective is something else entirely.

Another source of difficulty with MBO programs is that objectives sometimes conflict. We go to work every day with two sets of objectives: organizational and personal. Organizational objectives are those we are ostensibly paid to accomplish. When our personal and our organizational objectives coincide, everything is fine. When they don't coincide, problems may arise. The more significant the objectives and the more distance between our personal and professional goals, the greater our problems.

Another problem with MBO systems is that they often fail to connect longer-range objectives to day-to-day living. We don't live in the long run; we live one day at a time. Long-range objectives must be accomplished within a daily context.

THE OBJECTIVES PYRAMID

Objectives should be related to one another. Long-range objectives build upon short-range objectives. They exist in a hierarchy, as shown in Figure 10. The accomplishment of daily objectives should lead to the achievement of weekly objectives; the accomplishment of weekly objectives should lead to the achievement of monthly objectives; and so on up to long-range objectives.

How often should objectives be considered? Every day. How far into the future should objectives be projected? As far as possible. The further objectives are projected into the future, the easier it is to know what to do right now. Personal objectives might be projected for a lifetime. On the job, some objectives should be projected at least several years into the future.

An example will help clarify the objectives pyramid. Suppose a company establishes the following objective for next year: "De-

Figure 10. The objectives pyramid.

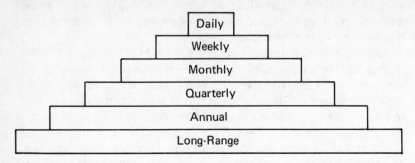

| Daily |
| Weekly |
| Monthly |
| Quarterly |
| Annual |
| Long-Range |

velop, complete, or revise, and have approved 12 standards of customer service." This objective could be a reasonable attempt to provide standards for continuity in customer service activities. To do that, the company will have to document the process, establish the levels of personnel required for the activities or procedures, and make this documentation available to appropriate personnel. The manager with primary responsibility for customer service now has a well-clarified objective. By the end of the year, 12 standards of customer service should be approved, ready for use.

If the manager understands the objectives pyramid, he or she will first break down the annual objective into quarterly objectives of perhaps three standards per quarter, or one standard per month. Breaking this down into weekly objectives might yield the following action plan:

> Week 1: Determine top-priority standard for review.
> Week 2: Review and revise standard.
> Week 3: Review and approve revised standard.
> Week 4: Prepare final version of standard.

To break these weekly objectives down still further, the manager will have to identify each step necessary to accomplish the objectives and how much needs to be done each day. Action may not be required every day during the week. However, action will be required on some days during the week if the weekly objectives are to be met.

Figure 11 shows how weekly objectives fit together into an action plan. Note that in order to meet the monthly objective, the manager must plan to work on it 5 hours the first week, $12\frac{1}{2}$ hours the second week, $7\frac{1}{2}$ hours the third week, and 5 hours the fourth week. Other

Figure 11. Weekly schedule for achieving target objective.

Objective: Revise and have approved the customer service standard relating to time required for call-backs.

Target Date: January 31

Week	Activity	Time Required
1	Review current standard	1 hour
	Analyze performance variances	1 hour
	Discuss variances with customer service reps	3 hours
2	Collect new customer data	4 hours
	Develop proposed standard	2 hours
	Discuss proposed standard with customer service reps	2 hours
3	Revise proposed standard	1 hour
	Discuss revised standard with customer service reps	2 hours
	Discuss revised standard with VP services	1 hour
4	Prepare final proposed standard	2 hours
	Present to VP services for approval	1 hour

obligations will dictate which hours of the week are devoted to this task, but the time must be spent if the manager hopes to meet the monthly objective.

Again, if weekly objectives are met, monthly objectives will be met. If monthly objectives are met, quarterly objectives will be met, and hence annual objectives will be met.

George Odiorne, in his book *Management and the Activity Trap,* discusses the concept of "activity traps." According to Odiorne, we fall into an activity trap when we become so engrossed in an activity that we lose sight of its purpose. We fall into activity traps in the absence of objectives. When there is no objective to serve as a focal point, the activity itself takes on the main emphasis. Why? We must focus on something. If there is no objective, the focus must be on the activity. Unfortunately, this inversion of means and ends is unlikely to produce the results we desire.

Activity traps can occur even in an organization that manages by objectives. It's interesting to see how this develops. Suppose a manager begins writing annual performance objectives. We know that whenever objectives are written down, the probability of achieving them increases. The result, however, does not happen automatically. The manager must still take action in order to accomplish the objectives. But when does the manager become concerned about whether progress is being made toward the objectives?

Pause for a moment and recall our discussion about people's tendency to wait until a deadline approaches. When did you do your homework? At the last minute. When does our manager tend to become concerned about accomplishing an annual objective? Toward the end of the year, of course. Becoming concerned toward the end of the year is certainly better than never becoming concerned at all. However, the more frequently the manager becomes concerned, the more likely it is that an objective will be achieved.

Suppose the manager breaks down each annual objective into quarterly objectives. The manager will probably become most concerned about accomplishing quarterly objectives toward the end of the quarter. But now the manager is spurred to action four times a year, not just once. If quarterly objectives are broken down into monthly objectives, the manager will obviously become concerned about the accomplishment of monthly objectives toward the end of the month. But now he or she is excited 12 times each year. If monthly objectives are broken down into weekly objectives, the manager will become excited about the accomplishment of objectives 52 times each year. And if the manager can break down weekly objectives into daily objectives, he or she will have made long-range objectives operational on a daily basis. When will the manager become concerned about daily objectives? Probably toward the latter part of the day. But when concern occurs this frequently, results are bound to follow.

Approaching objectives in this interlocking fashion is one way of making our habits work for us instead of against us. By habit, most of us put things off until deadlines approach. By breaking objectives down into subparts as small as days or weeks, we change the structure of the deadlines. The old habit will work in the same fashion, but the results will now be beneficial instead of detrimental.

WRITING "GOOD" OBJECTIVES

Developing objectives is not easy. A "good" objective is one that motivates you to take action and provides direction for that action. Several criteria can be used in developing objectives. These criteria will help you improve your efforts and enable you to develop objectives that really work for you.

1. *Objectives should be your own.* You are more likely to work at and accomplish objectives that you set for yourself. This does not

mean you cannot accept an objective that your boss, friend, or spouse wants you to accomplish. But your motivation will be higher if you consciously consider the advantages and disadvantages of the proposed course of action and then make your own decision. You should own at least some part of the objective. You should be willing to listen and talk to others, but you must do your own thinking and deciding. The more the objective is your own, the greater your commitment to its accomplishment.

2. *Objectives should be written.* Many people think that writing objectives is unnecessary. They often say they keep their objectives in their head, and as long as they think about them it doesn't matter if the objectives are written down or not. This is dangerous reasoning. The purpose of writing objectives is to clarify them. There seems to be a special kind of magic in writing objectives. Once an objective is written, you have more invested in it than before. As your investment increases, your personal commitment increases.

Written objectives have other advantages too. They are less likely to be forgotten in the midst of daily routines and pressures. When objectives are written, it is easier to integrate several of them simultaneously and to identify and resolve conflicts among them. If you are serious about using your time more effectively, you must write down your objectives.

3. *Objectives should be realistic and attainable.* Setting an objective is the first step in attaining it. If the objective is unrealistic or unattainable, it is not an objective at all. Fantasies, daydreams, aspirations, good intentions, and generalizations won't suffice. This doesn't mean that you should set your objectives low. Objectives should make you stretch and grow. They should be challenging, but they must also be attainable. They should be set at a level at which you are both able and willing to work. In general, your motivation increases as you set your objectives higher. But if an objective is so high that you don't believe it can be achieved, you will probably never start.

Attainability is difficult to pin down. Ultimately, each person and each organization must judge what is truly attainable. History is filled with examples of people achieving "unattainable" objectives. If it feels right to you and if it makes sense to you, then it is probably possible. The danger to avoid is being so optimistic that you set too many objectives to be accomplished in too short a time.

4. *Objectives should be specific and measurable.* When objectives are stated in vague terms, they provide very little direction. It is difficult to know exactly where to start and in what direction to

proceed. For example, a manager bothered with excessive turnover in the personnel department might set this objective: "Reduce turnover of personnel employees." While this may be an admirable intention, it is not nearly as good as if the manager had said: "Reduce turnover of personnel employees from 65 percent to 25 percent within six months." The latter objective is specific and measurable.

Objectives should be quantified whenever possible. If numbers can't be attached directly to the objective, try using an indirect measurement. When you simply can't quantify objectives directly or indirectly, you will have to make a subjective judgment about your progress. The best approach may be to restate the objective in such a way that measurement is possible.

5. *Objectives should have time schedules.* Assigning target dates for accomplishing objectives increases motivation, commitment, and action. Objectives without time schedules quickly become daydreams under the pressure of daily affairs. For each step along the way you should set a realistic target date that can, and should, be adjusted if conditions change. As each target is reached, you gain a sense of accomplishment and greater confidence in your ability to achieve even higher objectives.

6. *Objectives should be compatible.* Your objectives must be compatible with one another. If they are not, accomplishing one objective may prevent you from accomplishing another. This leads to indecision and uncertainty about which objective to pursue, and you may end up pursuing no objective at all.

Anyone can improve the clarification of objectives by checking them against these six criteria. The more closely the objectives match the criteria, the more they will add direction and purpose to your use of time. Remember that writing objectives is a skill. Like any skill, it will improve with practice.

A good starting point is to write down your significant objectives for a 30-day period. Compare each objective with the criteria listed above to determine whether it is well written. Then break each monthly objective into a set of weekly objectives. Look at the first week of the month. Estimate how much time you will need to meet each weekly objective. When you have estimated the time for each objective, add up all the estimates to obtain the total time required to meet your weekly objectives. Always estimate a *minimum* time requirement. This does not mean that you will be able to accomplish the objective within the minimum time, but it does provide a starting point. In practice, the objective may require more time, but it is not likely to require less than this minimum. Keep a record of your time estimates. They will provide useful comparisons with later exercises in this book.

The importance of objectives cannot be overemphasized. Consider this example. A survey was conducted recently to determine how word processing systems might change executive secretarial jobs. It was noted that the average executive secretary spends approximately two hours on routine typing each day and six hours on other items. A good word processing system should eliminate nearly all the routine typing, thereby freeing the executive secretary to use those two hours for other activities that would make a greater contribution.

However, the survey noted that many of the organizations which had implemented word processing systems failed to realize the two-hour potential gain. What happened? Parkinson came in when they were not looking. According to Parkinson's Law, "Work expands to fill the time available for its accomplishment." Without realizing it, the executive secretaries allowed their remaining job assignments to expand, filling the entire workday.

The survey team also discovered that the same organizations which failed to realize the two-hour potential gain failed to do two other things: They failed to clarify specific objectives for the use of those two hours, and they failed to engage in careful planning to make sure those objectives were achieved. Again, when you don't know where you're going, you'll probably wind up somewhere else.

PRIORITIES

Once objectives are clarified, some time management concerns are almost automatically solved. Those people who have only one objective can rest easy, because for them most of the hard work is over. However, most people have more than one important objective in their work (and in their life as well). What is the next step for them? The answer, of course, is that they must set priorities.

Most of us have a fuzzy grip on priorities. We use the word "priority" to describe an important project or responsibility connected with our jobs. Under this definition, we would say that a small portion of our time is devoted to priorities. We would be correct in stating that it is simply not possible to always work on the basis of priorities.

The dictionary defines "priority" as something given prior attention—in other words, something done before something else. This definition gets right to the heart of spending time. Everything people do during the day involves a priority decision. Unfortunately, many priority decisions are not made consciously and do not reflect stated objectives. Nevertheless, the dozens of priority decisions made each day, consciously or unconsciously, go a long way toward determining what the entire organizational team considers to be important.

When we examine how managers allocate their time, we find many complex answers that reflect priority decisions. The average manager may be involved in 60 or 70 incidents every day. A study of priorities is a study of time allocation—of how the manager decides to engage in any particular action at any given time.

Managers seem to use a wide variety of criteria in deciding how to use their time. A list of these criteria was presented in Chapter 3. All of them have some merit, and most have awesome implications for allocating time. Six deserve further comment:

1. Demands of others.
2. Closeness of deadlines.
3. Amount of time available.
4. Degree of enjoyment.
5. Order of arrival.
6. Degree of familiarity.

Demands of Others

All people may be important, but certainly not everything that people want you to engage in is important. Nor are all "others" equal. For instance, the boss probably has a greater impact on how you use your time than any other person in this category. Yet not everything the boss requests is of utmost importance, nor should all things requested by the boss necessarily be done. Nevertheless, many subordinates unthinkingly carry out all requests from the boss.

Consider a typical example. Charlie is walking down the hall one day and notices that the wallpaper is coming loose near one of the elevators. This section of the building has been undergoing extensive renovation, and Charlie is peeved that this eyesore has not been repaired. On returning to his office, Charlie dictates a memo to his assistant manager responsible for maintenance and repairs. When the memo is received by the assistant manager, it will move rapidly to the top of his activity list, whether it should or not. Why will it be escalated? Because Charlie keeps a record of how long it takes his assistant manager to respond to a memo of this type. Charlie saves the memos and notes the responses they receive. When it is time to conduct a performance review with his assistant manager, he will retrieve the memos and discuss those items even before he talks about the assistant's primary responsibilities.

Charlie believes that what he is doing is beneficial. He believes this because his predecessor thoroughly indoctrinated him in the need to stay on top of details at all times. Charlie's assistant manager is learning the same lesson very well. Even though he realizes that many of these memos are relatively unimportant, he will respond to them promptly because he wants a positive evaluation from Charlie.

Consider the consequences. The assistant manager may be doing his job very capably and may even have been aware of the peeling paper. He may have already scheduled repairs in the normal course of maintenance. He may have weighed the job relative to other needs and scheduled it according to some rational priority system. But when Charlie's memo arrives, the job is likely to be escalated to the top of the list. As a result, a more important job will be delayed. While this may be a good personal strategy, enabling the assistant manager to receive positive evaluations from Charlie, it is not necessarily a good strategy for the company. If too many of these incidents occur, the company could be in big trouble. At the very least, there will be more crises taking place than need be.

Charlie and his assistant manager need to find some rational way of dealing with this type of problem. Each one needs to understand how the other responds and the kinds of actions that cause a response. This approach requires some dialogue between Charlie and his assistant manager about the best way to utilize their time. Unfortunately, it never occurs to Charlie to initiate such a dialogue. And the assistant manager is often too intimidated to bring up the subject; he simply assumes that what the boss says is "top priority." Given the subordinate's eventual objectives, he may or may not be correct.

Closeness of Deadlines

Waiting until the eleventh hour to begin working can often lead to trouble. The closer we get to a deadline, the more likely we are to engage in the activities necessary to meet the deadline. We rationalize this by saying that we do some of our best work under pressure. This is often true. Just as often, however, it is not true. Sometimes, the last-minute rush results in poor performance or no performance. Deadlines are often missed. Managers who put things off until the last minute often find themselves working at a much more frantic pace than necessary. It is far better to develop the habit of starting well before the deadline, thereby ensuring steady and solid progress. Remember the Law of Thermodynamics: "Things get worse under pressure."

Amount of Time Available

Using available time as an allocation criterion creates much wasted time. People tend to tackle jobs with short time demands first, putting off jobs that require large investments of time. Unfortunately, short jobs are not necessarily important jobs. It would be better to work on more important jobs in small pieces than to continue to do less important tasks simply because they are short.

A prime example of this is the person who tackles a lot of little things first to get them out of the way so he or she will have "time to do bigger things later." Of course, later seldom comes. This type of behavior is guaranteed to generate more crises than anyone needs.

Degree of Enjoyment

All of us have tasks we enjoy and tasks we do not enjoy. Most of us do the tasks we enjoy more readily than the ones we do not enjoy. Unfortunately, not everything we enjoy doing is the most important thing to be done. Nor should we always tackle tasks we like before handling tasks we dislike. Some people turn this situation around. If the disliked activities are more important, they will do them first, at the beginning of the day, before allowing themselves to take on things that bring them greater enjoyment.

Order of Arrival

Performing tasks in the order of arrival may work for a clerk in a shoe store, but it is a poor strategy for a manager who wants to be effective. Taking telephone calls on a first-call, first-response basis, doing paperwork as it arrives, or seeing visitors in the order they drop in will guarantee that you waste a great deal of time on unimportant, trivial items. You must have some way of sorting out tasks so you can handle the more important ones first.

Degree of Familiarity

People are more likely to work on familiar tasks than on unfamiliar ones. Few people are eager to tackle jobs they do not know how to do. Nevertheless, many of the responsibilities that will require new skills are the very items that should occupy people's time.

DETERMINING WHAT IS IMPORTANT

Establishing priorities is difficult for many people. "How," they ask, "can you say one item is more important than another item when everything is important?" We agree that setting priorities is a difficult task, but it is necessary nevertheless. The alternative to consciously setting priorities is unconsciously reacting to demands as they occur. Reacting seldom brings best results. Initiating action requires control coupled with decision-making abilities. Actions initiated on the basis of carefully thought-out decisions are almost always better than actions initiated haphazardly. You may not always establish the best priorities, but your odds are greater with careful thought.

In your efforts to establish priorities, ask yourself the following questions:

1. What are my objectives? If I had to identify my primary objective, which one would it be?
2. By what criteria do I now establish priorities? (Review the 20 points listed in Chapter 3.)
3. How can careful timing and coordination of my goals help me become more effective? Since I feel all my goals are important, how can I make sure that the activities required for one goal are attended to at a time that helps another goal or, at least, doesn't hinder that goal?
4. Do I have a good understanding of the cause-and-effect relationships on my job? Do I thoroughly understand what activities lead to the results I need? If I don't understand, where can I get some answers?
5. Which of my goals will bring the greatest value to the company?
6. Which of my goals will bring me the greatest personal satisfaction? Which are beneficial to the greatest number of people?

Remember, too, that as difficult as it is to set priorities, you make a priority decision even when you decide not to set priorities. By default you allow any urgent activity to control your time while items of greater importance go unattended.

PERSONAL AND PROFESSIONAL OBJECTIVES

The value of an activity is measured by its contribution to an objective. Those activities that lead directly to objectives are the most important. Important activities can lead to organizational objectives or to personal objectives. When conflicts arise between personal and organizational objectives, personal objectives tend to take precedence. In some cases people pursue personal objectives to the detriment of organizational objectives.

How do organizational and personal objectives differ? Organizational objectives are carefully and logically determined. Frequently we must discuss them with other people in order to define them exactly. An organizational objective is one that we understand and commit to intellectually. A personal objective, on the other hand, is a private and often purely emotional commitment. It need not make sense to anyone except us. No one else may even know what it is. But we have committed ourselves to it on an emotional level.

Thus a conflict between organizational and personal objectives is a conflict between an intellectual commitment and an emotional commitment. The emotional commitment is the one that usually prevails, other things being equal. In the event of truly significant conflict, emotional choice comes out on top every time.

Some conflict between personal and corporate objectives is inevitable. To the extent that you can avoid it, your life becomes much simpler. To the extent that you cannot avoid it, you must learn to come to grips with your own set of values and your sense of right and wrong. The old question "What is a fair day's work and a fair day's pay?" remains.

By all means, share objectives with those around you. Keep your subordinates informed about what you are trying to accomplish in your unit. Better yet, get your subordinates involved in setting unit objectives. The more they participate, the greater their commitment will be. Post your objectives where everyone can see them as a constant reminder of what you are trying to achieve.

Develop the objectives habit. Set at least one major objective each day and achieve it. If you do this, you will become more goal-oriented. You will learn to think in terms of objectives at all times.

As you accomplish objectives regularly, daily, you will gain a tremendous amount of confidence in your ability to accomplish still greater objectives. You will find it much easier to drop trivia out of your life as you focus on significant objectives. To paraphrase an old adage, "An objective a day keeps confusion away."

Objectives and priorities are extremely potent. They are powerful because they work. They lead to accomplishment. Once people begin achieving things that are important to them, they become addicted to achievement. Establishing objectives and priorities on a daily, weekly, monthly, yearly, and long-term basis becomes an established habit, a way of life. Reaching objectives is infinitely rewarding and often inspires us to set our sights on objectives we once considered unattainable.

7
Planning Your Time

FEW OF US spend as much time planning as we know we should, even though planning is crucial to using our time effectively. Planning becomes increasingly important as we move up the executive ladder, because with position comes responsibility for long-range goals. For middle, upper-middle, and top-level managers, it is virtually impossible to achieve carefully determined objectives without planning.

Because we fail to plan as we should, we are constantly bumping into Murphy's Laws:

1. Nothing is as simple as it seems.
2. Everything takes longer than it should.
3. If anything can go wrong, it will.

People who spend an adequate amount of time planning run into these problems less often than people who fail to plan.

THE IMPORTANCE OF PLANNING

Most of us agree that proper planning is vitally important. Why, then, do we not give more time to this important function? Ironically, many of us simply don't have enough time to plan. There are too many other jobs that must be done, and planning can wait for another day. Yet if we took more time to plan, we would gain more time for our other job functions as well.

Another problem is that in the past most of us have been reasonably successful without planning. In the positive business climate of the last ten to twenty years, we have run up a series of impressive successes. Resources seemed to come from an ever-blooming tree. Many of us even surpassed our greatest goals. Clearly, it was possible to do well without planning. Whether or not we could have been more successful if we had engaged in planning is a moot point.

Life is different today. The business climate is not as positive and predictable as it once was. Today, if we hope to be successful, we *must* plan. Regulation and control from local, state, and federal government units demand it. The ability to develop new programs and services, keep up with the competition, finance operations, maximize reimbursements, and simply survive depends on our planning skill.

In an earlier chapter, we discussed people's tendency to engage in urgent affairs before they attend to important affairs. Planning is one of those important matters that often must wait until urgent demands have been settled. Of course, by then matters have often become far more complicated than they need be. Planning then becomes even more difficult and time-consuming. We will have even greater reason to put it off "until later."

Most of us are very action-oriented. We prefer to be in the thick of things, doing instead of thinking. As a result, we adopt a reactive pattern. We react to whatever happens around us. Reacting requires very little prior thinking. *Pro*acting, on the other hand, requires a great deal of prior thought and planning. This is difficult to do in a reactively patterned day. Therefore, most of us continue to react rather than carefully plan as many things as we could.

Most of us like to gain a sense of closure from our tasks. Planning does not provide immediate closure. We may not see the results of our plans for weeks, months, years, perhaps even never. Realizing the long closure time, many people are unwilling to plan. They are reluctant to engage in any activity that does not provide reasonably rapid feedback. Lack of feedback or closure increases the amount of ambiguity and uncertainty in their lives.

Many people also seem to pride themselves on being spontaneous. There seems to be a special status attached to spontaneity and a feeling that if someone plans carefully, he or she will miss the important things in life. This, of course, is nonsense. Life is too complex to "wing it" all the time. If you want things to happen right, you must plan at some point. If your time is to be spent well, it must be planned. The better you plan, the more time you will have for taking advantage of opportunities as they arise.

Some people seem to have a block about planning. They view it as a complex, time-consuming activity. The task of planning becomes so enormous in their minds that they are unable to take the first step. Planning need not be a complex undertaking. Planning simply means thinking about the future in some systematic way. It requires thinking about the events that should be happening and the conditions under which they should be happening.

Planning bridges the gap between where you are now and where you hope to be at some future point. Where you are now is one side of the chasm, and your objectives are the other side. Unless there is some way to bridge this separation, you will never be able to reach your goals.

Often people plan activities but fail to plan time. Planning time means setting a time frame or a time limit to the planned task. For example, an activity plan might include the following:

1. Write monthly summary.
2. Meet with John.
3. Develop new plan.

With a specific timetable, this list would be far more useful:

1. Write monthly summary—$1\frac{1}{2}$ hours.
2. Meet with John—$\frac{1}{2}$ hour.
3. Develop new plan—1 hour.

It is important to assign specific time frames to your tasks. Tasks or activities are never ending. There is always something else that can be done. Time is the limiting factor. There are never enough hours in a day for all the things that could be done. Therefore, a plan must be built around the most critical element—time.

Planning is the way we connect future points with today. It has often been noted that the further into the future we can project our objectives, the easier it is to know what to do today. However, that future point does not have to be very far off in order to be of benefit. Winston Churchill once reportedly complained, "One must always look ahead, but it is difficult to look farther than one can see." It is only when we have a purpose for tomorrow that today has substance—whether we are talking about the future of a country or the direction of an individual life. Most people think one to two weeks in advance for most of the things that engage their time. Even a one- or two-week time horizon can be valuable.

A SYSTEMATIC APPROACH TO TIME PLANNING

You can begin to master time planning by approaching it on a weekly basis. The important element in the process is to plan consistently, every week. Plan those weeks that seem to be too simple to require planning as well as those weeks when you think you're going to be too busy to plan. If you plan your time regularly every week, you will soon develop a habit of planning.

Once a week, write down your objectives for the following week. If possible, do this at the end of the preceding week. For instance, you might take time out on Friday afternoon, or perhaps on Saturday, to make a note of your significant objectives for the following week. Make sure these objectives are well clarified before you proceed. As you write down your weekly objectives, you should also look ahead to monthly, quarterly, or annual objectives in order to keep your week in perspective.

Once you have clarified your objectives for next week as precisely as possible, you are ready to ask yourself six key planning questions:

1. What has to be done?
2. When should it be done?
3. Who should do it?
4. Where should it be done?
5. What priority should it have?
6. How much time will it require?

Remember, you cannot *do* an objective. An objective is a result achieved over time. You can only do activities. If you do the right activities, you have a good chance of reaching your objective. If you do the wrong activities, you will probably not reach your objective. Determining what has to be done requires that you think through all the activities necessary to accomplish each objective. Suppose, for instance, that one of your objectives is to have a new wage policy approved by the end of next week. What activities are required to accomplish this objective? If you do these activities with a reasonable amount of skill, you should have an approved wage policy by the end of the week. If you do not do these activities, the wage policy will probably not be approved by the end of the week. In that case, you will carry things over to the next week and fall further behind.

As you consider the question of when things ought to be done, remember that there is a proper sequence for events. If things are done in the proper sequence, they take less time and produce better results. If they are done out of sequence, they inevitably create a great deal of wasted time before they are finally accomplished.

Where things are done can also have a major impact on whether or not they are achieved. For instance, a discussion taking place in your office is subject to any number of interruptions. If the discussion were to take place in a conference room, many of those interruptions could be avoided.

Effective delegating will also help to ensure that your planning will be successful. Whenever the question arises of who should perform a particular task, think about what you must do yourself. Consider what can be done by others. (Delegation is discussed in detail in Chapter 11.)

Setting priorities for all your activities is mandatory. Plans will not always work out in the way they are written. When changes become necessary, they should be built around the highest-priority items. If you fail to establish priorities, you may forget important actions in your rush to modify the plan.

Most of us are hopelessly optimistic about planning. We are poor judges of time and generally underestimate how long a task will take. When we try to estimate the time for a total project, we tend to make our greatest errors.

A better approach is to break the project down into specific activities and estimate the completion time for each activity. When estimating completion times, you should always think in terms of absolute minimums. If you could work at a certain task without interruptions or distractions, how long would it take? This estimate should then form the basis for your time plan. Try an experiment using the objectives and the time estimates you wrote in Chapter 6. Break each objective down into specific tasks. Estimate the time to complete each task. Is your total time estimate the same as your estimate from Chapter 6? Most people find that the process of estimating time by tasks yields a higher total than an overall time estimate for the project. The process is also more accurate.

Figure 12 shows a sample weekly time plan based on points discussed earlier. The objectives are noted at the top. Actions necessary to accomplish these objectives are listed at the bottom. Next to each activity is a priority value, an estimate of how much time the activity will take, and a note about when each activity should be done. When the activity times are added, the total for this example is 35 hours. Assuming that the manager will work an average of 50 to 55 hours next week, how likely is he or she to achieve the objectives?

Figure 12. Weekly planning sheet.

weekly plan

January 21

OBJECTIVES (what I hope to have accomplished by the end of the week)

1. Complete preparation for Personnel Committee meeting 1/30.
2. Finish first draft of year-end Performance Report.
3. Review final plans and cost estimates for West Building.

	ACTIVITIES REQUIRED TO ACCOMPLISH OBJECTIVES	Priority	Time Needed	Which Day
1.	Meet with Personnel Director to plan agenda	1	1 hr.	Mon
2.	Review format of YE report with PR staff	3	1 "	Mon
3.	Briefing with Acctg. on data display	2	1 "	Mon
4.	Complete reviews of all Dept YE reports	1	6 "	Mon
5.	Review report and pension plan recommendations with actuaries for presentation to Per. Comm.	1	2 "	Tue
6.	Review presentation and approve final PC agenda	3	1 "	Wed
7.	Brief Chm. Pers. Comm. and Pers. Director	2	2 "	Fri
8.	Dictate first draft of YE report	2	2 "	Tue
9.	Edit first draft of YE report	3	1 "	Wed
10.	Approve draft of YE report for printer	2	1 "	Fri
11.	Meeting on remodeling with Controller	3	2 "	Wed
12.	Meeting with architect, Controller, Bldg. Comm.	1	8(all day)	Thu
13.	Meeting at bank with Pension Trust officer	2	2 hr.	Tue
14.	Walk through and visit with employees of units to be remodeled	1	2 "	Tue
15.	Misc. time for problem areas encountered on walk through	1	3 "	Wed
			35	

The answer to this question depends on how much time the manager can hope to control. Observation indicates that the range of controllable time varies from 25 to 50 percent of a manager's total time. This means a manager working a 50-hour week can assume that 12 to 25 hours are within his or her control. If the manager needs 35 hours to accomplish the objectives for next week, the weekly plan is clearly in jeopardy.

The problem with the plan shown in Figure 12 is that it does not take the uncontrollable into account. It shows no time for interruptions. It allows no time for unexpected events or crises. It doesn't consider the impact of telephone calls and drop-in visitors, or requests from the boss. It does not allow for absence of staff members or changes in the weather. All these things will continue to happen. In spite of them, however, the manager has a set of objectives to accomplish.

Whenever the time required to accomplish objectives is greater than the probable time available to accomplish them, something has to give. The manager is often tempted to say, "Well, they've all got to get done, so I'll just have to spend less time on each activity." However, if the minimal times estimated for the activities are accurate, this is not a possibility. You simply can't do things in less time than they actually take. In addition, Murphy's Second Law reminds you that an activity may not be accomplished within the estimated time.

Faced with this kind of difficulty, the manager has several options. He or she could revise the original plan, rescheduling some things for another week. The manager could delegate more tasks. Or the manager could work more hours than normal, utilize more staff than normal, or under certain conditions add temporary staff. If none of these options is feasible and the activities simply must get done, the manager will have to find some way to create more available time than normal.

At this point an important difference should be noted between having a plan and not having a plan. Assume that the manager did not prepare a weekly plan. When would the manager be likely to discover that he or she had tackled more tasks than could actually be handled during the week? Probably Thursday or Friday. By then, however, it would be too late to do much about it. The purpose of thinking through the week and writing up a plan is to discover potential problems far enough in advance to do something about them.

The value of weekly planning cannot be overemphasized. The weekly plan is the backbone of any strategy to control time. Managers who consistently prepare a weekly plan seem to get more accomplished than managers who don't plan each week. Ironically, the fact that planners consistently produce better results than nonplanners has not been sufficient to cause managers to plan more often.

DAILY PLANNING

Once the weekly plan is completed, daily planning is the next step. For most people this will take the form of a things-to-do list. (See Figure 13.) Many people use to-do lists, but most experience difficulty in making the lists work.

One reason many lists don't work is that people prepare them poorly. Their lists tend to be a random collection of activities. Some lists are several pages long. Many of these activities relate to objectives, but many do not. They are simply random events that have appeared in people's day. The lists include everything from the key activities of the day to unimportant reminders such as "Buy a loaf of bread on the way home from the office." (Granted the bread may be important at dinner time.) Very few lists have any indication of priorities or estimates of how long it will take to accomplish the various tasks.

As a result, very few people consistently accomplish all the items on their to-do list by the end of the day. Most people complain that they carry more and more things over to the next day. In this case, of course, people can rightfully say that preparing a to-do list seems to make very little difference in the results they achieve.

A to-do list prepared in a haphazard manner is actually demotivating, guaranteeing the preparer a future of frustration. Seldom does the preparer accomplish all the items on the list. Thus each new list is simply a reminder of the disappointments to be faced by the end of the day. This strengthens people's conviction that writing things down has nothing to do with accomplishing them. It is frustrating to realize at the beginning of the day that all your intended work will probably not be finished. Further frustration results when, in fact, a number of the items are not finished by the end of the day. To continue to write out a to-do list under these conditions is a futile gesture.

A better approach is to base your daily to-do list on a weekly time plan. Each day, determine which portion of the weekly plan you wish to achieve. Establish your objectives for the day. Write out all the planned activities for accomplishing the day's objectives. Rate them according to priority, and estimate the amount of time required for each one. Now add the other events that will occur in your day to

Figure 13. Daily plan.

things to do today   Monday   1-21

Item	Priority	Time Needed	Done		Scheduled Events
Meet with Bob	1	1 hr.	☐	8:00	
Meet with Fred	2	30 min.	☐	8:15	
Meet with PR staff	3	1 hr.	☐	8:30	
Review dept. reports	1	2 hr.	☐	8:45	
Letter to Bill Smith	2	5 min.	☐	9:00	
Letter to bank	1	10 min.	☐	9:15	
Call Betty	2	15 min.	☐	9:30	
Call about recruiting	3	10 min.	☐	9:45	
Complete trip expense report	1	15 min.	☐	10:00	
Check on Steve's bicycle	—	5 min.	☐	10:15	
			☐	10:30	
			☐	10:45	
			☐	11:00	
			☐	11:15	
			☐	11:30	
			☐	11:45	
			☐	12:00	
			☐	12:15	
			☐	12:30	
			☐	12:45	
			☐	1:00	
			☐	1:15	
			☐	1:30	
			☐	1:45	
			☐	2:00	
			☐	2:15	
			☐	2:30	
			☐	2:45	
			☐	3:00	
			☐	3:15	
			☐	3:30	
			☐	3:45	
			☐	4:00	
			☐	4:15	
			☐	4:30	
			☐	4:45	
			☐	5:00	
				5:15	
				5:30	
				5:45	
				6:00	
				Evening	

Notes

Keep door closed today ! ! !

the list. In all probability, many of these other activities will not relate directly to objectives. You may have to do them anyway. However, preparing a to-do list in this fashion gives you the opportunity to compare important activities with unimportant activities.

With things spelled out in black and white on a list, you may find it easier to let the unimportant things go until you have attended to the important things first.

When should you do your daily planning? Preferably at the end of the previous day. Your daily plan should be completed before you arrive at the office in the morning. There are at least three good reasons for this.

First, it helps to review the day you have just completed when preparing the list for the next day. What went right today? What went wrong? Were things in control or out of control? How can you do better tomorrow? This quick review at the end of the day helps you prepare a better list for tomorrow. Second, a list prepared in advance gives you a psychological head start. While you are preparing for your day and commuting to the office, you can go over all the points on your to-do list for today. You will be ready to swing into action the moment you arrive at the office.

Third, a list prepared in advance gives you a comparison base right from the beginning. Without such a list, you are likely to be trapped by half a dozen things that are already coming unglued the moment you walk through the door. You will tend to get engaged in them immediately. With a list, however, you might pause to say, "Is this item more or less important than what I have on my list?" If it is more important, by all means do it. If it is less important, think for a moment about how you might ignore it, say no, reschedule it for later, or otherwise avoid it. A to-do list is a useful curb on extraneous activities. It keeps you on track of your goals. Of course, you can still "jump the curb," but you have an extra measure of protection if you conscientiously prepare the list daily.

Planning is a central factor in all time management success stories. It is a roadmap to accomplishment and an exercise in freedom. Planning leads to results, for it gives us control over our most valuable resource—time.

8
Scheduling Activities

PLANNING IS DECIDING what to do. Scheduling is determining when to do it. Each day, as you schedule the events that will fill your hours, you must carefully chart a path between Parkinson and Murphy. Parkinson reminds you that work expands to fill the time available for its accomplishment. This means that if you allow too much time for a task, the task will take up all the time that you allow. Murphy, though, cautions you that everything seems to take longer than you think it will. This means that if you do not allow adequate time for a task, the task will take as much time as it needs anyway. In either case, your schedule will be upset. Your challenge is to allow enough time, but not too much time, for every task you undertake.

CONSTRUCTING A SCHEDULE

A schedule is more than a to-do list, although many people assume it is the same thing. A to-do list is an itemization of all the activities that must be done today, with appropriate priorities assigned to them and a time estimate for each activity. However, the list says nothing about what time of day each activity is to be done. That's where scheduling comes in.

Figure 14 illustrates the relationship between a to-do list and a schedule. The to-do list portion is on the left-hand side; the scheduling portion is on the right-hand side.

Your schedule should start with activities on the to-do list, or daily plan. This is derived from the weekly plan, as discussed earlier. With

Figure 14. Scheduled daily plan.

things to do today Monday 1-21

Item	Priority	Time Needed	Done
Meet with Bob	1	1 hr.	☐
Meet with Fred	2	30 min.	☐
Meet with PR staff	3	1 hr.	☐
Review dept. reports	1	2 hr.	☐
Letter to Bill Smith	2	5 min.	☐
Letter to bank	1	10 min.	☐
Call Betty	2	15 min.	☐
Call about recruiting	3	10 min.	☐
Complete trip expense report	1	15 min.	☐
Check on Steve's bicycle	—	5 min.	☐
			☐
			☐
			☐
			☐
			☐
			☐
			☐
			☐
			☐
			☐
			☐
			☐
			☐

Scheduled Events

8:00	Review dept reports
8:15	
8:30	
8:45	
9:00	Meet with Bob
9:15	
9:30	
9:45	
10:00	
10:15	
10:30	Letters – bank + Bill
10:45	
11:00	
11:15	
11:30	Meet with Fred
11:45	
12:00	
12:15	
12:30	Review dept. reports
12:45	
1:00	
1:15	
1:30	Expense report
1:45	
2:00	
2:15	
2:30	
2:45	
3:00	Call Betty
3:15	Call about recruiting
3:30	
3:45	
4:00	Meet with PR staff
4:15	
4:30	
4:45	
5:00	
5:15	
5:30	Steve's bicycle
5:45	
6:00	
Evening	

Notes

Keep door closed today !!!

both the weekly plan and the daily to-do list, you should relate actions to carefully developed objectives, with the focus on important things first. To begin with, note appointments, standing meetings or committees, and similar items that you know, in advance, will have to be done at a particular time. Block these out of your schedule. These items are fixed unless you realistically have the option of not doing them.

When you consider possible options, remember to keep your objectives in mind. You may be required, for example, to attend a particular staff meeting. You know from past experience that the meeting is usually unproductive. Attending the meeting will hinder your efforts to achieve good results from your day. On the other hand, you want to survive in the organization. What do you do? You can try to make the meeting worthwhile (see the section on meetings in Chapter 9). If that is not possible, you may be able to skip a meeting from time to time without serious consequences. It is usually unwise, though, to miss all the meetings. Therefore, you will have to consider some unproductive meeting time as part of your job. You may as well block it out on your schedule and work around it. Concentrate on using the balance of your time effectively.

FLEXIBILITY

The biggest mistake people make in scheduling is to allocate every minute of their day. This approach is guaranteed to fail. You can seldom control the entire day. Even if it is possible occasionally, you cannot count on its happening very often. There are just too many unexpected things that make demands on your time. You must leave room for the unexpected when you are constructing your schedule. Most people know that they will be interrupted during the day, but very few actually plan for interruptions. Remember, interruptions are a part of your job. Planning for interruptions means leaving room in your schedule for them.

How much flexibility should you allow? There is no definite answer to this question. You will have to determine the appropriate amount of flexible time for yourself. Most managerial jobs require between 25 and 50 percent flexibility. This means that in an eight-hour day you should leave two to four hours unscheduled to absorb unexpected events. Keeping a time log of your job for a week or two can help you determine how much flexibility your job demands.

The amount of flexibility required in your job depends on several factors. The more people there are around you and the more you interact with others, the more flexibility you will need. Self-discipline is another factor. If you are highly disciplined in your work habits, you will probably need less flexibility than a less disciplined individual. The amount of "noise" around you also affects flexibility. The more you work in isolation, the less flexibility you will need, since you are less likely to be interrupted.

There are several ways to arrive at the flexibility factors in your schedule. Figure 15 illustrates several common scheduling patterns. Many people prefer Pattern A, which offers a distinct advantage over the others. With Pattern A, if things do work out according to schedule, you have a large block of unscheduled time available in the afternoon. With the other patterns, even when things work out well, your gained time is scattered throughout the day.

An entire afternoon would allow you to tackle another special project, analyze parts of your operation, catch up on your reading, or do any number of things that you simply couldn't do as well in little blocks of time. An available afternoon may give you an opportunity to work on your long-range plans or explore a new opportunity. Occasionally it may even allow you a round of golf. An increasing number of people are gaining additional personal time by finding ways to accomplish their goals earlier in the day than usual.

Remember Parkinson as you're trying to decide which flexibility pattern to use. Work does expand. Even if you do find yourself with

Figure 15. Scheduling patterns.

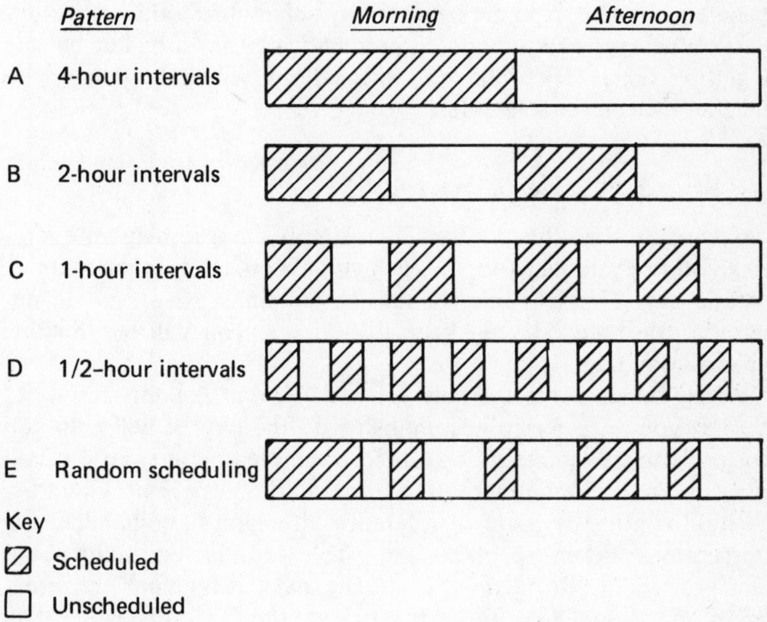

a slack period, you may waste the time trying to decide what to do next. Therefore, you should always have at least one alternative plan prepared for those days when the unexpected—surprisingly— doesn't happen.

One thing you might do on those occasional days is gain on tomorrow's list. You may also want to develop an "opportunity" list ahead of time. On most days you will need all the time you have just to take care of the unexpected, but on those days when the unexpected doesn't happen, you should have plans for adequately using that gained time. If there isn't anything *significant* for you to do, maybe you should take a long lunch hour instead. If you hang around the office when you don't have anything to do, you may "goof off" and prevent other people from accomplishing their goals for the day.

Whatever you do, match your schedule to the realities of your job. Try to schedule the morning as tight as possible. Make sure the first hour of your day is a productive one. The first hour sets a pattern for the day. If you get a good start, things will go better all day. If you get a poor start, you'll be trying to catch up all day.

SCHEDULING TIPS

If you want things to happen, you must create space for them. Space equals time. You create space by scheduling a time for every event. Whatever gets scheduled automatically has a higher chance of getting done. The following suggestions will help you create realistic, successful schedules.

Put Your Schedule in Writing

A schedule should be written. You simply can't remember everything you're planning to do, or when you plan to do it, in the midst of a hectic day. The schedule should be on a single sheet, not on numerous little notes. If you keep little notes, you will be shuffling paper all day long.

Writing things down will help you clarify your thoughts and focus on what you're trying to accomplish with the day. It will help you spot problems or faults in logic before they lead you astray; it will increase your commitment to your daily objectives. A written schedule is a handy point of reference after you have handled the interruptions and unexpected events. You won't have to think about what you should do next; you already have it on your schedule. Simply go to it and do it. Be certain to keep the schedule visible at all times. Don't tuck it in a drawer, your pocket, or your briefcase. Keep it on the desk in front of you or tack it to the wall overhead. Put it in a spot where you'll be sure to see it frequently. The list should be a constant reminder of what you ought to be doing and how your day should be progressing.

Group Related Items

Don't make your day any more fragmented or hectic than it already is. If you have a number of phone calls to make, try to handle them all at the same time. If you have to write a number of letters, try to dictate all of them at the same time. If you group related items in your schedule, you will not have to make as many psychological shifts during the day. Even if your phone calls relate to different things, handling all the calls at one time will put you in a telephone frame of mind. If you intersperse telephone–letters–telephone–meeting–letters–telephone, you will have much more difficulty focusing your activities and your efforts.

Schedule Thinking Time Every Day

More thinking never hurt anyone. You should develop the habit of thinking regularly about what is happening and what ought to be happening. If you do not build time for thinking and planning into your schedule, you will have great difficulty doing an adequate amount of either.

Make Transition Time Productive

Transition time is the space between events, consisting mostly of waiting time or travel time. Your time log will show how much time you normally spend in each category. (Travel time is discussed in Chapter 13.)

Many people think of waiting time as a gift, an uninterrupted spot of time they had not planned on. They use it for catching up on their reading, doing some planning, or reviewing things that they never seem to find the time for. You should always have alternative activities in mind so that when you are faced with waiting time you won't waste it trying to figure out what to do.

Carry reading and writing materials with you at all times. As you walk from office to office, try to use the time productively. Return reports to the file, water a plant, or even conduct a walking meeting with another person.

Focus on Objectives

Do anything you can to avoid activity traps. Don't engage in random activities. Before you put an activity into your schedule, think about its purpose. Most people are far too casual in their work habits. Use your schedule as a way to help you develop better habits.

When something unexpected arises, do not automatically take off after it. Stop and ask yourself, "Is this unexpected event more important than what I had planned to do instead?" If it is more important, go right ahead and pursue it. You should always focus on the most important items before you tackle the less important ones. But if the unexpected event is not more important, try to reschedule it for another time, ignore it, say no, or do anything else that will enable you to engage in more important activities. Whenever possible, stay on your planned course.

Have Others Schedule Your Time

Secretaries frequently schedule managers' time. There are two good reasons for this. First of all, another person can be more objective about your time use than you can. Second, another person can say no much more easily than you can. If you have staff available who can schedule your time, why not let them try it?

Schedule a "Quiet Hour"

Many people have found quiet time so helpful that they come to work early to be sure they have at least one private hour to themselves. While coming to work early is certainly valuable, it isn't necessary.

People in busy offices often assume that finding a quiet time is impossible. This assumption, like many other assumptions, has kept them from implementing an extremely useful time management tool. Almost anyone can find a quiet hour—an uninterrupted block of time for concentrating on important tasks. Here are some guidelines for making your quiet hour successful:

1. No telephone calls.
2. No paging.
3. No unnecessary talking.
4. No excessive movement.
5. No interruptions.
6. No distractions.
7. No visitors.
8. An appropriate time.
9. An appropriate place.

Michigan Miller's Mutual Insurance Company has enjoyed the benefits of a companywide quiet hour for many years. In 1962, Charles McGill, president of the company, noticed that many of his employees began the workday with nonproductive chatter. "They rehashed the soap operas and the ballgames," he remembers. "Other workers would complain that it was difficult for them to concentrate." So, long before quiet hours became a well-known idea, Mr. McGill instituted a quiet hour policy from 8:00 to 9:00 A.M. and from 1:00 to 2:00 P.M. in one division of his company. The experiment worked so well in the division that in 1966 the quiet hour became a policy throughout the organization. The afternoon quiet hour was dropped but the morning policy is still in effect. At 8:00 A.M. sharp a simple announcement is heard over the public address system: "Good morning." All conversation and idle chatter quickly stop—people get to work. "We all do it," one employee reported, "from the president to the custodians. That's what makes it work so well; we all do it together!"

Company employees appear to be as enthusiastic about the quiet hour as the company president. "We were told about the policy during our first employment interview," one secretary explained. "At first I thought it was a little childish, like being in elementary school; but now I know it works and I like it a lot." Frequent callers to the office are aware of the quiet hour each morning and voluntarily refrain from calling unless absolutely necessary. Of course, emergencies are handled when they need to be. As one employee pointed out, "This isn't a rigid system. It just helps us all get something accomplished with our day."

Experiment on your own. Pick a time when things are normally slower. Most offices experience a relatively slow period at three times during the day: between 8:00 and 9:00, 11:30 and 1:30, and 4:00 and 5:00. Discover the activity patterns in your own office. Then close the door and get something accomplished. If you don't have a door to close, you may have to remove yourself. Go to the library or a conference room or any isolated spot you can find. One man who works in an open office space simply dons a red baseball cap to signal that his "door" is shut. It works.

Consider Body Time

Most of us think of ourselves as either morning people or night people. It is true that our bodies are in better position to tackle certain kinds of tasks at particular times of day. For instance, morning people seem able to do creative work best early in the day, while night people prefer to do creative work in the evening. If it is possible for you to schedule your day to take advantage of your natural moods, by all means do so.

Be sure, though, that you really are a morning or night person and have not simply talked yourself into it. It is possible that your behavior has become a self-fulfilling prophecy. If you state a belief and then act according to it, you justify the belief. You act to fulfill your own expectations. Rearranging your expectations may allow you to discover new "truths" about yourself.

If you do not function well in the morning, ask yourself if you are starting your day properly. Many people begin their workday with inadequate sleep and inadequate nutrition. They wake up tired. Breakfast consists of a cup of coffee and perhaps a piece of toast. Then they attempt to start the day successfully.

Under these conditions, the body's blood sugar level is at its lowest point. You need protein in the morning to bring your body up to full functioning capacity. If you sleep more and eat better, you may discover that you can be extremely productive and creative in the early morning.

Prepare Your Schedule Before Arriving at The Office

You should prepare your schedule before you arrive at the office in the morning. If you do not prepare your schedule beforehand, you run the risk of beginning your day by reacting to things already taking place when you arrive. You will lose your psychological head start. With a schedule already prepared, you have the opportunity to stop and think for a moment before reacting.

There is another advantage to having your schedule prepared the evening before. As you go through your morning exercises of dressing, eating, and commuting to work, you can begin rehearsing the day around your schedule. With these preliminaries, you are far more likely to have the day work out as scheduled. For example, many salespeople have discovered that they consistently sell more when they know who their first call will be before leaving home in the morning.

Schedule Around Key Events

If you have one major goal, work that goal into your schedule first, then schedule everything else around the activities necessary to accomplish that goal. If, for instance, you know that an evaluation team from the home office is going to be in and out of your office over the next two or three days, build those activities into your schedule first. Then work all the other things that you hope to accomplish during the same period into your schedule. If you do not do this, the key event will be far more disruptive than it need be.

Learning to schedule is a skill. The more often you do it, the more likely you are to become good at it. The better you are at scheduling your time, the more likely your day will work out according to schedule.

DEVELOPING YOUR SCHEDULING SKILLS

To develop your scheduling skills, compare what you have scheduled for a given day with what actually happened. How did you do? What went right? What went wrong? Why? Could you have reasonably anticipated some of the unexpected events that threw your day off? Should you have used contingency plans during different parts of the day? If things were out of control, was it your fault or someone else's? For example, were you late getting into the office or did you take too long for lunch? Begin to examine the difference between how you think the day ought to go and how the day actually goes and you will develop more skill at determining how to make things happen right. You will automatically accomplish more each day.

The key to scheduling is the belief that there is a time and a place for everything. Scheduling allows you to consider the appropriate time and place ahead of time, while you still have an opportunity to do something about it. Scheduling allows you to operate purposefully rather than randomly. You are likely to get more accomplished in less time and have more time left over for yourself to do other things that are also important.

But remember, you cannot control everything. Many things are simply beyond your control. If you can consistently control 25 to 50 percent of your day, you will be in the upper echelon of effective managers. If you fail to control whatever time you can, you will diminish your effectiveness. Whether you can take charge of eight hours a day or one hour a day is, in a sense, irrelevant. The idea is to control whatever time you can control. Remember, too, that you can manage much more of your day than you realize. Scheduling helps you to determine exactly how much of your day is controllable and helps you discover ways to approach time with authority—to achieve the results you desire.

9
Eliminating Time Wasters

YOU KNOW TIME is important. You have adopted a systematic approach to time management. You have analyzed your time habits, clarified your objectives, established priorities, planned carefully for appropriate results, and scheduled your activities.

But things go wrong. Just when you begin work on your top-priority task, your assistant knocks on the door requesting help with a complex itemization. By the time he leaves, you and he have been interrupted three times by your telephone. At least one call requires action on your part within the next two hours. Your secretary informs you that a special meeting has been called for 2:00 P.M., and as you head out the door you notice the growing pile of paper in your in-basket. Yes, you believe in a systematic approach, but the system just doesn't seem to work!

Successful time management depends on more than a carefully planned system. You must also take positive action against the time wasters that threaten to destroy your plans. By improving your planning techniques *and* eliminating many of your time wasters, you take a double-barreled approach to getting on top of your job and using your time effectively. The formula for good time management looks like this:

Systematic time planning + positive action against time
wasters = effective time utilization

If either part of the formula is neglected, you will not be successful in your attempts to manage time properly.

You must also accept the fact that even if you are a paragon of self-discipline, you will not achieve total time control. When you work with other people, you must resign yourself to their unpredictable actions, which create demands for you at inopportune times. You can't control everything. The trick is to accept the noncontrollable and control the controllable.

WHAT IS A TIME WASTER?

What is a time waster? There is no absolute definition. Life would be easier for all of us if we could make a list of 100 guaranteed time wasters followed by 100 guaranteed ways to eliminate them— uncomplicated by people, events, and human frailty. But that's not the way it is. Time control depends on you (a unique individual), your environment (a unique situation), and what you're trying to accomplish with your time (a unique objective). You waste your time whenever you spend it on something less important when you could be spending it on something more important. Importance is determined by measuring your activities against your objectives.

Time wasters can be divided into two groups: external and internal. External time wasters are generated by someone or something else. They often involve co-workers, family, salespeople, and customers. They sometimes involve paperwork, traffic jams, and electrical blackouts. Many external time wasters are beyond your control.

Internal time wasters come from within. They are often difficult to identify and conquer. Many people spend years passing the blame for their time problems to others when the true source of their dilemma is internal. Procrastination, socializing, lack of planning, and an inability to say no are examples of internal time wasters. As one man lamented when he looked in the mirror on his forty-third birthday, "I have finally met the enemy, and he is me."

Everyone wastes time. Even the most self-disciplined people have wasted moments now and then. But there is a difference between people who consistently produce good results and people who don't. The producers manage to hold their wasted time (whether internally or externally generated) to a minimum. They are able to control a larger percentage of the time killers than their frustrated, underachieving colleagues.

Careful identification of your objectives is the first step to conquering your time wasters. Without objectives, there is no such thing as time waste because any activity is as good as any other activity. It is when you have objectives, when you know what you want to accomplish, that wasting time is an important issue. What is a waste of time for one person may be a valuable use of time for another person.

Nearly everyone wastes at least two hours each day. Furthermore, few people attempt to identify their time wasters. They "don't have the time" to find the source of their problem. Even when they sense that an activity is a time problem, they seldom analyze the situation carefully. Often they simply find a scapegoat. It's simpler to pass quick judgment than to define the problem, analyze the facts, and develop good solutions. Scapegoating only leads to additional time-consuming problems.

Many people do not truly want to identify their time wasters, because eliminating them often involves change. Change does not come easily. Generally, it requires a review of personal habits followed by a lot of hard work. Most people prefer to maintain the status quo, no matter how annoying or irritating it may be. They cite numerous reasons why things *can't* be changed and continue to complain about their problems. But they will not take the positive steps necessary to reduce or eliminate the problems.

A SYSTEMATIC APPROACH TO ELIMINATING TIME WASTERS

A systematic analysis of all your activities is the best approach to eliminating time wasters. How does each activity contribute to the objectives you are trying to accomplish? Which activities are a waste of time? Which ones are more important than others? This type of analysis will give you important insights. You will begin to discover the real reasons your time seems to disappear into thin air. A systematic approach to eliminating time wasters involves five steps.

1. *Obtain good data.* It is often necessary to collect information in order to understand the nature of a time waster. For instance, it's not enough just to realize that drop-in visitors are a problem. Before you can act on the problem, you need to know how many people drop in, how often, for what purposes, under what conditions. Objective data will often uncover the patterns and help clarify the true causes. Sometimes, too, you may be misperceiving the problem. You need to verify that what you think is a time waster is indeed a source of misspent time. This verification can best be done by keeping a time log. (See Chapter 5.)

2. *Identify probable causes.* Take each time waster one at a time

and list all its probable causes. Is the source of the problem your environment—the things other people do, or don't do, that end up wasting your time? Or is the problem you—the things you bring on yourself that waste your time? The culprit will be you more often than you want to believe. As you analyze your time problems, you will realize that even when others are wasting your time much of the blame can be traced to your actions, habits, and shortcomings.

3. *Develop possible solutions.* Take each cause, one at a time, and write down all the ways you might solve the problem. Many of the causes will carry the seeds of their own solution. If you can't think of solutions, ask others to help you. Be as creative and innovative as you can. You might even air your concern on an office bulletin board and encourage "brainstorming" by everyone in the office. Ask your co-workers to write down any suggestions they can think of and tack them to the board. Build on others' ideas.

4. *Select the most feasible solution.* Evaluate all the possible solutions for each cause. Which solution is best for you, in your situation? In each case, pick the solution that is most likely to be effective and develop your plan of action.

5. *Implement the solution.* When you find the best solutions, take action now. Nothing will happen until you act, and act in a positive manner. Be sure to evaluate your progress. Is the solution working? Don't be afraid to modify your plan if necessary.

You will discover that this systematic approach works: If you follow the steps carefully and act on your solution—knowing that it is the best possible solution for you—you will make rapid progress toward greater time control.

We all like to believe that we are unique, unparalleled in this universe. Our job is unprecedented as well, for our unique personality gives our position a special slant. We sometimes rebel at time management suggestions, claiming, "You don't understand—no one has a job like mine!" Indeed, we are unique; that's what makes time management so interesting—and so difficult. There just are no absolute guarantees when it comes to identifying time wasters or solving them.

After years of work in time management, however, we have discovered that managers do have certain time-wasting problems in common. What follows is affectionately known as Douglass' Dirty Dozen—twelve of the most frequently encountered time wasters. Each time waster will be introduced through a short vignette that illustrates the problem. Following the story, you will find suggestions for eliminating the time waster.

Your ability and willingness to utilize the suggestions will depend on many things, including your office environment, your position in the organization, your years of employment, and your ambitions. But one of the most important variables will be your level of assertiveness. By assertive we mean (in agreement with Webster) being "persistently positive and confident." An action that seems impossibly brash to a minimally assertive individual may make good sense to a highly assertive person.

Therefore, to help you identify the suggestions most consistent with your personality and lifestyle, we have devised a simple "asstiveness quotient" for many of the time wasters discussed. We do not pretend that this quotient is indisputable. When it seemed appropriate, we merely grouped some of our suggested time tips into three categories. From our experiences with thousands of people and their time problems, we believe this classification will help you develop your own personalized approach.

Nonassertive people will find acceptable time-saving ideas listed under Quotient 1. There is little risk involved in taking these actions. Still, if the suggestions are implemented, much time can be gained every week.

Quotient 2 suggestions require a more assertive personality. Though not aggressive suggestions, they do require a willingness to accept a little negative feedback. These suggestions should be used in addition to those listed under Quotient 1 for greater time control.

Quotient 3 suggestions require a highly assertive personality. As you read each suggestion in this category, ask yourself if you would feel comfortable implementing it. If your reaction is "I could never do that," don't do it! But if you think the idea would be useful to you, try it. You may get the results you want, save a great deal of time, and become more productive.

Consider each idea carefully; give each suggestion a fair chance. Think in positive terms—how the general idea *can* work in your situation. Use the five steps for eliminating time wasters discussed earlier to customize the suggestions to your routine. When you merge the time techniques suggested with your job knowledge and efforts, those time wasters won't stand a chance!

TIME WASTER NO. 1: THE DROP-IN VISITOR

"Hi, Jake, what's new?"

It was him again. "Doesn't he have any work to do?" Jake thought. Without glancing up from his monthly report, Jake knew just what Ben would look like when he did: His left shoulder would be supporting his body against the door frame. His right hand would be cradling a steaming cup of black coffee while his left hand pulled at a strand of unruly hair. A lazy smile would be the focal point of his face.

"Whatcha up to?" he asked again.

"Hi, Ben, trying to get this monthly report pulled together," Jake said as he finally looked into Ben's curious eyes. "What's with you?"

"Oh, I had to take some tab runs down to Jefferson's office. Say, wasn't that some storm we had last night? Haven't seen one like it in a couple of years." He moved into the room and was standing in front of Jake's desk.

"Yes, it was something," Jake replied as he eyed Ben's movement while simultaneously looking for the West Mill summary.

"Yea, I shoveled for 45 minutes before I could get my car out this morning. Maggie has to go to the doctor this afternoon, so I thought I'd better get that snow cleared away." He took a sip of his coffee and pulled at that strand of hair again.

"Oh, no," Jake thought, "he's headed toward that green chair!"

"Did I tell you, Jake, about the pain she's been having in her left knee? It's been something! We're really worried about it," Ben continued as he lowered himself into Jake's green chair and took another sip of coffee.

"Hope everything will be OK," Jake responded as he searched for the North Mill summary.

"Thanks," Ben replied. "You know, it all began about three years ago when we were on our hiking trip in the Grand Canyon." He settled back into the chair, propped a wet boot on the corner of the end table, and tugged again at his hair.

Jake gave up. He knew he was in for a review of Maggie's medical history, the snowstorms from 1967 to the present, and a tour of the Grand Canyon. The monthly report? Well, maybe he'd get to it later in the afternoon.

People interruptions are a part of your job if your office routine is like most office routines. In addition to a considerable number of interruptions generated from outside the office, superiors and subordinates place constant, usually unplanned, demands on your time and attention. Consider these suggestions.

Assertiveness Quotient 1

Work on your attitude. Instead of being upset when an interruption occurs, think of it simply as part of the job. You'll be less frustrated and better able to stay in control of the situation.

You can't eliminate all your interruptions. Many are necessary, and some are even important. But if you do everything you can to keep them short, you'll solve half your problems. Examine the physical arrangement of your office. The arrangement may either discourage drop-in visitors or encourage them to consume more of your time. Remove the extra chairs. If your unexpected visitors never get seated, they will be less likely to linger. One manager correctly observed that the length of any meeting is directly related to the comfort level of the participant's chairs. No chair, therefore, encourages quick decisions.

While you're removing your extra guest chairs, rearrange the furniture. Move your desk so you do not face the flow of traffic. Your "front" is more inviting than your "side" or "back." Hang a large clock where it can easily be seen by you and your drop-in guests. The clock will serve as a reminder to all concerned that time is passing quickly. A casual glance at the clock will serve notice to your visitors that you are acutely aware of the time.

After you have removed those chairs and repositioned your desk, take one final decorative action in the name of time preservation. Remove all the interesting conversation pieces from sight. Beautiful photographs and delicate oil paintings are interesting, usually invite comments, and lead to lengthy discussions. Family pictures do the same thing. By displaying the smiling faces of your spouse and children, you give your visitor a glimpse of your personal life. You have encouraged comment, for most people know that positive observations about family are pleasantly received.

Meet people outside your office whenever possible. Use the hallways, reception area, or conference room. There's less chance for small talk in these places. If people call to say they must see you, volunteer to go to their office instead. You'll have more control over when to leave.

Of course, in some situations the physical niceties of an office are part of your business procedure. A lawyer, for example, may want to encourage small talk to put clients at ease. You alone can judge the value of such pleasantries. The important point is to know what your objectives are. Does the arrangement of your office help or hinder you in your effort to accomplish your goals?

Assertiveness Quotient 2

When planning your day, be sure to allow time for interruptions. Don't schedule activities back to back all day long so one interruption will completely throw you off schedule. Establish priorities, extract unimportant activities from your day, and schedule only valued items. On some days, of course, you will still be heavily booked, but on a good many days you will find some "breathing" time. Turn to your lesser priorities whenever time allows. If you don't get to them because of drop-in visitors, your day and your schedule won't be totally ruined.

Once your drop-in associate is in your office, do not add to the conversation unnecessarily. Do not offer personal advice, elaborate apologies, or lengthy explanations. If your guest offers you a compliment, a simple "thank you" will suffice. Forget about being right and winning arguments; you never really win what you think you win anyway. Don't try to analyze the actions of others; there are always factors involved that you know nothing about, so your conclusions may be wrong anyway. Be polite to your guest but do nothing to prolong the interruption. If you are sincerely interested in continuing the discussion with your visitor, set a luncheon date at a time convenient for both of you.

Learn to close your door. A closed door will provide a small roadblock to those wanting to intrude on your time. Most people will knock before entering. If they don't, ask them to do so the next time. The act of knocking will give the potential visitor a brief moment of second thought: "Do I really need to bother this person now?" Some people will decide to hold off until later—and you have successfully gained some time. Many people work better in an isolated environment. A closed door provides this advantage as well.

A physically closed door does not necessarily rule out an "open-door" policy. If you have instituted an open-door policy in your office, you can continue it even though your door is physically closed. You should, however, take the time to explain exactly what your open-door policy is. It is not a standing invitation for people to interrupt you when the mood strikes. To allow others to constantly control how you spend your time is a sure way to get very little accomplished. An open-door policy means that you are always accessible to those who really need you. This holds true whether your office door is open or closed.

You can modify your open-door policy in two ways: First, close your door *occasionally*. Establish a regular time when you will not be disturbed. Second, schedule regular times to see key people and staff. Much of the drop-in visitor problem is created by staff members who routinely need your advice. Have staff members save all items for your attention and go over them at one time. Show them the same respect and do not create a constant time problem for them. And be sure to keep all appointments made with staff.

Ask your subordinates to state their problems in writing, along with three or four ideas for solving each problem. Do the same when you take a problem to your superior. This simple action will help focus the discussion, clarify the issue, and set the course for a good problem-solving meeting. Set a time limit for these get-togethers.

Assertiveness Quotient 3

Keep two kinds of people out of your life; the ones who make unreasonable demands on you and the ones who constantly try to take advantage of you. This is not always easy to do. Begin by gathering written data that will verify or disprove your feelings about who these people are. List as many ways as you can think of to control the interruptions and choose your best course of action from the list. Initially this takes time, but the payoff is worth the investment.

Be candid when someone asks, "Have you got a minute?" Learn to say no. Only the most assertive people can say no easily. Since "no" is the most time-saving word in your vocabulary, however, you should strive to use it whenever appropriate. Each situation, of course, is a special case, but the nine guidelines below should help you.

1. *You can say no to the boss*. This suggestion depends on you, your boss, and your relationship. But don't automatically assume that your job will be in jeopardy if you question a request. Many superiors are eager for you to do a good job and will respect your decision not to overcommit.

2. *Develop priorities for the work you must do*. Decide whether an interruption is more or less important than what you had planned to

do. With priorities determined ahead of time, you will have more information to help you decide how to spend your time.

3. *Let others know that you are willing to help whenever you have the time.* When your work schedule permits, take the time to help others with their concerns and establish the reputation of being cooperative. When possible, give the person requesting your help an alternative idea.

4. *Lose the rabbit habit.* People who tackle any problem that comes before them are known as "rabbit chasers." They take off in any direction that beckons to them. This is a poor work habit and leads to ineffective time management.

5. *Level with people when you say no.* Let them know why a refusal was the most appropriate response in this particular circumstance.

6. *Learn to identify the danger signals when additional work is about to be passed to you.* For example, as soon as you hear the phrase "We have a problem," realize that the other person is about to transfer most or all of his or her concerns to you. Don't be overly defensive, but be sure the final responsibility remains where it belongs.

7. *Don't try to solve people's problems for them.* If you do, you only guarantee that people will bring you more problems in the future. Your function is to train your subordinates to handle problems themselves.

8. *Make sure you are not "ego tripping" when you attempt to handle all requests.* Does it make you feel good to have subordinates ask for your help? Of course we all have an ego, but how much time are you willing to sacrifice to feed it? Also, are you being fair to your subordinates when you fail to develop them adequately?

9. *Don't feel guilty when you say no.* Use the facts you have acquired to make the best possible decision. If the decision leads to a "no" response, accept it. At another time you may give a "yes" response. And remember, by saying yes to requests that should be turned down, you have said no, directly or indirectly, to something else more important.

Ask yourself if you *honestly* want to get your work done. Are you really procrastinating? Did the office "Ben" walk by at a convenient time to save you from getting on with your task? Do you find the work difficult and feel uncertain about where to start? Remember, it takes two to make a conversation. It takes only one to stop it. Practice being the one to stop when more important priorities are calling for your attention.

TIME WASTER NO. 2: TELEPHONES

Jane heard her phone ringing down the hall as she stepped into the office out of the rain. Maybe if she hurried she could catch it. She tossed her lunch and briefcase into a hall chair and raced past Charlie's office. "Why is the house key always on top when I'm at the office?" she wondered. Her fingers finally separated office key 234 from the rest. She got the key into the lock, and opened the door—just as the phone stopped ringing. "Another Monday morning off to a good start," Jane thought. "The beginning of another week with my friend the phone."

Throughout the week, Jane had more and more reason to resent that demanding little instrument sitting on her desk. It always seemed to ring when she had a client in her office, when she had an important report to finish, or when she was balancing her books. On the other hand, when she called out, no one seemed to be in. "If only I could throw that phone off the Spencer Street Bridge," Jane mused. "My job would be a snap. My work would be done and I would be at peace!"

The ironic truth about the telephone is that it can be your biggest helper as well as your biggest time waster. It can save a great deal of time if you use it appropriately. You can minimize the troublesome side of telephones by remembering a few important points.

Assertiveness Quotient 1

Evaluate your phone system to see if it's outdated. Many modern time-saving instruments are now available. Find out what steps are needed to get your system changed. A modernized system will save your company money in the long run. Remember that time is money too, and a streamlined system will save hours that were formerly consumed by bad connections, disconnections, or busy lines.

Use a phone log to identify people who call you frequently. Each time you receive a call, record the data, the caller's name, and the time. Take special note of the subject matter. Did you talk about the weather? A forthcoming vacation? Whatever the subject, make a note of it. Once you have identified the people who call you frequently, consider a special arrangement with them. Ask them to call you at a certain time of the day or meet them for lunch.

Screen and group your outgoing calls. Set aside a particular time each day to make three to five calls. Grouping similar activities is always a big time saver. With telephone calls, the results are especially gratifying.

Ask the people you call regularly for times when they are usually available as well as for times when they are always busy (for example, Monday morning meetings from 10 to 12). Record their availability time next to their phone number so it will be easy to find. Exchange the same information with them so they can note the most likely times that you will be available for a phone conference. When you report your "availability time" to them, be certain it is during hours that are acceptable to you. A good time to make calls is just before lunch or just before the end of the day. Why? People are less likely to engage in idle chatter when something exciting is just around the corner—like lunch or going home.

Before you make a call, prepare a brief outline of what you want to say. The outline will give your conversation focus and will keep you from forgetting that one key point—the main reason you called in the first place. Developing an outline will also give you an opportunity to think through your conversation. It will provide a logical plan that has been carefully considered by 50 percent of the people involved. With odds that good, your phone conversation will often be a useful time expenditure.

Assertiveness Quotient 2

Forgo the social small talk that accompanies 90 percent of phone calls. Never talk about the weather. Most people are bored by the weather yet they talk about it at least ten times a day. It always snows during the winter in Michigan and rains in Atlanta in the spring. Nothing's new. Small talk has a purpose, but question whether or not it's appropriate with each call you make.

When you have covered all the parts of your phone outline and have answered any questions from the person on the other end, bring your call to a prompt close. If the other party seems to be "drifting" in his or her conversation, serve notice that you are ready to hang up. "Before we hang up, Chris, I'd like to . . ." is a tactful way to indicate that you're finished with the conversation.

Your secretary can be the answer to many of your phone problems. Many managers follow an "answer your own phone" policy. While this egalitarian approach may be admirable, it usually wastes a great deal of time. The higher a person is in the organization, the greater the cost of that wasted time. Remember, though, that if others are to answer your telephone, they must be properly trained.

Otherwise, you will end up wasting additional time. You must work with subordinates to develop a telephone methodology. Which questions should be asked? How should they be asked? When and how should calls be referred? Which questions can subordinates answer themselves? Your local telephone company may be able to assist you here. Many companies will send trained personnel to your office (free of charge) to instruct your employees in effective use of the phone.

Assertiveness Quotient 3

Sometimes a caller will go on, and on, and on—and say nothing. Assertive action is called for if you hope to minimize your time loss.

You might lie a little and tell the caller you have a meeting in two minutes in the next building. You can even disconnect the caller while you are talking. Conversations seldom call for such drastic measures, but for some people subtle hints are not enough. Do not worry about offending people. Most people are not offended as easily as you believe. You are probably far more concerned about your actions than they are; they are not focusing on what you do. Don't be rude, but be confident and firm.

TIME WASTER NO. 3: PAPERWORK—READING AND REPORTS

The MacMillian family was tired of waiting for Dad. The picnic lunch, blankets, swimsuits, and beach balls were in the trunk and the kids were fighting in the back seat. Patty looked at her children, her watch, and the back door—hoping to see Wayne come through it.

Inside his home office, Wayne was hurrying. He grabbed the materials for his monthly report and the Johnson account as well. While he was at it, he threw two books on office procedures into his briefcase. Maybe he'd get to them on the beach; he certainly didn't have time at the office.

Patty watched her husband as he maneuvered his briefcase, files, and books through the door and hurried to the car. She shook her head.
"Might as well get something done," Wayne explained. "It's not that hard to combine business with pleasure!"

There are always too many journals to read and too many reports to write. To get through the volumes of paper requiring your time, consider the following ideas. How can they fit into your daily routine?

Assertiveness Quotient 1

In *Getting Organized* Stephanie Winston states that only three useful things can be done with a piece of paper: (1) it can be thrown away, (2) it can be acted upon as required, or (3) it can be saved for reading or action at a more appropriate time. There are also several useless things that can be done with paper. For example, paper can be shuffled and reshuffled from pile to pile with no evaluation. Winston's crucial point is that you must act on each piece of paper or nothing will happen. You should form the habit of making a decision each time you touch a piece of paper. You will soon discover that these brief decisions can save a great deal of time.

Question the value of all reading material you receive regularly. If the publications no longer serve a useful purpose, cancel them. It's useless to keep stacking piles in the corner to read "when you have the time." Scan your reading material for clues to important articles. Review the table of contents. Read summations when available. Look through the index. Read the first lines of key paragraphs. When you write reports, use short, simple, clear sentences. It takes more time to express your thoughts in complicated, erudite words and lengthy paragraphs. Long reports are a double time waster, for they also take longer to read. Say what needs to be said—but don't obscure your points in fancy verbiage.

Plan what you're going to say before you say it. Taking the time to prepare a good outline is always worthwhile. Prepare an outline even if you dictate your reports instead of writing them out. Once you have completed a good outline, 70 percent of your work is finished.

Give serious thought to using dictating equipment if you do not currently do so. Many people have been writing out their reports for so long that they are convinced it's much quicker to continue in their old habits than to try something new. Give one of the modern, portable dictating machines a chance. In a short time, you will find the machine almost indispensable. When you discover how much time it saves, you will become a believer. You'll wonder how you got anything done before you discovered your handy "portable brain."

Assertiveness Quotient 2

Have your secretary monitor trade journals and newspapers for items you should see. There are two advantages to this approach: Your secretary will gain a greater understanding of your business and at the same time will be helping you. She will become a greater help to you as her knowledge of your field increases.

Give your secretary careful instructions on screening your mail. Have her throw away useless items before they cross your desk. You will also find that some materials can be rerouted to a qualified assistant or, in some cases, to a person more appropriate than you. Some questions and reading materials are better handled by other people, and these items need not cross your desk.

Look into a speed-learning course or a speed-reading course. For the course nearest you, contact your local university. If you're not interested in a course, consider the following tips:

1. Increase your reading concentration by putting on earphones, turning on loud background music, and learning to zero in on the page—blocking out unwanted noise.
2. Stop saying words aloud or chewing gum while you read.
3. Use your finger as a guide, moving it faster and faster down the page.

Read only the index in magazines and books; do not read the articles or contents at all. Dictate a summary of the key topics. Your secretary can then transfer your summary to reference cards and file them by subject matter. In the future, if you ever need quick information about a particular topic, refer to your subject cards. At that time, read the article when it has a special meaning and purpose for you.

Distribute reading materials to your co-workers and exchange information with them. In this way, you can reap the benefits of the information without doing all the reading yourself. Make sure, however, that the reading materials are useful to your group.

A periodic office bulletin can also be valuable. Have someone who is skilled at condensing information read through all the materials and prepare abstracts for the office bulletin. This system will relieve you of the pressure to read everything and will point you to topics that you may wish to pursue.

If you receive a large number of reports, consider having some of them taped instead of written. Many employees would prefer this form of reporting, and a taped report may be more convenient for you. You can listen to the tapes while dressing or driving to work or at other odd moments.

Before you begin writing a report yourself, determine its purpose. Is it to influence or to inform? Do not write all reports in the same manner. Once you have determined the reason for the report, decide how much time it deserves. Act accordingly. Spend high-quality time on items that lead to top-priority goals. If you've been asked to "make a note of your ideas for the file," dictate your response quickly into your dictating machine and forget it.

Don't make revisions in the name of perfectionism if the added benefit is small. If it *really* must be perfect, take the time; but often quick, accurate information is more important than a flawlessly presented report.

Assertiveness Quotient 3

Ask yourself, "Is this report needed?" If it is no longer serving a useful purpose, determine who has the power to discontinue it. If it's you, discontinue it immediately. If it's a superior, present him or her with your reason for calling it "useless." Suggest a more expedient alternative. You won't always be successful in getting the report discontinued, but in some instances you will. If you're sure the report is a waste of time, getting it discontinued will be well worth the effort. If you're not sure, don't issue the report and wait to see who hollers.

TIME WASTER NO. 4: PAPERWORK—LETTERS AND MEMOS

Wayne MacMillian turned off The Tonight Show, *scratched his head, yawned, and collapsed at the foot of his bed. He glanced at his wife, peacefully sleeping, and wished that he too were cavorting in dreamland. He thought of the piles of paper clustered around his eight-year-old briefcase. His break was over; he had to get back to those letters, for tomorrow a new batch would arrive with the morning mail.*

Perry Como had made a rare guest appearance on The Tonight Show *and Wayne grimaced as he recalled a little tune from Perry's old show: "Letters. We get letters. We get stacks and stacks of letters!"*

Yes, letters. They seemed to demand nearly all of Wayne's time and there was no denying that they were important. After all, he was in the "people business"—and that meant keeping up with all the correspondence that came to him. But he didn't have time to get to it at the office; there were just too many things to do. So Wayne carried a briefcase home with him regularly. He considered it part of his job.

At 2:00 A.M. he could take no more. He had three more letters to go, but his sagging eyelids would not cooperate. Those letters would just have to wait. Wayne staggered into the bedroom, feeling guilty about the unfinished work on the dining room table. He was asleep by 2:05. He didn't get a good night's sleep, however. In his nightmare he was drowning in a pool of letters, letters, letters!

Correspondence overload can get the best of anyone. Remember, however, that we sometimes bring the overload on ourselves. When we write a memo or a letter, we gain an immediate sense of closure—a finished product. Other tasks do not have as much closure; the finish line is farther off. Therefore, instead of tackling a more time-consuming task, we write another letter. This is not to diminish the value of letter writing but rather to indicate that it is often a form of procrastination—a way of putting off other activities. Letters are usually important enough that we can rationalize writing them before we do anything else.

There is no need to suffer from a "nightmare of letter writing." Determine the importance of each letter you must handle and respond accordingly. Do not handle each letter in the same way. After establishing priorities for your letters, consider the following suggestions.

Assertiveness Quotient 1

Develop the in-today, out-tomorrow habit. Take immediate action to avoid letter backlog. Of course, there will be some occasions when a letter will take longer than a day to process, but these special cases can be handled faster when they remain "special cases"—and not normal practice of continual delays. Your in-today, out-tomorrow habit will come more easily if you handle each letter or memo only once before moving it on. Never set it aside without taking some positive action.

Write your letters with the receiver in mind, using a clear, concise, fact-oriented style. Verbose letters, with long and complicated sentences, take a lot of time to read as well as to write. Often they are not read at all. There is nothing wrong with one-paragraph letters. In some instances, one sentence will convey your message. Think before you write. What are the points you need to cover? A simple outline will give direction to your writing. Time is always saved by planning.

Assertiveness Quotient 2

Use the telephone more and write less. The phone is often quicker. Sometimes an immediate response by phone will enable you to complete a contact with a simple follow-up letter. Without the phone call, you may have to write a letter, wait for the reply, read and answer a second letter, and wait again for a response.

Make handwritten responses in the margins of some letters you receive. In many cases an instant response in the margin is just as useful as a carefully prepared letter. Some companies use a stamp that reads, "Handwritten message—so we can respond to you faster."

A dictating machine is as useful for letter writing as it is for report writing. A well-trained secretary can transcribe dictated letters quickly and can fill in the address, date, and enclosures through a quick review of the files.

Use form letters and form paragraphs for routine correspondence. Of course, form letters are not as personal as individualized letters, but they are appropriate in certain instances. Remember, too, that with modern typing equipment form letters can be personalized. The point is that a quick response is often worth more than a carefully developed, time-consuming reply.

Spend some time developing a number of good form paragraphs. Identify them by number or letter, and cite them as follows: "Dear Mr. Johnson: Paragraph 2. Paragraph 5." Your secretary can readily prepare the letter with this code. Remember, only your staff need know you are using form paragraphs.

Your secretary can also handle much of your correspondence. Consider having stationery printed with your secretary's name on it. This action will relieve you of some of your letter-writing chores and will give your secretary more responsibility. Additional responsibility often enhances a secretary's performance and job satisfaction.

Assertiveness Quotient 3

Consider using the simplified letter form suggested by the Administrative Management Society. (See Figure 16.) It has begun to catch on in many organizations. Motion analysis of the typing alone on a 96-word letter indicates more than a 10 percent time saving. Your secretary will benefit from this change and your reader will as well.

With the new, simplified form, every line starts at the left margin. This minimizes the use of the space bar and the tabulator key. The body of the letter is prepared in block paragraphs with the indentation omitted. The omission of the salutation solves the problem of addressing a person as Ms., Miss, Mrs., or Mr. The new letter is easy to read as well as easy to prepare. The addition of a "subject

Figure 16. Simplified letter format.

Old Letter Format　　　　　　　　　New Letter Format

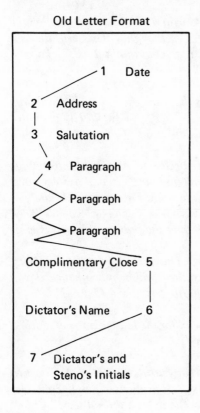
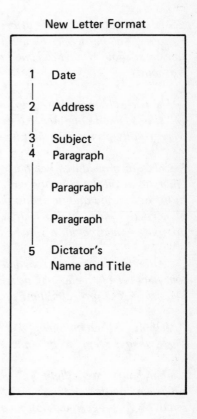

line" helps the reader categorize the letter in his or her mind—as well as in the files.

Consider these time-saving points for filing copies of your letters. You can diminish the number of papers in your file if you make the carbon copy of your reply on the back of each letter you receive. Not only will space be saved, but your response will be permanently attached to the original letter. Put a destruction date on all correspondence before filing it. This simple act will facilitate your file-cleaning efforts and thus keep those important items in your files readily available.

TIME WASTER NO. 5: TRAVEL

"Universal Flight 103 for Houston is now ready for boarding at Terminal 3, Gate 12. All passengers are requested to check in for seat assignment."

Al Jones glanced quickly at Fred Martin as they hurried through the airport. "Another week, another trip," Al thought. "Oh, well, that's a salesman's job. Hope Fred and I can reach our quota. Last week was a washout!"

The two salesmen slowed down as they saw the line in front of Gate 12. "Looks like 15 minutes to the check-in desk," Al said. His estimates were usually pretty accurate; he had had a lot of practice.

Check-in procedures behind them, Fred and Al settled into lounge chairs to await the boarding call. Each had purchased a mystery novel at the newsstand and turned to the first page. Fifteen minutes later, Al glanced nervously at his watch. Just as he began to wonder when boarding would begin, a voice came over the public address system:

"Attention passengers scheduled for Universal Flight 103 for Houston. Because of mechanical problems, there will be a two-hour delay in departure. The projected time of departure is now 4:15 P.M."

"Oh, no," Fred moaned. "Let's head for the lounge and get a drink. There always seems to be some delay!"

Four hours later Flight 103 was ready to leave Chicago. The two salesmen boarded and took their seats. "How about a game of gin, ole' buddy?" Al suggested. "Let's not let the day be a total loss!"

Fred agreed and a slightly less than vigorous game began. By the time they arrived in Houston, gathered their luggage, stood in line for a taxi, and waited for a porter to get them to their rooms, they were exhausted. Al sighed as he unpacked his suitcase, thinking about all the work that would be piled on his desk when he returned to the home office. "All that plus the work from this trip! How can they expect one guy to do it all? Airport delays, taxis, suitcases, hotels, reports, and more reports. What's a nice guy like me doing in a climb-the-wall job like this?"

People who travel in their job, particularly those who travel frequently, can save both time and energy if they learn to view their trips as "part of the job." Many people still consider these jaunts quasi-vacations. They are disappointed when the trips are not much fun and produce additional work as well. Once you honestly accept the airport, the plane, the taxi, and the hotel as part of your office, you will be able to get something accomplished while you travel. You need no longer waste those hours in transit.

Assertiveness Quotient 1

Before you leave your office, analyze your work to discover which tasks can most easily be done while you travel. Remember, too, that many of your most time-consuming tasks can be broken down into smaller steps; these steps will often be suitable for travel time activities. Listening to tapes is a valuable way to spend your time while traveling. Tapes have become a major industry. There are tapes available on all subjects of personal and professional concern. Some cassette machines are small enough to carry in your pocket.

Always take a small dictating machine with you on a trip. With this convenient device you can dictate reports, action notes, memos, and letters for your secretary to transcribe later. Use the newer dictating machines that block out background noises. You will be able to clearly dictate even in jet planes, and dictate all reports and correspondence generated by the trip before you return home. Consider the paperwork an integral part of the trip. Do it as you go along.

When your other work is completed, go over some of that secondary reading material you've been meaning to review. Many of the articles are short and can be read during brief waiting periods.

If you travel alone, take advantage of your opportunity for privacy. Learn to tune out travel noises while you focus on your most important business concerns. You will not be interrupted, no phone will ring, and you will not even have to speak to another person unless you happen to run into an old friend at the airport. Learn to utilize this unique "quiet time."

Accept the fact that there will be lines, delays, bad weather, and traffic jams. If you anticipate these problems, you will not waste time and energy, or lose your good humor, when they occur. If you occasionally have a trip without calamities, all the better. Your attitude is a main ingredient in using travel time productively.

Above all, remember to follow good time management concepts. Use a time log to determine what wastes the greatest amount of your time on trips, list solutions for overcoming these problems, and implement your best ideas. Identify your goals for each trip and list the subgoals that will lead you to achievement. Remember to plan your time around your scheduled activities for maximum accomplishment while you're away.

Assertiveness Quotient 2

Learn to forgo the fun and games that often accompany business trips. The steak, salad, and red wine are probably just as good in your hotel as they are in that special restaurant across town and no better than they are back home. Schedule room service often for your meals so you won't have to wait on breakfast, lunch, and dinner lines at the sandwich shops. Many hotels allow you to plan your meals ahead of time for delivery to your room.

Forgoing the fun and games may sound ridiculous to some travelers. Many executives feel that this is the best part of the trip. "So what's wrong with a little happy time, anyway?" Nothing's wrong with it, if that's what you feel is the best use of your time. Agreed, on many trips the cocktail or dinner hour is a vital time when deals are made and plans developed. By all means, continue to keep these appointments.

Your objective is effective use of your time. Question the added value of those nights on the town. Are they worth the time you spend? Would you be happier with yourself the next morning if you had completed a demanding report, watched the news, and gotten a good night's sleep? Don't feel obligated to do the town simply because you're out of town.

Assertiveness Quotient 3

Your ability to say no and mean it has a great deal to do with how well you control the use of your time. Peer pressure often forces many travelers out in the evening when they are tired after a full day's work. Saying no to a travel companion who wants to play cards is difficult, but after you've refused once or twice it will seem the natural thing to do. A new habit will take over—a habit that is more productive and useful to you. (Chapter 13 examines many special concerns for travelers.)

TIME WASTER NO. 6: MEETINGS

Jack Moynihan listened halfheartedly to what Hal Davidson was saying over the phone. With a "Yes" here and an "I see" there, he was secretly wondering how he would ever complete his marketing report by the fifteenth. His secretary walked in and handed him three notes about return calls. She reminded him that he had a staff meeting in three minutes.

With a final "I'll get back to you, Hal," Jack grabbed a pen and a blank pad of paper. He might as well jot down some notes for his monthly report during the meeting; nothing else ever seemed to get done.

Tuesday morning, 10:00 A.M. The Mandax Corporation's sales managers gathered for a meeting. Every Tuesday morning. They always did.

Bob Petrosky and Alan Parsons appeared at the meeting room door just as Jack sat down next to Marge Daniels.

"Good morning, all!" said Bob. "Certainly is a gloomy day today, isn't it?" "Say, let's grab a quick cup of coffee before the meeting starts. Barb brought some danish from the new bakery this morning. Besides, we're the first and only ones ready for the meeting!"

At 10:17 they returned to the meeting room. Five or six other managers had gathered, but there were still eight unfilled chairs. Rich Zimmer, director of sales and the meeting leader, was also missing, but his secretary had sent word that he would be there in a few minutes.

At 10:29 Rich darted in the door, coffee and notes in hand. A little coffee flew onto his notes as he seated himself. "OK, let's get going, gang. We've got a few things to discuss. Alan, what's the matter with John Johnston and the Willowbrook line? He seems to be in a real mess!"

"Johnston? What d'ya mean? Is he having problems?" Parsons gazed at his boss.

"That's what I hear through the grapevine," Zimmer responded. "Can't afford incompetence! Get the facts, Alan, and we'll talk about it sometime."

Zimmer continued, "OK, we have to talk about the Mason Mill line and how to get it going. Let's hear your opinions. Will it sell?"

"I doubt it," answered Marge Daniels. "It's just too frilly for today's women. They're getting interested in modern, geometric layouts instead."

"Oh, come on, Marge," Art Van Damm interjected. "That might be true of a few women, but most are still old-fashioned at heart! I say it's a winner!"

"That's a typical comment from you, Mr. Van Damm," Marge retorted. "It shows how much you know about women today! Your idea of progress is taking 15 steps backward! When are you ever going to realize that women are beginning to take their place in this world?"

A number of people in the room began to smile at the little miniwar developing between the two co-workers. This was beginning to be fun.

"OK, Marge," Parsons rebutted, "if women are beginning to take their place in the world, who's going to stay home and have babies?"

All laughed and the game was on. It was Marge's turn to take the brunt of the comedy this week. When Rich finally got around to calling a halt to the merriment, Janet Fleming pointed out that Dave Morgan wasn't at the meeting anyway, and he was responsible for any final decision on new products. Rich answered that he would talk to Dave later.

The meeting went on and on. A few items were left and everyone agreed to "talk about them next week." Besides, it was lunch time.

Jack Moynihan returned to his office. Eight more people had tried to contact him while he was away, and his report still glared at him with only the title on page 1. Mary Gilbert had left word that she needed an answer on the Flowerwood II line by 1:00 P.M.

"What a day," Jack thought. "But then, it's a typical Tuesday morning; nothing gets done. I may as well go to lunch and try again this afternoon."

Time wasted in meetings must be approached from two points of view: those meetings you call, and those meetings you attend. For both kinds you must consider activities before, during, and after the meeting.

Assertiveness Quotient 1

When you are responsible for calling a meeting, be certain you are prepared. Know what you hope to accomplish at the meeting and try to state your goals in terms of actions to be taken rather than points to be discussed. Although there are times when discussion is necessary, meeting discussions frequently lead nowhere and disintegrate into idle chatter. If you focus on the required decision, discussion becomes a step toward that decision. If you focus on discussion, the vital decision may never be made.

Be certain you have all necessary information and papers with you. Nothing is more embarrassing than to have "center stage" at a meeting and find that you failed to gather important data. If you proceed without the forgotten material, you will handle the subject awkwardly, confuse the members of the group, and generally waste a great deal of time as you attempt to explain your point extemporaneously.

Resist any interruptions and stay on course. In any group there are always people who would rather talk about anything except the business at hand. If you prepare an agenda before the meeting and keep your "roadmap" before you, you can easily note when the group is straying off course.

Make sure that concise notes are kept on the meeting. These minutes can be an important time-saving tool. It is usually best to assign the note-taking duties to a secretary rather than to one of the meeting members. The minutes should be distributed promptly to all participants and should include the names of those responsible for actions decided upon as well as time frames for these actions. For example, following a note that "all personnel are to be informed of the new Mayberry line" should be the designated informer, "Joe Jones." It should also be noted that Joe will complete this task by "May 30th."

Assertiveness Quotient 2

Discourage unnecessary meetings. This suggestion is not as easy as it sounds, for some meetings have become "institutionalized" over the years. If a meeting is called without a definite purpose, it becomes nothing more than a social hour. Many meetings will end before they begin if you ask the crucial question, "What will be accomplished at this meeting?"

When you must hold a meeting, be certain you have a prepared agenda. Distribute it a few days before the meeting and designate those who will be called upon to discuss certain points. This approach allows you to delegate responsibility for the meeting to others and give them time to consider the important agenda points beforehand. The participants can then bring their best ideas to the meeting. The agenda should also indicate the amount of time you plan to devote to each topic. This will help keep the meeting on schedule and give participants an opportunity to judge how detailed you expect their contribution to be. You will waste their time if they believe a one-hour presentation is required when you had a ten-minute summation in mind.

Set a time limit for all meetings. Start and end at the times indicated on your agenda. You will find you can accomplish just as much in far less time than you have in the past. Don't wait for everyone to show up before starting. If you delay a meeting by waiting for stragglers, you guarantee that people will be late in the future. They will plan on being tardy, for experience has shown them that your meetings never start on time.

Choose the participants carefully. Invite only those whose attendance is necessary. Extra people create extra confusion and increase the likelihood that your agenda will go astray. Be certain that all important decision makers are present. It is a waste of time, for example, to hold a meeting for final approval on a project when a key supervisor is away on a business trip. It is difficult to get everyone together at the same time, but realize that time-consuming problems are inevitable if crucial members are absent.

Be certain all participants know what contribution is expected of them. An agenda distributed before the meeting will serve this purpose. Allow people to come and go as their contribution is needed. There is no point in having people sit all the way through a meeting if only a few minutes of it are relevant to them.

Don't make people too comfortable during the meeting. In other words, don't give people two-hour chairs if you intend to keep them only 30 minutes. The length of a meeting is directly related to the comfort of the chairs and the amount of coffee available. You might even try holding some stand-up meetings. At the end of the meeting, present a short critique. Review the main points and consider how the meeting could have been better.

Analyze each of your meetings from time to time. Are the right people attending? Are too many people attending? Are people prepared? Is the meeting held at the proper time, in the proper place? How could your meetings be improved? Develop your skills as a meeting leader. Attend a seminar. Read a book. Practice new approaches. Experiment a little. You will quickly be rewarded for even the smallest effort to make your meetings more worthwhile.

Assertiveness Quotient 3

As frequently as possible, make responsible decisions without meetings. Gather necessary data and suggestions from your staff, but never use a committee if you can make the decision on your own. Individual decision making is often difficult when people are accustomed to making decisions by committee. Naturally, some decisions will still require the group, but many decisions can and should be made by the manager alone. Don't worry about achieving unity. You will end up discussing things forever without taking action. It is far better to make the decision, delegate it, and then ask for compliance from competent administrators. Managers are paid to make decisions and to act on them. Think through your own problems before carrying them to others.

As a meeting participant you can also make meetings more useful. If you have a particular grievance about a meeting, take your concern directly to the chairperson instead of complaining to others who have no control over the meeting. Know the purpose of a meeting before you attend and identify your role in it. Encourage the chairperson to distribute an agenda beforehand so all participants will be prepared, and find out what follow-up actions will be expected.

Come on time to the meeting and encourage others to do so. Don't contribute to unnecessary chatter—unless the "meeting" is a party.

Be the kind of participant you would like to see at your own meetings. If the chairperson appears to be losing control, you can even subtly take over the meeting. You can define goals for the group, bring a straying discussion back to the point, call for a decision, and summarize the actions planned. If you are particularly skilled, you can accomplish all this without antagonizing the chairperson. Undoubtedly, this calls for assertiveness quotient 3, but it may bring results from an otherwise aimless meeting.

In his book *You and I Have Simply Got To Stop Meeting This Way,* Richard Dunsing suggests that you take an inventory of your feelings about meetings. Make a list of your most frequent reactions as you take part in meetings. Dunsing notes that you should "trust yourself," because your feelings are probably shared by others in the room. Remember that your choices in improving a meeting are the same as those in other aspects of your life: You can change it, leave it, or drop it.

A person can breathe new life into meetings simply by changing his or her usual behavior. Dunsing suggests that, after carefully analyzing your current behavior, you consciously respond in a different way. If you are usually a silent participant, make an effort to voice your opinion. If you are normally assertive in meetings, sit back and quietly observe what is taking place. You will see others change in response to your change. The "new life" you generate may be the key to a more meaningful meeting.

Many people complain that they have no influence over improving meetings, but this is simply not true. If all participants requested improvements, very few meeting leaders would be able to resist those requests. It is precisely because participants accept ineffective meetings that many continue. It is your valuable time that is being consumed in meetings, and if the meetings are useless it is your time that is being wasted. You have a right to demand some value for the time you invest.

TIME WASTER NO. 7: INEFFECTIVE COMMUNICATION

Bonnie Logan, director of special projects for the Bensonway Corporation, buzzed her secretary, Anita Wesley. "Anita, please come into my office. I have a number of items I want to review with you."

"Mrs. Logan," Anita responded, "I'm right in the middle of the monthly report and it's due this afternoon. You told me to be sure it got out on time."

Ignoring Anita's dilemma, Bonnie continued, "Bring your note pad in with you." She put down the receiver and tried to remember whether John Burton had asked her to call this afternoon or Friday morning. Anita stopped her thoughts as she entered the room. "Ready, Mrs. Logan," Anita said as she pulled up a chair.

"Remember that communication from Alex Arkin a few weeks ago?" Bonnie said. "Get a memo to him immediately stating that we accept the terms of his agreement. Also call Shirley Masters and tell her yes on her proposal of the fourth—and do that right away because she's waiting for an answer. Also, tell Brian Ridgeway that—"

"Wait a minute, Mrs. Logan. Who's Alex Arkin?" Anita asked, looking puzzled.

Bonnie didn't hear Anita at all. Her mind was moving onward. "Tell Brian Ridgeway that I'll have that report for him on Friday, so he can call a meeting sometime that afternoon. And, Anita, get on that report right away; it has top priority!"

"Sure, right away." Anita sighed, looking slightly dazed. She pushed back her chair as Bonnie Logan reached for her phone. "Hello, Sam," Bonnie chatted into the receiver. "Where was it you told me you wanted to go for lunch?"

Proper communication is essential if we wish to conserve valuable time on the job. We all have days when we become so preoccupied that we fail to communicate well to our subordinates, peers, and superiors. We offer hasty instructions or explanations, only to find ourselves in a lot of time-killing trouble later. We never seem to have time to do it right at first, but we always find enough time to do it over. George Bernard Shaw noted that "the greatest problem of communication is the illusion that it has been accomplished." Those of us who have suffered through misdirection, misconceptions, and misinformation must heartily agree.

Over 90 percent of all communication is oral. When we consider that many people have a limited vocabulary, don't know how to use the vocabulary they have, are often preoccupied when they speak (to people who are often preoccupied when they listen), generally fail to think through their thoughts properly, and seldom say what they mean anyway—we must wonder how any communication is successful!

Before people can be successful as communicators, they must be clear themselves on what they want to say. One of the most common reasons communication fails is that people truthfully don't know what they are talking about. Obviously, managers will have trouble giving subordinates instructions if they have never defined those instructions clearly to themselves. In order to achieve that all-important clarity, managers should:

1. Get complete and accurate data on the subject.
2. Arrange the information in an order that makes sense.
3. Transmit ideas in simple, clear terms.

Managers have a particular responsibility to be effective communicators. Businesses have become so complex today that employees have difficulty keeping abreast of what is going on. Policies and practices are passed through multiple levels of command before they arrive at front-line employees. Managers at all levels, therefore, need to be certain that their people have an unclouded impression of what is expected of them. Managers are the crucial link in the chain between top management and employees. Their skill at communication and interpersonal relationships is a cornerstone of the company's success.

Successful communication cannot be achieved overnight. Before effective, open communication can take place, there must be an atmosphere of trust and understanding within the work group. The people you manage must feel free to exchange ideas and must be allowed to question and make mistakes. Only then will they be truly receptive to your messages. When people tense as their superior enters the room, they are not ready to receive communication. Their defensiveness will prevent them from hearing what the superior has to say.

Communication must be a daily habit. You cannot communicate only when things go wrong and people need to be told what to do. Effective communication must be nurtured each day. The seed of understanding must be carefully sown so that people respond effectively during times of crisis. The following suggestions can help you minimize communication problems.

Assertiveness Quotient 1

Simplicity is the key to clear communication. Do not be concerned that you are "talking down" to your employees when you state your instructions or ideas simply. Once you define the important concepts clearly, you can elaborate with supporting thoughts and data.

Take your time when you deliver crucial messages. Employees frequently complain that they are given instructions too quickly and do not have the time to absorb them. They are often afraid to appear "slow," so they say that they understand—and perform their assignments with a poor knowledge of what they should be doing. Take the time to give instructions carefully, particularly on new and unfamiliar projects.

When you are giving instructions, remember that concepts which are familiar to you may not be familiar to your subordinates. Wouldn't you be confused if someone told you to "get the SWP report to Sam's office a week before the staff meeting"—when you had never heard of SWP, Sam, or the staff meeting? Remember, what is perfectly understandable to you may not be clear to someone else. Take the time to carefully define your terms now in order to save yourself and your employees a lot of heartache later.

Hold regular get-togethers with your key employees. These meetings will not only establish a comfortable social atmosphere but will also keep your people informed about what you are doing. With this background, your people may become familiar with SWP, Sam, and that "staff meeting" which is so important to you.

Be certain that people are speaking the same language when they try to get their message across. Many a communications breakdown can be traced to the fact that the communicators are talking about two different things—and scratching their heads because the other party fails to understand. When problems develop, take the time to define important terms carefully—and start over. A subordinate who fails to see a marketing strategy clearly may quickly understand the idea if it is presented in football terminology. Again, learn to communicate for the listener's benefit, not for your own.

The more an employee knows about the company in general, the less difficulty he or she will have in handling office communications. You can keep everyone informed in many ways—through newsletters, bulletins, special magazines, press releases, public memos, and so on. Forget about the antiquated policy of secrecy among those in top management. This policy can lead to misinterpretation and guessing on the part of employees. It can also make people feel "shut out" from the crucial matters of the company. Nothing is more embarrassing or annoying to employees than having to learn from an outsider or the newspaper information that they should have known months ago. Make sharing of information a major goal in your office.

Be aware of the fact that there is such a thing as "communication overkill." This means that, as a manager and a trainer, you can overdo your efforts. People can take in and learn only so much; they soon reach the point of diminishing returns. How do you know when that point has been reached? If you develop an open relationship with those crucial "others" who must receive your communications, you will soon sense when "enough is enough." If your second sense fails you, in an open office environment employees will feel free to say, "Whoa!"

As a good communicator you will hear that "Whoa!" and quickly turn into a good listener, for listening is another crucial aspect of effective communication. Communication is a two-way street. Speaking is simply no good without listening. Here are a few guidelines for being a good listener:

1. Listen totally—with all your faculties. Look at the person, listen closely, and keep your mind on what is being said.

2. Listen to meaning as well as to words. Realize that the person may be unclear about the message.

3. Keep an open mind to new ideas. Refrain from passing judgment on what you *think* the speaker is saying until the thought is completed. Remember that even if the idea is unclear or impractical, it may be the beginning of a valuable idea.

Good listeners show respect for the ideas of others. Good listeners are also astute. They know that only by listening carefully can they hope to get their own ideas across.

Assertiveness Quotient 2

We have already stressed the importance of being clear about your message before you attempt communication. We have also suggested that you use clear, concise words and phrases to get your meaning across. Still, we must ask again, "Are you sure you said what you meant to say?" Sometimes your mind plays tricks on you and your words come out with a great deal of difficulty. You believe you said one thing—when actually you said something quite different.

One way to guard against such miscommunication is to restate your idea in a variety of ways until you are certain it has been communicated clearly. You may want to ask your listeners to repeat what you said in order to confirm that they understand. Following your verbal message, a written communication may be in order.

Putting words on paper can clarify misunderstandings before they become major crises.

Remember the value of praise for creating an atmosphere of positive communication. Most managers forget to give their subordinates a word or two of praise for the good work they perform and thus pave the way for more difficult, less pleasant messages later. Everyone understands "You did a good job" or "Good work!" A smile is a good signal that the message has been happily received. That same smile will lower the defensive barriers later when there are more serious ideas to discuss.

Assertiveness Quotient 3

Encourage "back talk" from your subordinates. This suggestion may go against your need to be right as often as possible, but it will bring about clearer communication between you and your staff. Through back talk (or "questioning" if you prefer) all dimensions of an idea can be explored. New angles on old ideas will become apparent, and your initial ideas may take on real strength as they survive the verbal teeter-totter. A strong leader is interested in the best idea for the project, not in seeing that his or her idea is implemented.

We use the term "back talk" in a very positive sense, to indicate the free back-and-forth flow of information to improve new ideas. Back talk is not possible in a closed work environment. It requires an open atmosphere of trust and respect.

Use your power with words over your subordinates with care. If you are a significant person in their lives (and many "bosses" are), a misplaced comment in a moment of spite may severely damage the lines of communication for a long time. Of course, it is your duty to correct errors, but offer criticism with care. Be particularly careful not to criticize an employee in front of others.

Remember, too, that nonverbal communication is a significant part of your message. Your walk, expression, dress, movements, and general attitude all color any message you present. Try to have all nonverbal communicators working for you. These communicators enhance the message you send, they don't detract from it. You owe it to yourself and your company to project your best in all your communication efforts—whether you are dealing with your staff, your boss, or an important client. In all cases, your best will draw the best response from your listeners.

Open communication is part of good time management. It is a tool that will allow you to work more efficiently. Without careful attention to effective communication, you will waste endless hours correcting wrong ideas, redirecting misguided efforts, and soothing hurt feelings. It is only when you begin to appreciate the value of clear communication that real progress becomes possible. This value will be apparent in the amount of time saved, the improved morale of employees, and the resulting increase in productivity.

TIME WASTER NO. 8: PROCRASTINATION

As Chris stirred the nondairy creamer into his plastic cup, he looked around the lunch room to see if he knew anyone. "Not many people here at 9:20 in the morning," he thought, "too early for coffee break." He spotted Nellie Jensen coming through the west door and remembered a conversation he had had with her last spring. "Wonder how that interview worked out," he thought.

Forty minutes later he left the lunch room. He now knew that Nellie did not get that new job she had hoped for and that she was burned up about it. "Too bad for Nellie," he thought, "but I doubt she could have handled it anyway."

His report was still there on the corner of his desk. No one had finished it in his absence. It was now almost 10:30 and he had a meeting at 11:00. Chris thought to himself, "Maybe I'd better make a couple of phone calls and tackle that report right after lunch. I'll be fresh then and ideas will come easily."

His meeting came and went. Lunch hour with Sally Harvey and Joe Girard was fun, but he had two Southern Comforts too many. It was now 1:00 P.M. and he was relaxed—a little too relaxed to tackle anything as heavy as that report. "Why do we have to do those useless reports, anyway?" he thought. "No one reads them. What a waste of time."

He glanced again at the mimeographed directions for completing the report. "Two pages of instructions!" he observed. "Better start making notes on my ideas."

He was close to getting something written when there was a knock at his office door. "Hi, Chris!" Nat Arnold began. "How'd the meeting go this morning? Was Sugarman up to his old tricks?"

"You guessed it." Chris smiled. "He's always been like that. Did I ever tell you about the meeting last year when Sugars and Baxley locked horns over the new plant? You should have seen him then!"

The conversation was on. Nat sat down and both enjoyed a little fellowship. By the time Nat left at 2:30, Chris had decided to clean his desk of a number of "little items" and get to that important report first thing in the morning. "After all," he told himself, "tomorrow is another day."

Thousands of people will jokingly admit to being procrastinators. There was even talk of a Procrastinators Club. The club planned to meet but decided to put off the organizational process until next year. Kidding around is fun for everyone, but when the time comes to get things accomplished, procrastination is not a laughing matter. Many people think procrastination is a harmless little hang-up. It's not. Marriages fail because of it. Businesses fold because of it. People die because they keep putting off that trip to the doctor for a checkup. Still, many of us smile at procrastination because it's "such a human quality."

Perhaps the most valuable thing you can do when you are procrastinating is to admit it. Once you acknowledge that you are indeed procrastinating, you can examine your situation and determine why. Procrastination can become a habit. Procrastination breeds procrastination. Analyze your habits and make a list of all the things you tend to put off. Use this knowledge to change your do-it-later tendency into a do-it-now habit. Chapter 14 is devoted exclusively to the topic of procrastination.

TIME WASTER NO. 9: INEFFECTIVE DELEGATION

Delegation! Delegation!
*   What a source of consternation!*
Hesitation! Aggravation!
*   Think I'll take a long vacation!*

Harry, will you please come here?
*   Bring your pad, pull up a chair.*

> *We have this big report to do.*
> 　　*And so I thought I'd count on* you!
>
> *On second thought, why not forget it?*
> 　　*It's pretty tough—so let* me *hit it.*
> *I'll have to find the time to do it.*
> 　　*I really doubt that you'd get through it!*
>
> *Delegation! Delegation!*
> 　　*What a source of consternation!*
> *Hesitation! Aggravation!*
> 　　*Think I'll take a long vacation!*

On the surface, delegation appears to be simple. All you have to do is tell someone else what to do. What's so difficult about that?

Many things are "difficult about that." Self-confidence and assertiveness are crucial in proper delegation. If you lack confidence in your own ability, or if you are not assertive enough, you will delegate poorly. And if you are overly assertive, or aggressive, you will also have problems with delegation.

Delegation is an art that is mastered only through practice. No one automatically delegates well, and a great deal of time is wasted by ineffective delegation.

A major portion of Chapter 11 is devoted to this topic. For now, let's simply say that effective delegation is possible. In this area, too, we favor a systematic approach!

1. Clarify objectives for the work you're delegating. Focus on taking the time to communicate clearly. Ask for feedback from subordinates to check on the message received. Whenever possible, put the objectives in writing.

2. Define responsibility and authority. Your subordinates need to know what they are expected to do, how well they are expected to do it, and how their performance will be judged. Remember to delegate the authority necessary to implement decisions. If your subordinates must check with you for each move they make, your time will be wasted—and you will have delegated very little.

3. Create a motivating environment for your subordinates. A positive atmosphere takes time to develop, but it will ultimately save you much time and enable you to get better results. Good delegation requires a minimal level of trust between manager and subordinate.

4. Require completed work. Set an acceptable standard for performance but don't ask for perfection.

5. Provide adequate training. Training takes time, but it is an important duty of a good manager. Too often, training is put off "until later."

6. Establish adequate controls. As the manager, you are ultimately responsible for what happens, even when you effectively delegate tasks. You, therefore, need a good follow-up system to stay on top of things. This does not mean that you should constantly look over your subordinate's shoulder; it means that you must make timely checks on progress made.

As you work on your delegation skills, keep in mind the words of Lao-tzu: "Of all the best leaders, when their task is accomplished, their work done, the people remark, 'We have done it ourselves.' "

TIME WASTER NO. 10: THE CLUTTERED DESK

I had it here just a few minutes ago!" Jay Allen bellowed in exasperation. "So where is it now? It was right between the minutes from last January's cost meeting and April's Business Week. *It couldn't disappear into thin air! Barbara! Come in here. Do you have that Jackson letter? I need it now!"*

Barbara Clark quit typing in midsentence and rushed into her boss's office. He needed immediate help in situations like this. She shook her head as she took in the familiar sight of his desk—stacked high with correspondence, magazines, and reports. Occasionally, he'd restack the materials and set them in piles across the top of his desk. By the next morning, the desk was a mess again.

Barbara picked up the Jackson letter from the floor and handed it to Jay. "Here you are, sir," she said. She hesitated before she added, "I thought you told me last week that you were going to clear that desk. It would be a good idea, you know."

"Yeah, yeah, that's what I said, all right," Jay responded. "I'll do that soon. Now let me get to work!"

Barbara closed the door behind her as Jay stared at the Jackson letter. "Clear my desk, huh?" he thought. Suddenly a bright idea hit him. He smiled. Then he smiled wider as he decided on a course of action. With two well-executed shoves, he redistributed the mess to the floor. "There," he said triumphantly, "it's clear! Maybe now *she'll leave me alone!"*

Organizing your desk and staying on top of the paper flow is one of the most difficult things in any office. But if you intend to be effective and manage your time well, you must get organized.

Since your desk is usually your own, an assertiveness quotient does not fit this time waster. Of course, your secretary might have a vested interest in the condition of your desk, but then it is she who must decide how assertive she wants to be in her efforts to get it cleaned up. *Your* assertiveness is not the question.

Over the years, we have observed thousands of offices. We have formulated Douglass' Law of Clutter: "Clutter tends to expand to fill the space available for its retention." If you are a disorganized person and have a small desk, your desk will be cluttered. If you get a desk that is five times larger, it will still become totally cluttered.

Why do desks become cluttered so easily? There are a number of reasons. People have no criteria for determining what goes into or on top of the desk; they use the desk for the wrong purpose; they have sloppy work habits; or they fail to think through the problem. Solving the problem will require a certain amount of discipline, the development of a few new habits, and mastery of the Eight Principles of Desk Organization outlined below.

PRINCIPLE 1: *If you don't really need a desk, get rid of it!* Not everyone who has a desk really needs one. An increasing number of executives are finding that they get more accomplished without a desk. You can read reports and correspondence just as easily in a comfortable chair. Any absolutely necessary writing—writing that can't be dictated—can be done at a small table. If the desk isn't there, it can't become cluttered and you might become more effective.

PRINCIPLE 2: *If you must have a desk, pick the right one.* Desks come in all sizes, shapes, and designs. Aside from considerations of esthetics, status, or company policy, there are several things to keep in mind when selecting your desk.

Begin at the top. How wide is your desk? The most convenient work area is generally an arm's length from your chair. If your desk is any wider than that, it's too wide. Stay away from glass tops and highly polished surfaces. They may look good in magazines, but the glare will cut your productivity dramatically. Try to keep the brightness of paper and desk reasonably close.

Next, consider your desk drawers. If you don't really need them for frequently-referred-to items, get a desk without drawers. To determine if you really need them, open your desk drawers and inventory the contents. What percentage are miscellaneous, unnecessary objects?

Pull-outs can add to the usefulness of a desk by providing additional, close-in work areas. If you need more space, check with your purchasing department for help. But remember, pull-outs are for temporarily expanding the working area of your desk; they are not for permanent storage.

Many people have no say in selecting their desks. Often the furniture is chosen by a purchasing agent or, even worse, by an interior decorator who never works at a desk. If this is the case in your company, your first move is to educate the interior decorator. There is no reason why a desk can't be both attractive and functional.

PRINCIPLE 3: *You should always be able to see the top of your desk.* You can only work on one thing at a time. Everything else should be put away, easily retrievable when you need it. When you have several jobs in front of you, you can quickly become distracted. You will not concentrate as efficiently. To be really effective at your desk, you must clear it off. Work on only one project at a time.

PRINCIPLE 4: *Never clear off your desk simply by putting things in a drawer.* Have a rationale for everything that goes into your desk drawers. There is no rule that says you must have each drawer filled to capacity. Don't store anything in your desk just because you can't think of anything else to do with it. Consider throwing it out.

A desk is not a general store. If you insist on keeping a supply of aspirins, instant coffee, soup, and other miscellaneous items in your desk, at least try to confine them to one inconspicuous drawer.

PRINCIPLE 5: *Files should not be obstacle courses.* Files were invented to provide fast retrieval of information. Make sure you have a good filing system, suited to your requirements. Files should be clearly labeled and simply arranged so that your seven-year-old child could use them. If it takes you more than a few seconds, on average, to put your hands on filed material, you'd better call in a consultant to help you rearrange things.

To begin weeding out your file cloggers, categorize your records into active, inactive, and discard. Active records are those you will need in the regular course of business. Inactive records are those you must keep even though you may never use them. Discards are items you don't need to keep at all. Once you've sorted everything out, keep only active files in your office or desk. Relegate inactive files to lower-cost space. Transfer discards to the wastebasket.

Periodically clean out your files. Experts estimate that 95 percent of all filed materials over a year old are never referred to again.

PRINCIPLE 6: *It's never too late to turn over a new desk.* What can you do if your desk looks hopeless? Start by changing the appearance of both the outside and the inside. If you are an average desk owner, it will take you between two to four hours to reorganize your desk. Plan to stay late or work Saturday—it is best to have no interruptions when you undertake this task.

Get yourself a large wastebasket. Then take everything out of the desk drawers and stack it wherever you can find room. Analyze the stack one item at a time, being as critical as you can. Ask yourself, "Why do I need this? What have I used it for in the past week? The past month? What does this add to my effectiveness? Could it be thrown away?"

You should have a rationale for everything you put back into your desk. And you must be ruthless. Throw away all unnecessary clutter you have accumulated. Send all inactive materials to the appropriate storage files. Develop a priority-sort system for determining what to put back into the drawers. Put the system in writing. It will be useful in the future for keeping things out of your desk drawers and for preventing your desk from becoming disorganized again.

When you finish with the drawers, turn to the desk top. Stack all papers in one big pile. Dispense with all items other than paper with the same ruthless analysis you used on the drawers. Anything that distracts you or gets in your way should be removed. Now you are ready to tackle that pile of paper.

PRINCIPLE 7: *There are only three kinds of paper.* As you sort your stack of paper, separate it into the following categories:

1. Things that require some action.
2. Things that must be read and passed on, or filed if absolutely necessary.
3. Things that can be thrown away and forgotten.

Put papers in the first category on the right side of your desk, papers in the second on the left side of your desk, and papers in the third category in the wastebasket. When you have finished sorting, take the first group of papers and analyze each item in turn. What kind of action is required? Who must do it? Don't set aside an item until you have taken some action or at least scheduled initial action.

Prepare for some quick reading on the second group of items. Read one item at a time and don't set aside anything until you have noted whether it is to be filed or sent on. Your secretary may hate you the next day, but in the long run you both will enjoy your new efficiency.

Follow this system each day. Throw out discards immediately. Keep paper moving, and never put a piece of paper that requires action into a pending file without initiating some action.

PRINCIPLE 8: *Wastebasketry is an art.* The wastebasket is a functional link in the paper flow process. Many people never think about their wastebasket and never learn to use it well. Here are some tips to help you transform your wastebasket from a piece of furniture into a valuable tool.

Get a wastebasket that is big enough to hold all you can feed it without being an eyesore. It should be convenient for your use, not placed to suit the whims of the janitor or interior decorator. Set up your own rules for what goes in and what stays out. Your objective is to throw out as much as possible. Think about the kinds of paper coming through your office. Make a list of what should be discarded, what must be kept, and how long things must be kept.

For some people, throwing away things in a decisive act; for others, it creates an unusually high level of apprehension. For these people, the wastebasket achieves only a fraction of its potential value. Try to get over your emotional attachment to paper. And don't avoid your trauma by routing your junk to someone else.

As you learn to master these eight principles of organizing your desk, you will notice a significant increase in both the quality and quantity of the work you accomplish.

TIME WASTER NO. 11: PERSONAL DISORGANIZATION

As she put on her coat, Carol Borden noted with satisfaction that she was on time. By leaving the house at 8:30 A.M., she could easily be at the office by 9:00.

"Wait a minute," Carol thought. "Where'd I put that report I was reading last night? I'd better get those figures for the 11:00 A.M. meeting too. Where'd I stash that accounting folder?"

Ten minutes later, Carol headed for the door, somewhat disgruntled over her ten-minute loss. Her anger was compounded by her annoyance at her daughter Susan. "Why'd she spill that chocolate milk on Pete's notes! Can't leave anything on that TV table without someone messing things up!" Carol thought.

As she turned right at the stoplight on Fourth Street, she glanced at the gas gauge. "Almost empty!" she moaned. "I suppose it's running on air now. Can't possibly make it all the way downtown." She spotted Frank's station just in time and glided in—behind two other cars.

By 9:30 A.M. Carol was finally seated at her desk. She was late, yes, but then she usually was late. "Those interruptions weren't my fault," she rationalized.

As soon as she finished her first cup of coffee and read the morning paper, her thoughts turned to work. "So many important things to do," she thought. Behind her on the credenza was a stack of magazines five inches high. She planned to read them today; you never know what important information might be in them. Carol also noted four plant proposals she had hoped to review and remembered her promise to Jeff Adams that she'd write an opinion on each proposal.

To the right, stacked on her yellow straight-back chair, were two files for the accounting meeting. "Where'd I put that third section?" she wondered. "It has to be somewhere!"

As she noted six more projects around the room, she felt a panic switch turn on inside her. She worked for ten minutes on the Butler letter, but a fourteen-minute phone conversation with Betty Azner disturbed her thoughts and she switched to the Harrington file. That effort lasted seven minutes. As she reached for the first sip of her second cup of coffee, her thumb slipped on the leftover danish that still clung to the cup. The hot coffee saturated the Harrington file and Carol's new blouse as well. Carol spent the next half hour wiping the coffee from her shirt and the report and the tears from her eyes. "Another one of those days," she sighed.

Personal disorganization is a trap. It is in the same family of time wasters as the disorganized desk, but it reflects a far more serious problem. Nothing short of aggressive action against your old ways will make a difference. Why is aggressive behavior needed? Because personal disorganization is a deeply ingrained habit. It will take extraordinary effort to break this self-defeating habit, turn it around, and change it into self-enhancing behavior.

People who suffer from personal disorganization are missing the boat—ever so slightly. Most of them have remarkable talents and abilities, or they would not have achieved the level of success that is already theirs. They simply lack what it takes to go that extra inch. That extra inch involves a personal organization strategy.

The idea of "personal organization" suffered a setback during the 1960s and 1970s, when the notion of "doing your own thing" came into vogue. Many people considered organization an evil, a form of manipulation—particularly organization that attempted to influence an individual's life. Little did these people realize that chaos is quite different from freedom. Anarchy and aimlessness are not fun; people become frustrated when they do not have a clear-cut purpose.

Ambitious people who are personally disorganized continually find they have too much to do. They feel swamped by the weight of it all and often opt to do nothing. They hope some of the pressures will go away. They also find themselves leaving tasks unfinished because a part is missing, something "more important" turns up, or they must "wait for inspiration." They are plagued by indecision as they consider the tasks at hand. "What should I do first? Everyone wants everything right away!"

These people spend a lot of time complaining about their burdens. They seem to enjoy sharing their troubles with co-workers or friends in the hope of eliciting sympathy, admiration, or help. They seldom receive any of these and succeed only in wasting everyone's time.

Personal organization is possible only if you believe that organization is worthwhile. You must know for yourself that your activities are getting you nowhere; you must recognize the need for improvement. Unless you have a need for organization and truly want to adopt organizing ideas, you will not benefit from the ideas suggested here.

If you honestly want to be an organized person, you must establish goals. Get a piece of paper and a pen, and write in large letters the word GOALS. Goals are the secret of personal organization. Without specific goals in your job, or your life, you have no direction. Randomness reigns. With goals, you have direction. Goals give you a yardstick to measure each activity that demands your time.

Write down your goals and set your priorities. Then identify some of those little personal quirks that continually get in your way. Start with your morning ritual at home. Missed morning alarms, a misplaced toothbrush, an empty cereal box and sour milk, scattered papers on the TV table, and an empty gas tank are all signs of disorganization. Some people believe small things aren't important. They are wrong. Small things set the tone for the entire day. Next, think about your activities at work. If you begin with chatter, coffee, and the newspaper (while vaguely remembering all the work you have to do), you have already determined that little will be accomplished during the next eight hours.

If you have tried to change one or two of these little quirks and have been unsuccessful, you may think that change is impossible. Perhaps you have resigned yourself by saying, "That's the way I am. You can't teach an old dog new tricks!" Yes, you can teach an old dog new tricks. But it isn't easy! You must look ahead. Envision that organized person you want to be. Forget all the reasons you have been disorganized in the past. Focus only on the way you want to be.

Don't try to change your habits casually. Habit change must be planned, in detail, with determination. And remember that a change in behavior usually precedes a change in attitude. Once you force yourself to replace your old habits with self-enhancing behavior, your attitude will eventually follow your actions. Soon your new behavior will become you—and you will be the person you want to be.

Plan your behavior carefully, minutely at first. Be certain all the materials you need for work are ready before you go to bed. Have them by the door. If you usually pack a lunch for work, do that the night before. Pick out the clothes you will wear the next day and save yourself the decision at dawn's early light. Be sure the car has a full tank of gas before you put it to sleep for the night. In fact, get in the habit of keeping the tank more than half full; in emergency situations you will have at least half a tank of fuel to get you to your destination. If you usually sleep through your alarm or push the "doze" button five times before getting out of bed, try getting up the first time the alarm goes off—just this once. Anyone can do it once!

Examine your routine for small habits that are robbing you of time and effectiveness. Ask yourself which habits would help you become a more organized person. Start with a few important habits and plan to make positive changes tomorrow. Do not allow yourself to be swayed from your prescribed course of action until your new habits have become established. Your organized habits will foster your goals in the same way that your disorganized habits once hampered your goals.

TIME WASTER NO. 12: LACK OF SELF-DISCIPLINE

Tom Connors was excited about the time management course he had just attended in Chicago. The two-day program was exactly what he needed. It gave him numerous insights into his time problems, many ideas for setting goals, and the confidence that he would soon be saving "at least two hours a day." As he got into his car to drive back to Springfield, he promised himself he would get busy on his time management ideas "as soon as things settle down."

The weeks flew by and Tom continued to be frustrated. He'd be "time-conscious" tomorrow, but the proverbial tomorrow never came.

"What's wrong with me?" he thought. "I know the things I'm supposed to do—so why don't I do them? I seem to be my own worst enemy!"

Most of us have discovered that there is a big difference between knowing what to do and doing it. We go to great lengths to acquire accurate information on a variety of activities in our business and personal lives only to disappoint ourselves by failing to use this knowledge. We indeed become our own worst enemy as we create a bigger and bigger gap between what we want to do and what we actually do. We know the bridge is called "self-discipline," but we can't seem to cross it.

Self-discipline involves personal organization, but it goes beyond the physical dimension of organization to include all the powers of the mind. It is the significant difference between winners and losers in this life. It is the difference between those who dream and those who achieve. You can't beg, borrow, or steal self-discipline. All you can do is achieve it. And the only way to achieve it is to plan your time carefully and then act on your decisions.

Many of us fight the idea of self-discipline. We still remember the externally imposed discipline of our youth. We try to get away with what we can. We remember our mother's admonition to do it "because I told you to do it," and the child that's still in us smiles a little—because now we don't have to. We fail to realize that external discipline and self-discipline are not the same thing. External discipline is confining. It asks us to do things whether we want to or not. It forces us to spend our time achieving goals that are important to others. It boxes us in and makes us uncomfortable.

Self-discipline is quite different. It is a tool for achieving objectives of our own. It releases us to spend our time in a way that will help us accomplish our own goals, not the goals of others. It puts us in charge of our lives. Self-discipline is the key to personal freedom. It paroles us from the prison of our habits and releases us to fulfill our lives. In a world where we often feel we control nothing individually, self-discipline helps us define that part of the world where we *can* make a difference.

Many of us know in our hearts that we can be self-disciplined— and we promise ourselves that someday we will be. We have a vision of that perfect day when all our dreams will come true: Everything will be done on time and done well. All our potential will become actual. We will come into full bloom as disciplined, proud human beings. We are no longer children with the future before us. We are the grown-up generation that is making things happen. If ever there is a time, it is now. The future is today!

Where do we find that golden key known as self-discipline? Philosophers and poets, inventors and executives have searched for it throughout the centuries. They can tell us only that it comes from within. Each of us must find it for ourselves. We are the only ones who can unlock our potential and make time management techniques work for us.

There are no six easy steps to becoming disciplined. Self-discipline is a mental process. Consider the following thoughts, which have worked for others.

Dwell on this formula:

> Almost
> Nearly
> Just about
> Not quite
> Planning
> Hoping
> Wishing
> Wanting
> Yearning

Now add self-discipline:

> Strike!
> Arrive!
> Success!
> On the mark!
> Achievement!
> A Winner!
> Satisfied!
> Victory!
> Triumph!

The point? Those of us who dream and wish, those of us who aspire to anything great, those of us who want to become more than we are—we are only one step away. Without that step, we fail. With that step, we achieve. That one, all-important step is self-discipline. Remember:

"Potential" counts for nothing unless you're under eighteen.

"Almost" counts only in horseshoes.

"Wishing" is for those with a lucky star.

You will not be able to gain control over all your time; indeed, many of the time wasters that plague your days are an important part of your job. But strive to control an increasing percentage of your time on the job. Would a 10 percent increase in the amount of time you have available be useful to you? Would a 20 percent increase be useful? How much more would you get accomplished each day if you had an additional one or two hours to spend on important things? There is little doubt that the effort you exert to eliminate your time wasters would be worth it to you.

You can control many of your time wasters if you choose to do so. It takes dedication on your part to implement our time-saving ideas. It takes careful planning and a realistic knowledge of your work situation. It takes self-knowledge and the ability to push yourself a little beyond your former limits.

Decide today that you will be prepared for the time-consuming interruptions in your life. Your attitude, your preparedness, and your willingness to take action will enable you to turn your new knowledge of time management into a daily habit.

10
Managers and Secretaries

MANY MANAGERS AGREE that good secretaries can double their bosses' worth to the organization, while poor secretaries can reduce it by half. A good secretary can facilitate a meeting, rescue you from an unwanted visitor, and develop your small concept into an action plan. A poor secretary can ruin a meeting (by losing the agenda, fouling up the meeting-room arrangements, or misinforming the participants), can invite four Whitchit salesmen to talk to you further, and can make you lose track of any idea you ever conceived. Clearly, a good secretary is an office treasure—and is increasingly difficult to find.

Unfortunately, the word "secretary" carries negative connotations for many people. Some misinformed eccentrics seem to think that secretaries are a necessary evil, and even some secretaries describe their jobs in pejorative terms. An occasional dandy will treat secretaries as the lowest form of corporate life.

We believe that secretaries should be, and can be, much more than clerk-typists and coffee maids. A secretary has a unique relationship with a manager. It is doubtful that anyone else has as close a relationship to the manager's thoughts and actions as the secretary. She* has professional access to everything happening. Yet, in spite of the potential afforded by this relationship, many secretaries are poorly treated and underutilized.

---

* We acknowledge the fact that as women move increasingly into managerial positions, men are also expanding their numbers in the secretarial force. In this chapter, however, we will generally use feminine pronouns, since there are still far more female than male secretaries.

Think of the manager–secretary team as a single job unit, rather than as two separate jobs. The only rationale for having a secretary is to enable the manager to accomplish more. Thinking of the manager and secretary as a team will help you focus on how both professionals can use time more effectively, whether alone or together, to achieve a common purpose.

THE SECRETARY'S JOB

Exactly what is a secretary? What should a secretary be? Certainly not everyone who is labeled "secretary" actually functions as a secretary. Many people who are given this label have a single job function: typing, filing, or greeting office visitors. Each of these activities is important to an organization, but these functions alone do not fulfill the meaning of the word "secretary."

The National Secretaries Association (NSA) has invested much effort in defining the secretary's position. According to the NSA definition, a secretary is "an executive assistant who possesses a mastery of office skills, demonstrates the ability to assume responsibility without direct supervision, exercises initiative and judgment, and makes decisions within the scope of assigned authority."

To help organizations implement this definition, the NSA developed the following prototype job description for a secretary:

1. A secretary relieves an executive of various administrative details; coordinates and maintains effective office procedures and efficient work flows; implements policies and procedures set by employer; establishes and maintains harmonious working relationships with superiors, co-workers, subordinates, customers or clients, and suppliers.
2. A secretary schedules appointments and maintains calendars; receives and assists visitors and telephone callers and refers them to executive or other appropriate persons as circumstances warrant; arranges business itineraries and coordinates executive's travel requirements.
3. A secretary takes action authorized during an executive's absence and uses initiative and judgment to see that matters requiring attention are referred to delegated authority or handled in a manner to minimize effect of employer's absence.
4. A secretary takes manual shorthand and transcribes from it or transcribes from machine dictation; types materials from longhand or rough copy.
5. A secretary sorts, reads, and annotates incoming mail and docu-

ments and attaches appropriate files to facilitate necessary action; determines routing, signatures required, and maintains follow-up; composes correspondence and reports for own or executive's signature; prepares communication outlines by executive in oral or written directions.

6. A secretary researches and abstracts information and supporting data in preparation for meetings, work projects, and reports; correlates and edits materials submitted by others; organizes material which may be presented to executive in draft format.
7. A secretary maintains filing and records management systems and other office flow procedures.
8. A secretary makes arrangements for and coordinates conferences and meetings; may serve as a recorder of minutes with responsibility for transcription and distribution to participants.
9. A secretary may supervise or hire other employees; select and/or make recommendations for purchase of supplies and equipment; maintain budget and expense account records, financial records, and confidential files.
10. A secretary maintains up-to-date procedures manual for the specific duties handled on the job.
11. A secretary performs other duties as assigned or as judgment or necessity dictates.

If all secretarial jobs matched the description suggested by the National Secretaries Association, there would be many more effective managers than there are today. The kind of secretary described by the NSA is clearly a thorough professional with crucial responsibilities. Such a secretary would indeed be the best aid a manager could have to focus and use time well.

In practice, though, the manager–secretary relationship is rarely so harmonious. Typically, the manager and the secretary make problems for each other, almost as if they were on competing teams. They sometimes act as if their jobs were totally unrelated and believe that each could probably do a better job if the other would simply "go away." Fortunately, not all manager–secretary relationships are this way. In the past few years a new respect has developed for the role of secretary. There are several reasons for this:

1. Increased pressures and demands on the manager have forced a search for additional help. When given the opportunity, many secretaries proved themselves. Soon responsibilities came to them on purpose—not by default.
2. More and more women are planning lifelong careers. With these long-range plans comes a professional, growth-oriented attitude toward their jobs. Women in secretarial positions have begun

to use their knowledge and experience more effectively. As secretaries remain longer in their positions, their knowledge and abilities increase, as do the expectations of their supervisors.

3. With more and more working women moving into positions formerly held by men, the number of available secretaries has decreased. The scarcity of good secretaries has forced employers to increase the salaries offered to secretaries. More money, predictably, has found its way to employees with greater skills.

4. Many managers have made sincere efforts to upgrade the secretary's role. The increased stature and responsibility has improved perceptions of the secretary.

THE MANAGER–SECRETARY TEAM

As a manager, how well do you use your secretary? Are you and your secretary pulling in the same direction? Perhaps you are reasonably happy with your joint efforts but feel they could be improved. To initiate improvement, test yourself with the following quiz:

The Perceptions of Your Secretary Quiz

	Yes	No
1. Do you always tackle things on the basis of priorities?	____	____
2. Do you frequently switch signals or priorities on your secretary?	____	____
3. Do you take enough time to provide good instruction and keep communications flowing freely between you and your secretary?	____	____
4. Do you have confidence in your secretary's ability to handle routine activities and keep trivia away from you?	____	____
5. Do you delegate as much as you could to your secretary?	____	____
6. Do you use a dictating machine instead of dictating personally to your secretary?	____	____
7. Do you always keep your secretary informed about what is happening?	____	____
8. Do you and your secretary review your daily objectives and priorities?	____	____
9. Is your secretary a good sounding board for ideas and problem solving?	____	____

	Yes	No

10. Is your office well organized and free of clutter?

11. Do you frequently interrupt your secretary?

12. Do you always treat your secretary as an important and unique team member rather than as an office fixture?

13. Do you always take the time to listen well?

14. Do you compliment your secretary more than you criticize?

15. Have you discussed the specific responsibility, authority, and accountability factors of your secretary's job?

16. Have you discussed your secretary's career goals within the past six months?

17. Do you encourage your secretary to express initiative and resourcefulness?

18. Can you easily accept constructive criticism from your secretary?

19. Do you consistently encourage and support your secretary's efforts to improve and develop?

20. Do you complain about your secretary to co-workers or others?

If you answered yes to all the questions above except for questions 2, 11, and 20, you're in good shape. You have a healthy, thriving relationship with your secretary. If you answered no on a number of questions, read the following pages carefully. These suggestions were developed with you in mind. If you act on any of these ideas in areas where you were formerly negligent, you will gain some pleasing results from your efforts.

ASSESSING CURRENT PROBLEMS

How do you begin to transform your present relationship with your probably underused and generally unfulfilled secretary into something better, something that will benefit both of you in your careers, in your utilization of time, and in your achievement of job satisfaction? Tradition and habit, as we have frequently pointed out, are powerful forces in people's lives. People often choose the status quo, no matter how depressing, over efforts that may lead to positive change. The first step toward the professional team relationship we advocate here is the biggest one. It involves taking a second look at your current secretary and realizing that perhaps she does want "something more." Not all secretaries, of course, want or can handle additional responsibility. But most of them do, and can.

Unfortunately, there are limited materials available for teaching managers how to use secretaries effectively. Where do we learn? Most of us have learned by observing how other managers deal with their secretaries. This can be good or bad. If we have a positive role model, we learn good things. If we emulate a bad manager, the results are negative.

A better road to results begins with self-analysis. The following questions will help you develop a better team relationship with your secretary:

1. How, specifically, has your secretary helped you most?
2. How could your secretary best help you in your most important responsibilities?
3. What are you doing that could be done by your secretary?
4. What do you wish your secretary were doing that she is not now doing?
5. What prevents those things listed in questions, 2, 3, and 4 from happening?
6. What prevents you from delegating more to your secretary?
7. What suggestions from your secretary do you resist most?
8. What are your secretary's strongest points or skills?
9. What specific steps can you take to upgrade your secretary's skills?
10. What actions can you take immediately to begin creating a better relationship with your secretary?

These ten questions will help you focus on the particular needs of both you and your secretary. Try to be as specific as possible in your responses. If you have difficulties, your personal time log may be helpful. It will routinely point to rough spots in your day-to-day activities and provide direction for your efforts.

Your time log will also help you initiate a dialogue about time wasters and effective time use with your secretary. If your secretary has also kept a time log, your potential benefits are increased. With two logs, you can make comparisons for greater insights into time problems.

Whenever we suggest more manager–secretary dialogue, a question usually arises: "How do you organize it?" The following exercise has proven extremely useful in helping manager and secretary understand the time problems they share and what can be done about them. Set aside some time to develop the following profiles; you will recover your investment many times in the months to come.

MANAGER–SECRETARY TIME WASTER PROFILES

The profile forms in Figures 17 and 18 are designed to help you and your secretary find the best approach to handling your time management problems. The manager's profile is developed as follows:

1. Identify and rank your top six time wasters in column 1.
2. Weight your top six time wasters in column 2 as follows:

> No. 1 time waster = 30
> No. 2 time waster = 25
> No. 3 time waster = 20
> No. 4 time waster = 15
> No. 5 time waster = 10
> No. 6 time waster = 5

3. Have your secretary identify and rank your top six time wasters in column 3. Your secretary should do this independently, without looking at your ranking. Weights should be assigned in column 4 on the same basis as above.

4. Add the weights in columns 2 and 4 for each time waster identified. Record the total weight in column 5.

5. Record the final ranking for your time wasters in column 6. The time waster with the greatest combined weight is No. 1, the time waster with the second-highest total is No. 2, and so on. In case of equal weightings, use the secretary's rank order as a guide.

The secretary's profile is developed in similar fashion. The secretary identifies and ranks her top six time wasters in column 1, and you identify and rank your secretary's top six time wasters in column 3. Weights and scoring are the same as for the manager's profile. This procedure will provide both an independent and a joint assessment of where you and your secretary are wasting time.

When the profiles are completed, analyze them carefully. Look for relationships between the manager's profile and the secretary's profile. Does each person seem to create problems for the other? Generally, improvement for one will be very difficult unless the other also improves. This is especially true for your secretary. Unless you begin to use time well, it may be impossible for your secretary to do so.

Quite often, solutions as well as problems will be evident from the profile. Managers and secretaries commonly cause time problems for each other. This need not be. Identifying the problems makes it easier for each person to change. By combining the suggestions in this chapter with the ideas presented in Chapter 11, you will be able to develop workable solutions to your joint time problems.

THE SHARED SECRETARY

Not all managers have a private secretary. How much easier life in the office would be if they did! In many cases, however, a private secretary is simply not justified. The shared secretary is becoming commonplace. As you might expect, though, this leads to further complications in the secretary's role.

First of all, if more than two people share a secretary, the secretary will seldom be able to function as she ought to function. You may call her by any title you like, but she is not likely to be a secretary in the sense described earlier. She simply has too many "bosses" to serve any one extensively. Also, when a secretary works for several managers, conflict is inevitable. Many managers who share a secretary expect the secretary to resolve conflicts between them. They leave her to decide whose work is most important and whose work should be completed first. Naturally, since there is always a great deal to do, each work assignment is accompanied with a "hurry up" request. The secretary cannot possibly do everyone's "urgent" work first!

It is not the secretary's job to resolve conflicts between office managers. This job belongs to the top manager or to the team of managers themselves. Many bosses hesitate to make the tough decisions required; often they simply don't know how to handle the question of whose work should receive top priority.

There are three approaches to resolving this problem. Let's consider first the situation where all managers are equal in status.

1. *First come, first served.* This is, by far, the easiest approach. Whoever gets to the secretary first gets his or her work done first. Managers can take a number, date their work assignments (with times indicated), or simply put their work at the bottom of the pile. The first-come, first-served system is used in many offices because it dictates an order that is usually indisputable. However, many managers try to "beat the system" and push their projects ahead—

Figure 17. Manager's time waster profile.

FREQUENTLY IDENTIFIED TIME WASTERS (If any of yours are missing, add them below)	LISTING BY MANAGER		LISTING BY MANAGER'S SECRETARY		MANAGER'S COMBINED LISTING	
	RANK (1)	WEIGHT (2)	RANK (3)	WEIGHT (4)	COMBINED WEIGHT (5)	FINAL RANKING (6)
1. Telephone calls						
2. Interruptions, drop-in visitors, distractions						
3. Meetings— scheduled or unscheduled						
4. Crises, fire-fighting						
5. Lack of objectives, deadlines, priorities, daily plans						
6. Cluttered desk and office; personal disorganization						
7. Ineffective delegation						
8. Doing routine tasks						
9. Attempting too much at once						
10. Unrealistic time estimates						
11. Ineffective communication						
12. Procrastination, indecision, daydreaming						

Figure 17. *Continued.*

FREQUENTLY IDENTIFIED TIME WASTERS	LISTING BY MANAGER		LISTING BY MANAGER'S SECRETARY		MANAGER'S COMBINED LISTING	
(If any of yours are missing, add them below)	RANK (1)	WEIGHT (2)	RANK (3)	WEIGHT (4)	COM-BINED WEIGHT (5)	FINAL RANK-ING (6)
13. Inability to say no						
14. Leaving tasks unfinished; jumping from task to task						
15. Failure to listen						
16. Involved in too much detail; "doing it yourself"						
17. Socializing, idle conversation						
18. Lack of self-discipline						
19. Constantly switching priorities						
20. Paperwork, mail, reports, reading						
21. Failure to do first things first						
22. Travel, waiting, commuting						
23.						
24.						

Figure 18. Secretary's time waster profile.

FREQUENTLY IDENTIFIED TIME WASTERS	LISTING BY SECRETARY		LISTING BY SECRETARY'S MANAGER		SECRETARY'S COMBINED LISTING	
(If any of yours are missing, add them below)	RANK (1)	WEIGHT (2)	RANK (3)	WEIGHT (4)	COM-BINED WEIGHT (5)	FINAL RANK-ING (6)
1. Lack of objectives, deadlines, priorities, daily plans						
2. Attempting too much at once						
3. Inability to say no						
4. Lack of established office procedures						
5. Socializing, idle conversation, drop-in visitors						
6. Procrastination, indecision, daydreaming						
7. Cluttered desk and office; personal disorganization						
8. Leaving tasks unfinished; jumping from task to task						
9. Telephone calls, interruptions, distractions						
10. Mistakes; ineffective performance						

Figure 18. *Continued.*

FREQUENTLY IDENTIFIED TIME WASTERS (If any of yours are missing, add them below)	LISTING BY SECRETARY		LISTING BY SECRETARY'S MANAGER		SECRETARY'S COMBINED LISTING	
	RANK (1)	WEIGHT (2)	RANK (3)	WEIGHT (4)	COM-BINED WEIGHT (5)	FINAL RANK-ING (6)
11. Lack of independence; overcontrol by manager						
12. Switching priorities; confused priorities						
13. Unclear or incomplete instructions						
14. Inadequate filing system						
15. Not being kept informed by manager						
16. Interruptions by manager; disorganized manager						
17. Equipment problems						
18. Errands						
19. Failure to listen						
20. Redoing work because of incorrect dictation or unclear instructions						
21. Ineffective communication						
22.						

either by slippery, fast-handed maneuvering or by bribing the secretary.

2. *Time division.* In this approach to sharing secretarial time, each manager is assigned a particular time slot for his or her work. For example, John Miller's material is handled from 8 to 10 each day; Marilyn Johnson's from 10 to 12; Harry Tompson's from 1 to 3; and Sue Smith's from 3 to 5.

3. *Topical division.* Each work group has certain activities that are more important than other activities. The secretary can, therefore, order her assignments according to the importance of the projects. If, for example, financial reports are the most urgent bit of paperwork in a particular office, the secretary always works on them before other projects. If developmental reports are of secondary importance, she works on them only after all financial reports are completed. Of course, within the topical division a first-come first-served system may be needed to determine whose financial report is completed first.

When managers of unequal rank share a secretary, some additional considerations come into play. The top manager may want to set secretarial priorities as though all managers were equal. This means that the boss stands in line just like everyone else, has an equal amount of time for his or her projects, or is subject to the same topical priorities as everyone else.

A more traditional supervisor may insist that his or her work come first. This is, perhaps, the supervisor's right, but such a policy should be clear to all other managers and to the secretary as well. The head manager may prescribe a large block of time for his or her work to be completed, with lesser amounts of time for the work of subordinates. The time schedule can be adjusted for special projects, unexpected requirements, or a change in staff routine.

The main concern, of course, is to have the secretary spend her time in a way that is beneficial to everyone involved. The secretary should not be pressured or continually beseiged by "rush jobs." With proper time management, last-minute emergencies can be held to a minimum. Your secretary should be treated as a respected member of the executive team.

One solution to the shared secretary problem is to hire a part-time private secretary. In many cases, this would clearly be an improvement over current conditions. At the very least, an additional part-time secretary would eliminate some of the status problems that result from sharing secretaries. Many organizations have found local high school or junior college students excellent part-time secretaries.

Another solution to the shared secretary dilemma is to use job sharing for secretarial functions. In job sharing, two people share one position, each working for approximately half a work schedule. Under this approach, each part-time person can "specialize" in a particular type of work or perform duties for one or two managers. More and more organizations are experimenting with job sharing and are finding it to be a valuable approach.

TOWARD EFFECTIVE TEAMWORK

Questioning your outdated perceptions about secretaries is a crucial first step toward building a new, mutually beneficial manager–secretary relationship. Carefully assessing your needs and discussing time management problems with your secretary will bring you closer to the partnership we advocate. The special team-building tips presented in this section will help you initiate your improvement efforts.

Talk with your secretary about what being an executive team means. Be sure that secretaries are included in meetings and development programs. Make certain secretaries receive the same kind of training and development opportunities that other key staff members are offered. Many organizations that have extensive budgets for staff training programs exclude provisions for secretarial staff. If secretarial training programs are offered at all, they are usually the first to be cut when budgets are tight. Yet, it is during tight periods that a secretary's role is particularly crucial to the welfare of the work group. Some organizations are finding it extremely valuable to have managers and secretaries attend training seminars together. Through this experience, the manager and secretary are exposed to joint concerns and have an opportunity to discuss how these concerns will affect their team relationship.

Organize for action. Both the manager and the secretary should prepare a weekly plan, a daily to-do list, and a daily schedule. Discuss objectives and priorities early in the day. A daily plan will cut down on the number of interruptions you create for each other. It will also help you spot potential problems so that you can resolve them before they become serious.

Keep your secretary fully informed. Let her know what is happening, what you're thinking about, what you're doing inside and outside the office, and how you can be reached. It is extremely embarrassing for your secretary to have to tell one of your superiors or customers that she simply doesn't know where you are or when you will return.

Share your ideas about upcoming objectives and new projects. If you inform your secretary fully about your affairs, you will find it much easier to encourage other people to deal directly with your secretary on many routine matters.

Delegate effectively. Ask your secretary what kinds of things she could do that you are now doing. Look for ways to continually improve her abilities and to delegate even more authority to her.

Take time to give your secretary good instructions. Providing good instructions also means being a good listener and encouraging your secretary to talk freely. Allow for individual initiative and individual differences. Don't expect your secretary to do things exactly as you would do them. And don't expect her to be just like your previous secretary. Do not continually compare her work with the way "Mary used to do it."

Ask your secretary how you can manage your time better and how she can help you become more effective. Your secretary frequently sees your problems more objectively than you do. Encourage her to organize and schedule your time to improve the systems in your office. Ask your secretary how and when she would like to schedule various activities, such as mail, telephone calls, visitors, meetings, calendars, and filing.

Habitually use the "best" principle. Hire the best, pay the best, expect the best, and use the best equipment and procedures. Many managers do not realize that their secretary and the equipment she uses are an investment. They tend to skimp or try to get by with less. Your chances of achieving the goals you've set are enhanced when you make an investment in the best. If, by chance, you don't get top results, you are entitled (and expected) to invest in someone else.

Choose a secretary whose personality is compatible with yours. This does not mean that she must be exactly like you. You will, however, work more effectively if you like her as a person, respect and value her differences, and accept her idiosyncrasies.

Treat your secretary with dignity and respect. Give her the support and backup she needs. Don't embarrass or abuse her. Be aware of the disrespect you express when you attribute your mistakes to "my incompetent secretary." Don't use her as an excuse. For example, if you fail to get your report finished on time, don't apologize by claiming, "My secretary just didn't get it finished!" At the same time, don't allow your secretary to abuse her position. Secretaries should not reinterpret messages to other staff members for their own purposes or overplay their own status and power.

Ask your secretary what she would like to know about your projects, objectives, and priorities. Ask her what she could do and would like to do that you are now doing. But do not automatically assume that she would love to balance your personal checkbook, type reports for your lodge, or write letters to your Aunt Hazel.

Protect your secretary's time as much as she protects yours. Help her find a quiet hour when she needs one. Don't hesitate to do some routine tasks when your secretary is engaged in an important activity. For example, you might set a rule that if the phone rings three times, the boss answers it.

Do anything you can to encourage your secretary's development. Give her credit whenever you can. Remember that there is no limit to what you can accomplish if you are not too concerned with who gets the credit. Mention your secretary's name in activity reports. Describe how she has contributed to different projects in your office. And if you must criticize her work, do it gently. Give her all the credit that she deserves.

Invest in trade journals that will help your secretary develop her skills. *The Secretary,* available from the National Secretaries Association, is excellent. Also, see that she has an opportunity to read some of the same journals you read so she can understand your function even better. Encourage her to join the National Secretaries Association or any similar organization that can help her in her professional development.

Encourage your secretary to become a Certified Professional Secretary. This designation is earned by passing a rigorous examination administered by the National Secretaries Association and by meeting certain experience criteria. Certification is not easy to achieve. At present there are only 14,000 Certified Professional Secretaries in the United States. However, anyone who has ever had the privilege of working with one will instantly recognize the value of certification. The National Secretaries Association, which has chapters in many cities, can provide a great deal of information about this program.

As the business environment continues to change, the secretary's role will undoubtedly change with it. Word processing equipment and sophisticated information systems will bring with them additional secretarial responsibilities and pressures. At the same time, secretaries will continue to gain in terms of financial rewards and job fulfillment as managers learn to develop, rely on, and profit from their expanding capabilities.

11
Working with Others

MANAGING IS NOT a do-it-yourself job. No one works in a vacuum. Many people must cooperate if things are to happen right. Working with your staff, however, can be both rewarding and frustrating.

In this chapter we will focus on five questions that managers frequently ask in working with others:

1. How can we balance our priorities with those of others?
2. How can we extend time management concepts to others?
3. What can we do if the boss is our time problem?
4. How can we become more effective delegators?
5. Who is responsible for improving productivity?

BALANCING PRIORITY CONFLICTS

Conflict is a way of life in any organization. The conflict is not usually intentional, but it arises anyway. Superiors and subordinates frequently have differing views of what is most important and what ought to be done first. Unfortunately, there seems to be very little dialogue between superiors and subordinates about these differences. Little honest effort is made to resolve the conflict in a way that will enable both superiors and subordinates to function more effectively.

Much of this conflict stems from activity traps. We tend to become so engrossed in our activities that we lose sight of the purpose behind them. We fall into activity traps by focusing on activities when we should be focusing on objectives. If we were to observe any two individuals, one a superior and the other a subordinate, we would find many activity traps. Left to their own devices, both of them are likely to be so busily engaged in activity that they have lost sight of the purpose behind it.

When this happens, the following exercise, suggested by George Odiorne in *Management and the Activity Trap,* may prove helpful. First, the superior should make a list of the major responsibilities of the subordinate. For each area of responsibility, the superior should define the expected results. The subordinate should make a similar list, independent of the superior. In preparing such a list, the subordinate should consider his or her job in terms of the following question: "What are my major areas of responsibility, and in each area of responsibility, what results do I think the boss expects?"

Next, the two lists should be compared. According to Odiorne, the average superior and subordinate, caught in activity traps, will fail to agree at least 25 percent of the time on their recurring, ongoing responsibilities. As a result of the failure to agree on regular responsibilities, superior and subordinate will disagree at least 50 percent of the time on what major problems exist and which ones should be solved. Worst of all, superior and subordinate will disagree 90 percent of the time on what needs changing or improving.

Discovering the nature of disagreements between superior and subordinate will not automatically resolve them. With this information in hand, however, superior and subordinate can better define the next step. The goal is to reach a consensus on the important issues, important results, and appropriate priorities for working on them.

Ultimately, the only way to resolve differences in priority perceptions is to establish an ongoing dialogue with your superiors, your peers, and your subordinates. You must regularly discuss objectives, intended results, perceived priorities, and appropriate methods. These discussions must involve a great deal of give-and-take. They should not be one-way communication.

Effective managers discover many ways to develop a continuing dialogue with their staff about how to use time best. They find ways to talk about time waste without blaming others. They realize that it is pointless to complain to outsiders about how time is wasted by people in their organization. They talk directly to the people who are both part of the problem and part of the solution.

Groups exhibit complex, dynamic behavior patterns. Group behavior is more than simply the sum of each member's actions. Because of their constant interactions, group members often create time problems for one another. Many of these time problems are best resolved on a group basis. When group members tackle their time problems together, they can encourage and support one another.

GROUP TIME WASTER PROFILE

To approach time problems together, you and your staff must have a common starting point. You want to make sure that group efforts are directed at solving the most important time wasters first. Figure 19 is a form for preparing a group time waster profile. Refer to this form as you review the five steps below:

1. Have each member read over the list of time wasters and select his or her six biggest time wasters. Each member should rank these six time wasters in order of importance.

2. Assign each member's six time wasters the following weights:

> No. 1 time waster = 30
> No. 2 time waster = 25
> No. 3 time waster = 20
> No. 4 time waster = 15
> No. 5 time waster = 10
> No. 6 time waster = 5

3. Record the rank and weights for the time wasters identified by each group member on the profile sheet.

4. Add the weights across all columns for each time waster identified. Record the total group weights in the "combined weight" column.

5. Determine the final ranking for the group time wasters. The time waster with the greatest weight is the No. 1 group time waster. Continue in this fashion until all time wasters are ranked for the group.

With this procedure, you will be able to identify individual time wasters as well as time wasters shared by the group. The profile provides an excellent basis for group discussion on the causes of each time waster and possible solutions.

You are now ready to attack time problems on a group basis. Start with the biggest group time waster. Review the systematic approach to eliminating time wasters presented in Chapter 9.

One word of caution. It may be wise to verify the time wasters before trying to resolve them. Most of us don't know how we actually spend our time. Consequently, we sometimes identify time wasters incorrectly. Time spent trying to solve the wrong time waster is a waste. An easy way to verify time wasters is to have each member of the group keep a record of his or her time for a week or two. The time logs may produce some changes in the group time waster profile.

Discuss time problems with your staff without pinning the blame on anyone. In a nonthreatening atmosphere, people will generally discuss time waste openly. Such a discussion will quickly produce ideas about how time wasters might be eliminated or reduced. At this point, you have the beginning of a group action plan.

The group time waster profile can also be valuable in discussing good time use with your staff. In other words, if some wasted time could be recovered, how should it be spent? Why should time be spent on those particular activities? The discussion should emphasize intended results and planning. When you focus on plans for accomplishing objectives, you will discover ways in which everyone can use time more effectively. That, after all, is what priorities are all about.

Frequently, conflicts over priorities result from different opinions about cause-and-effect relationships. Many of us attempt to solve problems by treating symptoms rather than by identifying underlying causes. As a result, we often develop fuzzy perceptions about what truly causes a particular event. The solution to this problem is to dig a little deeper before drawing any conclusions. The first thought is not always the best thought. The real problem and the specific objective should be identified before any attempt is made to resolve different opinions about causes and effects.

Remember that you can't really motivate another person to use his or her time effectively. In fact, you can't motivate another person at all. The best you can do is help create an environment that fosters individual motivation. Motivation is an internal process. If you create the right kind of environment, people will indeed become motivated. They will become achievers; they will become more productive; and they will inevitably use their time in better ways.

IMPROVING GROUP TIME

A good part of this book has focused on you as an individual. The question from the individual standpoint is "How can I use my time better?" When you begin thinking about other people, however, the question changes to "How can we use our time better?" Realize that

Figure 19. Group time waster profile.

FREQUENTLY IDENTIFIED TIME WASTERS (If any of yours are missing, add them below)	1. MANAGER		2.		3.	
	RANK	WEIGHT	RANK	WEIGHT	RANK	WEIGHT
1. Telephone calls						
2. Interruptions, drop-in visitors, distractions						
3. Meetings— scheduled or unscheduled						
4. Crises, fire-fighting						
5. Lack of objec-tives, deadlines, priorities						
6. Cluttered desk and office; per-sonal disor-ganization						
7. Ineffective delegation						
8. Doing routine tasks						
9. Attempting too much at once						
10. Unrealistic time estimates						
11. Ineffective communication						
12. Procrastination, indecision, daydreaming						
13. Inability to say no						

Figure 19. *Continued.*

4.		5.		6.		COMBINED GROUP RANKING	
RANK	WEIGHT	RANK	WEIGHT	RANK	WEIGHT	COM-BINED WEIGHT	FINAL RANK

Figure 19. *Continued.*

FREQUENTLY IDENTIFIED TIME WASTERS (If any of yours are missing, add them below)	1. MANAGER		2.		3.	
	RANK	WEIGHT	RANK	WEIGHT	RANK	WEIGHT
14. Leaving tasks unfinished; jumping from one task to another						
15. Involved in too much detail; "doing it yourself"						
16. Socializing, idle conversation						
17. Lack of self-discipline						
18. Constantly switching priorities						
19. Failure to listen						
20. Paperwork, mail, reports, reading						
21. Failure to do first things first						
22. Travel, waiting, commuting						
23.						
24.						
25.						
26.						
27.						

Figure 19. *Continued.*

4.		5.		6.		COMBINED GROUP RANKING	
RANK	WEIGHT	RANK	WEIGHT	RANK	WEIGHT	COM-BINED WEIGHT	FINAL RANK

in order to improve time use in your group, you will have to make several compromises. When compromise is appropriate, don't hesitate.

Suppose, for example, that you are doing very little while your secretary is extremely busy on an important job. The telephone rings. You believe that your secretary should answer the telephone, so you do not answer it. Your secretary must drop what she is doing and answer the phone. Since the phone call is probably for you anyway, why not answer it yourself? Under some conditions, it may be a good idea for a secretary to answer the manager's telephone. But if this policy is applied rigorously, the results can be disastrous.

Keep the group informed about what's happening and what's going to happen. Do everything you can to focus the group on results, not on the amount of effort being expended. Help people see how their activities relate to the objective you are trying to reach. Help them realize that it's not how much you do that counts, but what you get done. Think about whether what you are asking for will truly overcommit your staff. Don't expect unrealistic results.

Don't create busy work for your staff. If business is slack, realize that there will be a lot of unassigned time. If you create busy work during slack time, the work is likely to continue when business picks up. This will make it even more difficult for your people to focus on what they ought to be doing.

Periodically analyze the work flow through your office, especially the paperwork. Where does it come from? Who does what to it? Where do the bottlenecks occur? Do people generate too many copies? Is there some way that you could simplify things? Could you modify the process in some way? Work simplification analysis will frequently yield improved results and reduce the amount of paperwork processing that takes place in your office.

Continually think about how to do things better. Keep asking your staff for better ideas. Hold brainstorming sessions regularly. For example, you might have your staff brainstorm this question: "How might we develop more effective meetings in this office?" Walt Disney used to tack problems to the office bulletin board each day as a challenge to his staff. As any wild solutions occurred to people, they were to scribble the ideas on a piece of paper and tack it on the board. When various solutions had been collected, the staff would evaluate the ideas together and pick the best ones.

Keep subordinates informed about your objectives, your priorities, your plans, and your thoughts. If a boss frequently switches priorities, he or she is showing signs of disorganization. A boss who does not have a firm grip on objectives will continually send out confusing signals to the staff.

Realize, too, that in order to be effective, managers must learn to shift their sense of achievement from their own efforts to the efforts of others. As we begin to move ahead in an organization, much of our progress is based on our own ability to perform. Our ego is tied up in our ability to achieve. When we become managers, we must learn to shift our sense of achievement from what we can do to what others must do. If we fail to do this, we frequently wind up trying to do too much while our subordinates are doing too little. Indispensable managers should be fired immediately.

Hold a weekly planning meeting to coordinate activities and focus on the best use of everyone's time. Either on Friday of the preceding week or on Monday of the current week, meet with your staff to discuss weekly plans and priorities. This will enable your staff to focus on objectives and results daily and to match activities with objectives. It will also help group members spot future problems and assist one another in handling problems before they become serious. The meetings should be simple, informal, and small. You should have no more than five to seven people at a meeting.

Consider making an evaluation of time use part of your performance review, but don't discuss it from a punitive standpoint. Focus instead on the positive ways in which people are using time. Praise and reward people for improvement. If you encourage people to report honestly on their progress, they will openly discuss the weaknesses in their performance.

People tend to live up to what is expected of them. If poor performance is expected, poor performance will be delivered. If great accomplishments are called for, these too will be delivered. Learn to have faith in and respect for your employees; you will be the winner and so will they.

EXTENDING TIME CONCEPTS TO OTHERS

An important principle in managing group time is this: Don't expect subordinates to manage their time well if you're not managing your time well. In other words, don't try to extend time management concepts to your staff until you have first learned how to use them yourself. You must set a good example before your instructions will have any meaning.

Frequently, when managers discover a good time management concept, they immediately think of at least one subordinate who could benefit from it. A time log is a good example. You've just been thinking about time logs and it occurs to you that George could really use a time log to get hold of his job. But if you have never done a time log yourself, don't expect George to favor the idea when you discuss it with him. Do a time log on your own job. Discover your own problems and work out ways to solve them. Then tell George what you have done, how the time log was beneficial to you, and what you have learned from doing it. This approach is far more likely to encourage George to keep a time log of his own.

Extending time concepts to your staff should be part of your regular training and development effort. To develop your staff, you must understand time management concepts, use them, be committed to staff development, and actively make time for it. You must have your own time in control before you can hope to influence others. Training requires patience, knowledge, and good judgment about your subordinates' developmental needs.

Developing staff requires a tremendous amount of your time. Unfortunately, many managers let staff development slide to the end of the line, then try to improve staff performance by exhorting people to adopt good time management principles. If you do one thing and say another, subordinates will follow the example of your actions.

Before focusing on your staff, try focusing on yourself. Ask your staff, "How can I manage my time better?" Many of your staff members may see your time wasters more readily than you do. Seeing another person's problem is always easier than seeing your own. Be receptive to justified criticism from your staff. This requires a positive atmosphere—and a sense of security on your part.

To determine how you, as the manager, can be most beneficial in resolving group time problems, ask your staff the following questions:

1. What do I do that wastes your time and hinders your performance?
2. What could I do to help you make better use of your time and achieve greater results?

Every manager should regularly pose these two questions to subordinates. If you have never asked your staff such questions, don't expect miracles. The first time you do so, you are likely to raise people's anxiety level. They will probably think, "I wonder what the boss is up to now?" Don't worry unduly, just keep asking the questions. If you are sincerely interested in their responses and are willing to act positively on them, you will soon find a better dialogue developing between you and your staff. This dialogue will undoubtedly be focused on intended results.

The atmosphere of your organization is important in improving time management in your work group. You and your staff must be able to talk honestly with each other. In a positive, open atmosphere, this is not difficult. In a negative, hostile atmosphere, it may be impossible. Failure to develop an open dialogue with your staff will result in poor communication habits, time wasted in activity traps, scapegoating, organizational politicking, and staff members trying to outmaneuver one another.

There is good reason to extend good time management principles to your staff. If everyone in the organization used time in the best way possible, productivity would jump. You'd be able to accomplish far more than you do at present. Many managers, realizing the possibilities, become very excited about making everyone more time-effective.

This desire for improving staff time use has led many managers to attend time management seminars. A seminar provides an opportunity to break away from the hectic pace long enough to think about what is happening. Managers begin to understand work functions and time habits in new ways. They gain an insight into time problems and a commitment to improvement.

But what happens? They attempt to translate their commitment into action by presenting their new ideas to superiors, peers, and subordinates. They are met with responses that vary from "So what?" to "That sounds like a good idea—maybe we'll look into it sometime." The people back home may agree intellectually, but they haven't had the same emotional understanding or commitment that the manager has gained in attending the seminar.

Many managers have overcome this problem by exposing other people in their organization to time management workshops. They arrange for workshops off the premises and call in time management specialists to conduct them. Everyone hears the same material. Everyone has an opportunity to think about and discuss the main issues. People begin to develop a togetherness, with a focus on how to make better use of everyone's time.

The checklist shown will help you evaluate the pros and cons of holding a time management workshop for your staff. Would the benefits of conducting such a workshop be worth the costs for you? If the workshop is done well, people will usually emerge with a list of several things to implement immediately—things that will make a

Possible Results of Holding a Time Management Workshop for Staff

Probability of This Happening

Positive	*High*				*Low*
1. Staff would favor the idea.	___	___	___	___	___
2. It would raise everyone's awareness of the importance of using time more effectively.	___	___	___	___	___
3. A quiet hour could be implemented for everyone.	___	___	___	___	___
4. It would lead to greater coordination and cooperation.	___	___	___	___	___
5. Time spent in meetings would be reduced.	___	___	___	___	___
6. We could initiate priority-setting conferences.	___	___	___	___	___
7. We could reduce interruptions for everyone.	___	___	___	___	___
8. People might start planning better.	___	___	___	___	___
9. Morale would be improved.	___	___	___	___	___
10. We would get rid of unproductive activities.	___	___	___	___	___
11. Other offices would be impressed.	___	___	___	___	___
12. Productivity would be increased by at least 10 percent.	___	___	___	___	___
13. If successful, the workshop would help me personally.	___	___	___	___	___
14. Other:	___	___	___	___	___
15. Other:	___	___	___	___	___

Negative					
1. Upper management might be hard to convince.	___	___	___	___	___
2. Some people might find it threatening.	___	___	___	___	___
3. If not successful, I would be blamed.	___	___	___	___	___
4. Other:	___	___	___	___	___
5. Other:	___	___	___	___	___

significant difference in your operation. Further, they will be committed to these actions and to supporting one another's improvement efforts. Morale will be improved as people feel more in tune with the total operation. And there will usually be an increase in productivity of at least 10 percent.

PROMOTING CHANGE

Much of the work in extending time management concepts to your staff will involve individual change. You will usually be working one on one with people in an attempt to change their behavior. However, many people resist change, for a variety of reasons. To encourage people to successfully change their behavior, you must help them answer the question "Why should I?" People change when they discover how the change will benefit them.

The following matrix will help you understand what motivates people to change their behavior:

	Unproductive Behavior	Productive Behavior
Positive Consequences	1	3
Negative Consequences	2	4

To change other people's behavior, you must help them move from the unproductive to the productive side of the matrix. Any form of behavior has both positive and negative consequences. Therefore, no matter how much you may think the other person should change, realize that the current behavior is supported by some positive feedback.

In seeking to help a person answer the question "Why should I change—what's in it for me if I do?" you are essentially looking for positive consequences to support the new behavior. These may be tangible or intangible, monetary or nonmonetary. But they must be perceived as valuable by the other person.

Start with cell 1—what the other person is doing now that you want changed. List any favorable consequences to the person for remaining with the present behavior. In cell 2, list any negative consequences for continuing to behave in the same manner. In cell 3, list any positive consequences the individual will enjoy if he or she changes to the new behavior. List any negative consequences for the new behavior in cell 4.

Consider the following example. Your assistant seems to be busy all day but seldom gets much accomplished. Furthermore, he always has work to take home in the evenings. You've talked with him on several occasions but have been unable to obtain any significant improvement. The main problem seems to be that he is disorganized and spends too much time visiting with other people. You want him to change. The question: "Why should he?" The following matrix shows an analysis:

	Unproductive Behavior	Productive Behavior
Positive Consequences	Enjoys visiting with others. Prides himself on handling things as they come. Values spontaneous work style. Is making average career progress.	Better performance evaluations. More personal time available.
Negative Consequences	Has to take work home. Poor reviews from boss.	Less time spent talking with others. Doesn't like to plan. Peers may think he is snubbing them.

If your assistant wants to progress and values having more personal time, there is a good chance that you can persuade him to change. But what if he hates to go home because his life there is miserable? Or what if he doesn't really want to be promoted and likes the role of "jolly good fellow"? Your chances of influencing a change will be poor.

Remember, if the favorable consequences to the person for doing the right things are low, and the favorable consequences for doing the wrong things are high, and the unfavorable consequences for doing the right things outweigh the favorable consequences for doing the right things, wrong things will probably happen. This same result will obtain if there is very little difference between outcomes. You must strive to present the change in as positive a way as possible. The more appealing the change is to the other person, the more likely he or she will make the change.

TIME–TALENT ASSESSMENT

In our discussion of objectives in Chapter 6, we pointed out that people are more likely to dedicate themselves to goals that are their own. They will work on activities assigned them by superiors, but they will not have the dedication that they readily give to their own objectives. This concept is crucial to effective time management in the work group. Your subordinates will achieve more in less time and be happier over better work if they can match their individual talents and preferences to the needs of the organization.

Of course, you hope to achieve an accurate match when you hire people. The employment process is an important step in achieving a good fit between employee and job. But even when you believe you have a good system, problems and disappointments develop. One reason is that both the external environment and the environment of your business change, and your needs in an employee change in response. Your employee also changes, and the carefully documented employee application only vaguely resembles the person who now works for you.

Rigid job descriptions often become a barrier to the flexibility required to successfully utilize time. But job descriptions can usually be altered. The time–talent assessment (TTA) described below is a useful tool for managers who feel the need for some reorganization in work assignments for their work group. It may be the technique that can get your unit moving again when you seem to be stagnating. Here are some guidelines for performing the TTA.

Needs Assessment

Begin by analyzing your goals. Do not do this lightly, for it is the basis for all further action. Do not assume that goals are what they seem to be. What is your business all about? If goals have been set carefully, this step is not difficult. If goal setting has been neglected or attended to rather haphazardly, this will require considerable work.

Determine the activities that lead to your goals. Again, question the activities that have traditionally been performed by your group. Where do these activities lead? Do they lead to the *new* goals of your organization? Are they a waste of time because they lead nowhere? Determine the actions necessary to accomplish your organizational goals.

Talent Assessment

Have all your staff members review their talents as they perceive them. Ask them to carefully consider and list (1) special skills, (2) likes and dislikes in job activities, (3) attitudes, and (4) the pros and cons of the job they presently perform. In addition, have close associates review one another's work, sizing up the positive attributes of their co-workers. Other people can often see an associate more objectively—the good points as well as the bad. To avoid conflict or controversy, however, have people evaluate *only* the positive attributes of their fellow staff members.

As the manager, perform the above tasks yourself in private. Consider the negative characteristics of each staff member as well as positive qualities. Also, perform a self-assessment. Encourage your staff members to assess your skills.

Matching

Identify your needs on 3″ × 5″ cards of one color (for example, white cards). Then identify all your staff's talents on 3″ × 5″ cards of another color (blue cards, for example). To identify talents accurately, you must integrate your perceptions with those of your staff members and their co-workers. You can make a quick judgment to save time, but your conclusions will be more accurate if you discuss individual needs privately with each staff member.

As you list talents on the blue cards, do not include the names of staff members. Put names on the backs of the cards or use a coding system to match talents and people. This will prevent you from stereotyping people and roles.

Sort out the various activities required to accomplish your company's goals. Match the blue cards to the white cards. Then discuss reassignments with your staff. Develop your new organization carefully and discuss new activities with group members individually. You now have a basis for reorganizing your work group.

Conducting a TTA has many advantages:

1. Misuse of personnel will become readily apparent.

2. Any need for additional personnel will be evident.

3. Retraining needs of present personnel will become obvious. You will be able to identify the learning programs your staff needs to meet changing demands.

4. The people on your staff are considered as individuals; their wants and needs are carefully matched to your needs. They will begin to put forth their best effort as their skills and desires take on new importance.

5. A spirit of teamwork will develop as each person performs a specific and publicized work assignment that contributes to the goals of the group.

Repeat the TTA as often as necessary to meet the changing needs of your organization. Remember, change is certain and successful time utilization depends on having staff members who maximize their talents and pull together toward a common goal.

THE BOSS AS A TIME WASTER

Subordinates aren't the only ones who present time problems. Sometimes the problem is the boss. Although it is nice to think that the boss is aware of the problems he or she creates for the staff, this is rarely true. Most people are so enmeshed in their own problems that they are unaware of the problems they create for others. Your boss is probably as unaware of the time problems he or she creates for you as you are unaware of the time problems you create for your subordinates. Because of this lack of awareness, constructive change often depends on the subordinate's initiative.

Many of us are intimidated by the mere thought of attempting to change the boss. We worry that the sky will fall in, that we will be fired, that we will not get our next raise, or that any one of a dozen calamities will occur. Much of the intimidation we bring on ourselves. This doesn't mean that all bosses will welcome awareness raising with open arms. Clearly, there are still some arbitrary, negative bosses. If your boss is of this variety, there is very little you can do about it. Perhaps you should be looking for a better boss.

Most bosses have a much better attitude. They as well as their subordinates realize that "we are all in this together." They know that if anything is going to happen, people must cooperate to make sure that it happens, and happens right. Most bosses are approachable. They are willing to listen and to discuss issues. They are willing to admit that they too do things wrong. Think about it this way: What would you do to your subordinates if they attempted to discuss a time problem that you created for them? If the consequences to them would not be disastrous, there is a good chance that the consequences to you will not be disastrous if you try discussing the same thing with your boss.

Approaching the boss deserves a bit of thought. Some bosses act as though they can do no wrong. Everything they do or say suggests that you exist solely for their purposes. Any problems that exist are strictly your problems, and if a directive comes from the top, you do it and don't ask questions. In this case, there is no way to resolve a time problem created by your boss. Again, you either accept it or look for a better boss.

Even a more reasonable boss needs to be approached with caution. Very few of us have good, objective data about the nature of our time problems. We *think* something is a problem or we *feel* something is a problem. Discussion of the problem frequently boils down to our opinion versus the boss's. In this situation, the boss usually seems to have the best opinion. After all, the boss is the boss. Remember, the boss is not likely to be aware of the problem he or she creates for you. Thus the boss may find it difficult to understand or agree with your point of view.

We have found one approach to work extremely well in this situation. Instead of trying to talk the boss into changing, do a time log. Record your time for a week or two. If the boss really presents a time problem for you, it will show up in your time log. If the boss does not appear as a time problem in your log, you should reassess the problem.

However, let's assume that the boss is the problem and that it shows up in your time log. You now have some reasonably objective data about the nature of the problem. You are in a position to discuss issues rather than opinions. At this point, go to your boss and present the data from your time log. You might begin like this:"I have been concerned about making the best use of my time in this job. I decided to record a time log and analyze exactly where my time is being spent. I would like to share the results of that analysis with you." Very few bosses will refuse such a request.

As you discuss the results of the time log, point out your strengths and weaknesses. Indicate to your boss the steps you have already taken to solve some of your time problems. Then say to the boss, "Here is another problem which I will need your help to solve." Describe how your boss is presenting a time problem for you.

At this point, you will discover that your boss is either aware or unaware of the problem. The discussion will have solved the awareness issue. Once the boss is aware, he or she will be either concerned or unconcerned about improving the situation. If the boss is not concerned with improvement, you have just discovered another fact about your job. You can accept it and go on from there or look for a new boss. If the boss is concerned, he or she will either act to improve the situation or fail to act. Whether the boss acts will depend on how well you and the boss plan for action. Discuss how to implement your plan effectively.

Some people believe that this approach is no better than the subjective opinion approach. They feel that the boss will simply dismiss their time log data as irrelevant. We have never found this to be the case. Almost any objective information is better than no objective information. People will respond much more positively to objective data than to opinions. The very worst that might happen is that the boss will question the manner in which you collected the data. The boss may believe that you made a mistake in recording your time. This is highly improbable—but let us assume that it did happen. Your next step is to agree with the boss that you might have made a mistake and suggest that you and the boss both record your time for the next week or two. In this case your position will be strengthened, since the time problem will show up not only in your time log but on your boss's time log as well.

Sometimes, the boss may not really be guilty. The problem may lie with you. For example, a friend of ours was recently denied a promotion he felt he deserved. Another manager was given the job and wound up as Bob's superior. Unfortunately, the new manager did not understand the job nearly as well as Bob did. As a result, the new boss spent a great deal of time talking with Bob, relying on Bob, and interrupting Bob during the day in order to gain a working knowledge of the department. Bob interpreted this as the boss creating a time problem for him. In fact, whatever Bob's new boss did, Bob would probably have interpreted it negatively.

After a great deal of discussion, we suggested that Bob stop fighting and approach the new boss differently. On the assumption that the boss was not as qualified as Bob to hold the new position, we thought that Bob's best strategy would be to do all he could to make his new boss look good.

It took Bob several weeks before he would even agree to this approach. However, once he did, he discovered many ways to help his boss create a positive impression and, at the same time, make himself look much better. In a few months, Bob helped his boss look so good that the boss was promoted again and Bob himself was promoted to head the department—the position he wanted in the first place.

Frequently we get so engrossed in looking at a situation from our own point of view that we are reluctant to admit there might be another point of view. Sometimes looking at things from another perspective helps us realize that we are responsible for a greater portion of the problem than we thought. Other people are not always the culprit.

EFFECTIVE DELEGATION

Delegation is perhaps the greatest tool available for developing capable subordinates, accomplishing better results, and gaining more time. Yet many managers are ineffective delegators. How well do you delegate? Take the quiz below to assess your delegation skills. Be as honest as you can.

How Well Do You Delegate?

	Yes	*No*
1. Do you allow your people to make mistakes?	_____	_____
2. Do your people make most of the day-to-day decisions without your approval?	_____	_____
3. Do your people get promotions at least as frequently as others with equivalent responsibility in your organization?	_____	_____
4. Do you frequently take work home or work late at the office?	_____	_____
5. Does your operation function smoothly when you are absent?	_____	_____
6. Do you spend more time working on details than you do on planning and supervision?	_____	_____
7. Do your people feel they have sufficient authority over personnel, finances, facilities, and other resources?	_____	_____
8. Do your people think that more tasks should be delegated to them?	_____	_____
9. Is your follow-up procedure adequate?	_____	_____
10. Do you overrule or reverse decisions made by your subordinates?	_____	_____
11. Do you bypass your subordinates by making decisions that are part of their jobs?	_____	_____
12. Do you do things that your subordinates could and should be doing?	_____	_____
13. If you were incapacitated for six months, is there someone who could readily take your place?	_____	_____
14. Do your key people delegate well to their own subordinates?	_____	_____
15. Will there be a big pile of paper requiring your action when you return from a trip or absence?	_____	_____
16. Do your subordinates expand their authority with delegated projects without waiting for you to initiate all assignments?	_____	_____

If you are an effective delegator, you answered yes to questions 1, 2, 3, 5, 7, 9, 13, 14, and 16 and no to the other questions. Did you get all 16 correct? If you did, congratulations! You have learned the art of delegating. If, on the other hand, you missed several questions, this chapter may be very valuable in helping you learn to be a better delegator.

Why aren't more managers good delegators? Following are 20 common causes of ineffective delegation:

1. Lack of agreement on the specifics of the task being delegated.
2. Lack of performance standards or guidelines.
3. Lack of proper training for the subordinate.
4. Ambiguous organizational objectives.
5. Lack of confidence in the subordinate's capabilities.
6. Lack of self-confidence and unwillingness to take the necessary risks.
7. Fear that the subordinate will perform better.
8. Fear of punitive action by superiors.
9. Interference by the superior in the delegated assignment.
10. Interference by superior's superior in the delegated assignment.
11. Failure to understand the advantages of successful delegation.
12. Reluctance to delegate preferred tasks.
13. Mistaking delegation for work assignment.
14. Desire for perfection.
15. Belief that things are going well enough as they are.
16. Unclear understanding of job responsibilities.
17. Failure to establish adequate follow-up procedures for the delegated assignment.
18. Fear of criticism.
19. Unwillingness to make mistakes or to allow others to make mistakes.
20. Strong desire to be "liked" by subordinates.

Delegation can be defined as "appointing someone else to act on your behalf." It means that you are asking a subordinate to do something that is normally part of your responsibility.

Many managers do not understand the difference between delegation and job assignment. Consider the following statement: "Delegation should always include the results to be achieved as well as the activities to be performed." Do you agree or disagree? If you agree with the statement, you are probably assigning jobs when you think you are delegating.

Delegation focuses on intended results. Work assignment focuses on intended activities and only secondarily on results. Work assignment is simply instructing a subordinate to complete a particular task in a specific manner. When you assign work, do not expect the same results as when you delegate. Your subordinates may not become more motivated and may not improve their skills—and the assignment may not save you any time.

In delegating, you must give the subordinate three things:

1. Responsibility and accountability for completing the assignment.
2. Authority to make necessary decisions and take appropriate action to complete the assignment.
3. Freedom to complete the assignment properly.

If any of these three elements is missing, delegation will usually be ineffective. The result is usually frustration and disillusionment for both superior and subordinate. Some managers believe that when they delegate, they gain time and also relieve themselves of some responsibility. This is only partially true. You never delegate responsibility. Those things you were responsible for before delegation you are still responsible for after delegation. What you delegate is the authority to act.

The process of delegation actually creates more total responsibility within the organization. You are responsible to your superiors for some set of results. When you delegate to a subordinate, you are still responsible for ultimate results. However, now your subordinate is also responsible to you for some portion of the original set of results. Total responsibility has increased.

DELEGATION AND AUTHORITY

Delegating the authority to act is not simply a yes-or-no issue. Authority is normally delegated in varying degrees. In general, there are six levels of delegated authority:

Level 6: Take action—no further contact with me required.

Level 5: Take action—let me know what you did.

Level 4: Look into it—let me know what you intend to do; do it unless I say no (veto authority).

Level 3: Look into it—let me know what you intend to do; don't take action until I approve (direct authority).

Level 2: Look into it—let me know possible actions, include pros and cons of each, and recommend one for my approval.

Level 1: Look into it—report all the facts to me; I'll decide what to do.

The degree of authority you grant to a subordinate will depend on many factors, including the complexity or importance of the project, the subordinate's expertise, time constraints, and your confidence and trust in the subordinate. Each level of authority has a purpose. For instance, as you are training and developing subordinates, you will move from lower levels to higher levels. You should not delegate the same level of authority to an untrained subordinate as you would to a trained subordinate.

Many managers delegate "by rote" and often grant inappropriate levels of authority to subordinates. To discover your own delegation pattern, fill out the form shown in Figure 20. For each subordinate, list all delegated assignments. For each delegated assignment, indicate the level of authority that was granted to the subordinate. Do a chart for each of your subordinates. Look for patterns. Do you tend to delegate at low levels for some subordinates but at high levels for other subordinates? Why or why not? Have you consciously considered the appropriate level or authority for each delegated assign-

Figure 20. Delegation assessment.

SUBORDINATE'S NAME						
	DEGREES OF AUTHORITY					
PROJECTS–RESPONSIBILITIES	1	2	3	4	5	6

ment? Analyzing the charts will help you spot areas where you can improve your delegation.

Each level of authority requires a different time investment on your part. For instance, the contact required between you and your subordinate at level 1 will be considerably greater than the contact required at level 6. Many managers are surprised to find that increased delegation leaves them with less available time instead of more. In general, the time investment will be less as the level of authority increases.

If you have not delegated duties in the past, you will probably experience greater anxiety as you begin to delegate more. You worry a great deal more about delegated tasks. You tend to overcontrol subordinates. You spend more time than necessary checking up on what's happening. This will not save you time. It may, in fact, require much more time than if you had done the delegated tasks yourself. The solution is not to do the tasks yourself but to learn how to cope with your increased anxiety.

IMPROVING DELEGATION SKILLS

Managers tend to be like their managers, who tend to be like their managers, who tend to be like their managers, and so on. If delegation is ineffective at the top of the organization, delegation will probably be ineffective at the bottom. Therefore, improvement begins at the top. In order to improve the delegation patterns of subordinates, managers may first have to improve their own delegation habits.

The following symptoms are prevalent in organizations where many managers are poor delegators:

1. Poor planning.
2. Frequent orders to subordinates.
3. Overcontrol or undercontrol of subordinates.
4. A boss who works longer hours than subordinates.
5. Fat briefcases in the evening.
6. Constant pressure and confusion.
7. Criticism of subordinates.
8. Lack of policy or too much policy.
9. Inequitable workloads.
10. Lack of objectives.
11. Slow decision making.
12. Misplaced decision making.
13. Too large a span of control.

14. Aggressive empire building.
15. Money spent haphazardly.
16. Subordinates who quote the boss too often.
17. Lack of detailed job knowledge.
18. Lack of priorities.
19. Too many secrets.
20. Disorganized effort.

If many of these symptoms exist in your organization, improving delegation will be beneficial. Consider the following guidelines:

1. Analyze your job:
   What are your objectives?
   What results are expected of you?
   What do you do?
   Can anyone else do it for you now?
   Can anyone be trained to do it?
   Do your superiors agree with your job analysis?
2. Decide what to delegate:
   Review the decisions you make most often.
   Assess the functions that make you "overspecialized."
   Review areas in which your staff members are better qualified than you.
   Assess areas you dislike (but remember to delegate both the good and the bad).
   Consider areas in which subordinates need development.
   Think of tasks that will add variety to subordinates' jobs.
3. Plan your delegation:
   Strive for "whole job" unity.
   Review all essential details and decisions.
   Clarify appropriate limits of authority.
   Establish performance standards.
   Determine appropriate feedback controls, including what information is needed, how often, and in what form.
   Follow this rule: If you can't control it, don't delegate it.
4. Select the right person:
   Consider interests and abilities.
   Evaluate the degree of challenge.
   Determine who needs it most.
   Try to balance and rotate items.
5. Delegate effectively:
   Clarify the results intended and the priorities involved.

Clarify the degree of authority, time frame, and other operating parameters.
Stress the importance of the job.
Take time to communicate effectively.
Establish a follow-up procedure.
6. Follow up:
Insist on timely information.
Act promptly and appropriately.
Insist on results, but not on perfection.
Encourage independence.
Learn to live with differences.
Don't short-circuit or take back assignments.
Reward good performance.

Don't expect overnight success. If you are a poor delegator, you didn't get to be the way you are overnight; you certainly won't change overnight. Much of the problem may lie in your attitudes and beliefs. In order to change your behavior, you will have to change your way of thinking. Then you will have to work at delegation improvement slowly, deliberately, and systematically.

Effective delegation requires a minimal level of trust between the delegator and the delegatee. Trust takes time to develop. Delegation works best when the organizational climate emphasizes employee development, growth, innovation, creativity, and human dignity. If your organization does not stress these attributes, the climate will have to be improved before delegation can be truly effective.

Remember, too, that delegation should flow downward but not upward. Upward delegation is a fact of life in almost any organization. It begins innocently enough, and the result is always the same. The superior winds up making decisions and doing work that the subordinate should be doing. Bill Oncken described upward delegation in humorous detail in his classic article "Management Time: Who's Got the Monkey?" (*Harvard Business Review,* November–December 1974). It happens quite easily. You're walking down the hallway one day when you pass one of your subordinates who greets you with "Hi, boss. By the way, we have a problem with XYZ."

You must be careful of that "we." "We" may mean that the subordinate has a problem which he or she wants to shift to you. However, being a concerned superior and wanting to help, you listen. As the subordinate explains the problem, you recognize an impossible dilemma: You know just enough to get involved but not enough to solve the problem on the spot. You will probably say something like this: "You're right, that's quite a problem. I'll have to check into it and get back to you." This means the ball is now in your court. The next step is up to you, not the subordinate. In fact, several days later, the subordinate may pop into your office and say, "Boss, about that problem we were discussing the other day. How are you coming?" This is called supervision.

Your challenge, at all times, is to make sure that the people who work on a problem are the ones who should be working on the problem. When subordinates bring you a problem, your task is to help the subordinates become good problem solvers. You do this not by solving subordinates' problems for them but by helping them solve problems for themselves. If you are the victim of upward delegation, take steps immediately to send the problems back to the people who own them. Resolve in the future never to take a problem that is not your own.

GUIDELINES FOR WORKING WITH OTHERS

In working with others to extend time management concepts, you always face the temptation of procrastinating. Training and developing staff is seldom urgent. There are so many things that seem to crowd out developmental effort. Resist these temptations. Review the following guidelines regularly to keep yourself focused on utilizing group time effectively:

1. Don't expect subordinates to manage their time well if you're not managing your time well. Subordinates tend to follow your example.

2. Take time to properly train and develop subordinates; it's a key part of your job.

3. Examine and analyze the work flow through your office and look for ways to simplify it.

4. Develop a time waster profile for your staff members and discuss with them how to begin eliminating the top time wasters.

5. Make a discussion of time use part of the regular performance review and set improvement objectives.

6. Praise your subordinates' improvement; don't criticize what remains to be done.

7. Keep subordinates informed about what is happening—changes in objectives, priorities, plans, thinking.

8. Use the last few minutes of each staff meeting to discuss ways of spending group time better; focus on how meetings can be improved.

9. Discuss priorities with subordinates and encourage them to discuss their priorities with you. An ongoing dialogue is essential if group members are to balance priorities and focus on the most important tasks.

10. Keep everyone focused on objectives and intended results in order to avoid activity traps.

11. Ask your subordinates how you might manage your time better and eliminate some of your time wasters.

12. Ask your subordinates what you do that creates time problems for them and how you can help them use their time more effectively.

Practicing time management techniques as you work with others is a singular challenge. As a manager, you must believe in the value of a systematic approach to time management before you can instill those concepts in your subordinates. Remember, too, that teamwork is essential if any positive results are to be achieved. When each member of the team practices good time management techniques daily, there are multiple victories: The company excels; the manager looks good and is able to perform effectively; and group members gain the positive experience of working together to achieve a common goal.

PRODUCTIVITY

Experts tell us that the only permanent way to eliminate inflation is to improve productivity. Seeing that everything possible is done to improve productivity within an organization is the basic responsibility of the manager. Over the years, a variety of programs, procedures, and approaches have been developed to increase productivity. Some have helped; others have not. Some have had lasting effects; others have faded. But almost all the programs have had one thing in common—they have been directed toward people at lower levels in the organization, especially workers in production areas.

In a way, there's much to be said for this approach. Certainly the greatest number of man-hours are expended at lower levels. Furthermore, traditionally this approach has worked. From Frederick Taylor's scientific management to the sophisticated analyses of today's industrial engineers, and participative approaches such as the Scanlon Plan, many techniques have been successful in increasing worker productivity.

Today, however, the concern with productivity must be given new focus. The office rather than the plant has become the dominant work location. Most people today work in offices, and many more will soon. Furthermore, productivity experts estimate that most office employees waste at least 45 percent of the day. Clearly, there is much room for improvement. Some experts suspect that the often maligned factory worker has a better productivity rate than many of his or her office counterparts. Productivity is not an issue only at lower levels; it is an issue from the bottom to the very top of an organization. An optimally functioning organization demands effective, productive people in all positions—including management.

Attempts to "sell" productivity to office personnel and managers have met with limited success. Productivity and wages are not linked directly. Besides, we all believe we're OK—it's the other guy who's the problem. A great deal of "them-ism" is making the rounds today. "The organization would be in good shape if only they would improve." At times "they" are subordinates; at other times "they" are peers or superiors; at still other times "they" simply refers to things in general.

"They" are part of the problem. There's a glimmer of truth in almost any "they" statement, but there's also a big danger. As long as you focus on some outside force as the source of a problem, you never see the total picture. You actually begin to believe in your own immunity and nonresponsibility. When top management engages in this kind of fuzzy thinking, the results can be disastrous.

Consider this: Most managers tell us that they have no more than one to three productive hours in a day. Whose fault is it? In the beginning, these managers tend to fix the blame on outside factors. After some analysis, however, most agree that they are the problem. They complain that they need more time, yet they waste what time they have. They still attend unproductive meetings and generate unnecessary paperwork. They engage in an unbelievable amount of trivial work, oblivious to the fact that it decreases their productivity and that of others.

The question of productivity is intertwined with time management. Using time more effectively and efficiently will increase productivity. The best way to improve productivity within an organization is to have people focus on objectives and how they can best use their time to achieve those objectives. This focus must begin at the top. It is naive to expect subordinates to improve until the boss improves.

Most of the concern about productivity focuses on economic issues. While the economic gains are certainly significant, the psychological aspects of improved productivity are equally potent. Consider what increased productivity can mean to you personally. Think back to one of those days when nothing seemed to go right. The only way you could have made more mistakes was by getting up earlier. You ran in circles all day long, and by 5:00 P.M. you had accomplished exactly zero. How did you feel? Tired. Frustrated. Irritable. Cranky. Displeased with things in general. You probably went home, kicked the cat, yelled at the kids, crabbed at the spouse, downed two martinis, and collapsed on the couch. Your energy level was nil. You felt exhausted and drained.

In contrast, think of one of those days when everything seemed to go right. You piled success upon success. You were able to focus on important things all day long, and by 5:00 P.M. you had accomplished a great deal. How did you feel? Great. Exhilarated. Satisfied. Confident. You loved the world. You played with the kids, laughed with your spouse, and enjoyed your life. Your energy level was high. You could have danced all night.

Did you work longer on one day than the other? No. Did you work harder on one day than the other? Probably not. What accounts for the difference in the way you felt, in your outlook on life? Only your sense of accomplishment.

Productivity improvement would be worthwhile even if there were no economic gains. The psychological payoff alone is tremendous. People who accomplish more live better. Productivity is good for the psyche. It also raises profits and curbs inflation.

Whether you are motivated economically or psychologically, you need to become more seriously committed to productivity. Start by improving your own time management. Then get everyone below you, above you, and around you into the act. Become positively critical. Question everything. Keep asking about the best way to spend everyone's time.

12
Managing Sales Time

IN ONE WAY or another, almost all of us are in a selling function. We sell ourselves and our organization virtually every day of our lives. All time management concepts can be related to selling functions or to the jobs of people supervising others who are salesmen*—either directly or indirectly.

In this chapter we will focus on selling from the standpoint of people who actively call on customers to sell a product or a service. We will adapt some of our earlier concepts to the salesman's job. Some of our ideas will be merged with the excellent suggestions of Robert Vizza.†

"Time is money." Ben Franklin's old message has direct application to the people involved in selling. More than in any other profession, the salesman's personal and business fortune is directly affected by the way he or she spends time. Well-spent time is directly translated into additional revenues. Lost time or misused time results in lost opportunities—and a small paycheck. For this reason alone, the salesman has a powerful incentive to improve time management techniques. Nonetheless, many salesmen who say "Time is money" do not act that way.

---

* We have used the term "salesman" instead of "salesperson" throughout this chapter. We recognize, applaud, and encourage the increasing number of women who are succeeding in sales jobs and setting sales records. We trust that our use of the more traditional word will not get in the way of the concepts we advocate.

† *Time and Territorial Management,* R. F. Vizza Associates, 1975.

The basic system we have advocated throughout this book will be applied here:

1. Analyze your situation.
2. Clarify your priorities.
3. Set your objectives.
4. Plan for results.

ANALYZE YOUR SITUATION

Do you spend your time wisely? The following quiz will help you determine the answer. Consider each question carefully and honestly.

Salesman's Time Test

	Always	Usually	Sometimes	Rarely	Never
1. Do you do things in priority order?	—	—	—	—	—
2. Do you accomplish what needs to get done during the day?	—	—	—	—	—
3. Do you tackle difficult or unpleasant tasks without procrastinating?	—	—	—	—	—
4. Do you feel you are earning your potential?	—	—	—	—	—
5. Do you prepare a daily plan and set priorities?	—	—	—	—	—
6. Do you get your paperwork done on time?	—	—	—	—	—
7. Do you use your waiting and traveling time effectively?	—	—	—	—	—
8. Do you spend enough time planning?	—	—	—	—	—
9. Do you schedule your clerical work during low-value time instead of prime time?	—	—	—	—	—
10. Before you leave home in the morning, do you know where your first sales call will be?	—	—	—	—	—
11. Do you have a specific purpose for each call (not a social purpose)?	—	—	—	—	—
12. Do you have a list of the top 10 percent of your customers?	—	—	—	—	—
13. Do you have a list of the top 10 percent of your prospects?	—	—	—	—	—
14. Do you know how many calls per year it is economical to make on each account?	—	—	—	—	—
15. Do you take enough time to prospect and develop new business?	—	—	—	—	—

	Always	Usually	Sometimes	Rarely	Never
16. Do you find that you have to wait to see people?	—	—	—	—	—
17. Do you know how many calls, on average, you have to make to produce an order?	—	—	—	—	—
18. Do you set a dollar value on each minute of your time?	—	—	—	—	—
19. After each call, do you schedule the date of the next call on that account?	—	—	—	—	—
20. Do you set specific volume or dollar objectives for customer, prospect, and product?	—	—	—	—	—

Score yourself in the following manner:

Number of "always" answers	___ × 5 =	___
Number of "usually" answers	___ × 4 =	___
Number of "sometimes" answers	___ × 3 =	___
Number of "rarely" answers	___ × 2 =	___
Number of "never" answers	___ × 1 =	___
Total		___

If you scored between 90 and 100, you are probably a superstar salesman. You are using your time effectively, and your paycheck is probably the envy of all your associates.

If you scored between 75 and 89, you are doing very well. You have almost "arrived" but are in the difficult position of needing an extra boost to make you great. By the time you complete this chapter, you should be on the way to developing top time management habits that will lead you to the winner's circle.

If you scored between 50 and 74, you may be heading for trouble. Even if your present sales record is not bad, it is not nearly as good as it would be if you became serious about managing time.

If you scored between 20 and 49, you must be living on luck—or there must be some unusual factors that have kept you in the sales force. You, too, can improve. In fact, you could win the "greatest improvement award" if you made an all-out effort to change your present style. You face a real challenge. With the time techniques presented in this chapter you can meet that challenge head on—and succeed!

CLARIFY YOUR PRIORITIES

Everything you do is not equally important. Not even all your customers are equally important. One of your most difficult jobs is to treat all customers fairly, render good service to each, and yet give each account the amount of time it deserves. You must keep your objectives in mind at all times and match your activities to those objectives. Spending too much time with those safe, sure, friendly accounts that buy very little makes you feel good, but it also prevents you from developing accounts that buy more. Remember, big buyers can be just as friendly as small ones.

Most salesmen would be better off if they dropped 10 to 20 percent of their present customers and concentrated on those customers with greater potential purchasing power. But salesman can't do this arbitrarily. They must carefully determine the proper mix by comparing the potential value of all customers and prospects.

Calculate the potential value of each of your present accounts in this way:

	You	Sample
1. Past sales	$	$100,000
2. Future sales potential (plus or minus)	$	$ 50,000
3. Total sales potential (1 + 2)	$	$150,000
4. Probability of obtaining future sales potential (item 2)		.50
5. Potential value (1 + [2 × 4])	$	$125,000

Start with actual sales during the past period to a customer. Use a one-year period for all comparisons unless you have a special reason to use another time frame. To that figure, add any future sales potential for a similar period of time. Subtract future sales potential if the amount of business is likely to decrease. Record the combined figure on line 3. This gives you the total sales potential for that customer in the future period.

Next, determine the probability of obtaining the future increase (or decrease) in potential sales. For example, a high probability of obtaining the future increase (or decrease) might be .90; a medium probability might be .50; a low probability might be .20. Be as realistic as you can in estimating the probability factor.

Finally, determine the total potential value of the customer by multiplying future sales potential times the probability of obtaining that potential. Add this figure to the past sales figure.

Prospects should be handled in a slightly different manner, as shown below:

	You	Sample
1. Market potential	$_____	$100,000
2. Estimated share of market obtainable	_____	20%
3. Forecast (1 × 2)	$_____	$ 20,000
4. Probability of obtaining forecast	_____	.70
5. Potential value (3 × 4)	$_____	$ 14,000

Begin with the market potential of each prospect for a specific time period. Next estimate what percentage of that market potential you might be able to capture. Multiply the two figures together to obtain the forecast potential for the prospect. Next, determine the probability of obtaining the estimated market share. Finally, calculate the potential value of the prospect by multiplying the forecast by the probability of obtaining that forecast.

You can perform this analysis for every customer and prospect or for every group of customers or prospects. You might group your accounts by industry, by location, or by some other system that makes sense to you. Regardless of how you do it, you will gain valuable insights from performing this analysis.

Your next step is to compare the potential dollar value of both customers and prospects to determine how to classify them. Your accounts and prospects should be grouped into the following categories:

A = 10% Top customers or prospects
B = 20% Second best customers or prospects
C = 40% Third best customers or prospects
D = 20% Fourth best customers or prospects
E = 10% Least valuable customers or prospects

Focus your time on the top customers and prospects to maximize the returns on your selling efforts. Remember, what counts is not whether you like a customer, but how much business that customer may generate. Keep in mind that it may be better to call on an A prospect than on a D or E customer. While the prospect may require greater effort on your part, the potential value of your effort is much higher. Your best bet, then, is to call on the highest-value accounts or prospects first.

Figure 21. Sales time record.

Salesperson _____   Day _____   Date _____

TIME	CUSTOMER CALLS										PROSPECTS										TRAVEL	WAITING	PAPERWORK	TELEPHONE	EXPEDITING														
	SALES					SERVICE					SALES																												
	A	B	C	D	E	A	B	C	D	E	A	B	C	D	E																							
7:00–7:15																																						
7:15–7:30																																						
7:30–7:45																																						
7:45–8:00																																						
8:00–8:15																																						
8:15–8:30																																						
8:30–8:45																																						
8:45–9:00																																						
9:00–9:15																																						
9:15–9:30																																						
9:30–9:45																																						
9:45–10:00																																						
10:00–10:15																																						
10:15–10:30																																						
10:30–10:45																																						
10:45–11:00																																						
11:00–11:15																																						
11:15–11:30																																						
11:30–11:45																																						
11:45–12:00																																						

12:00–12:15																										
12:15–12:30																										
12:30–12:45																										
12:45–1:00																										
1:00–1:15																										
1:15–1:30																										
1:30–1:45																										
1:45–2:00																										
2:00–2:15																										
2:15–2:30																										
2:30–2:45																										
2:45–3:00																										
3:00–3:15																										
3:15–3:30																										
3:30–3:45																										
3:45–4:00																										
4:00–4:15																										
4:15–4:30																										
4:30–4:45																										
4:45–5:00																										
5:00–5:15																										
5:15–5:30																										
5:30–5:45																										
5:45–6:00																										
Total time in hours																										
Percentage of total day																										

Your next step is to determine how much time you invest in the various categories. One good way to discover how you are presently using your time is to keep a time log. In an earlier chapter we illustrated a diary time log. In this chapter, we will present another type of log, one that is less detailed than the diary, but much easier to keep. Salesmen seem to be particularly averse to paperwork. We therefore recommend the sales time analysis form shown in Figure 21.

The form is relatively simple. Each row represents a 15-minute segment of your day. The columns represent typical daily activities. There are additional blank columns for activities that are unique to your job. Simply place a check mark in the appropriate column as you proceed through the day. If you perform more than one activity during a 15-minute segment, record the predominant activity for that segment. At the end of the day, add up the check marks in each column. Four check marks equal one hour. You can then calculate what percentage of your day is invested in each activity.

Record your activities for a week or two and then analyze your time allocations. Are you spending your time productively? What changes should be made? Do you see any relationship between your time patterns and your level of results? Do you spend as much productive selling time as you thought you did? Do you see where your time is being wasted? Do you spend too much time on C, D, and E accounts and not enough on A and B accounts? Do you prospect enough? Do you prospect the most valuable accounts? Do you waste your time in needless travel? Are you spending too much time waiting? Are you doing paperwork during prime parts of the day?

SET YOUR OBJECTIVES

You are now ready to make changes in your time habits. The first step is to clarify your objectives. Objectives may be set in terms of dollars, volume, or any combination that seems appropriate to you. Recall the objectives pyramid discussed in Chapter 6. You will be most effective if you can break your objectives down into subunits. You should easily be able to break your sales objectives into weekly units and even into daily units.

PLAN FOR RESULTS

Remember that you cannot do objectives. You must do activities. Planning enables you to determine the activities necessary to reach your objectives.

When you plan sales time, you must determine how much time you will need to realize the potential value of each account. Presumably, you have already developed effective selling skills. This chapter is intended to obtain better results in less time. If your sales skills need improving, by all means take the time necessary to develop them.

Begin your planning with present accounts. The exercise shown on page 218 will help you compute the time you'll need to realize the potential value of your accounts. Use a one-year time period for your calculations unless a shorter time period would better serve your purposes.

Start with the number of calls required per account. This may be a figure set by company policy, or it may be the number of calls you need to make in order to maintain your present level of business with that customer. Regardless of the basis you use, begin with the number of calls you will need to make on that account during the time period in focus. Remember that A accounts may require more calls than B accounts, B accounts more calls than C accounts, and so on.

Next, determine the number of accounts in each category. Multiply the number of calls required per account by the number of accounts to arrive at the total number of calls required for all your accounts in each classification.

Calculate the length of the average call for each classification. Multiply the total number of calls by the approximate length of each call to determine the total number of call hours needed for your accounts.

Next, consider your average travel time per call. Multiply the average travel time by the number of calls. Add the total number of call hours to the total travel time to obtain the total field time required for your accounts.

After you have finished this analysis for your present accounts, focus on your prospects and follow the same procedure. Once you have determined the total field time for both customers and prospects, consider the total nonselling time required. The total field time plus the total nonselling time equals the total time required to handle both customers and prospects.

Compare your total required time with your available time. Clearly, if you need 90 hours a week but have only 60 hours available, you have a problem. If you see conflicts, try to resolve them. This is the place where planning really pays off. Is there any way to reduce the total travel time per call? Is it possible to reduce the length of the average call and still obtain good results? Is it possible

Time required to realize the potential value of accounts.

	YOU						SAMPLE					
	A	B	C	D	E	Totals	A	B	C	D	E	Totals
1. Number of calls required per account							9	7	5	3	1	
2. Number of accounts							10	20	40	20	10	100
3. Total number of calls required (1 × 2)							90	140	200	60	10	500
4. Length of average call, in hours							1	1	1	1	1	
5. Total number of call hours required (3 × 4)							90	140	200	60	10	500
6. Average travel time per call, in hours							$\frac{1}{2}$	$\frac{1}{2}$	$\frac{1}{2}$	$\frac{1}{2}$	$\frac{1}{2}$	
7. Total travel time (3 × 6)							45	70	100	30	5	250
8. Total field time required, in hours (5 + 7)							135	210	300	90	15	750

to decrease the number of calls on accounts in certain categories and still obtain results?

Again, this analysis can be performed on individual accounts, groups of accounts, or all of your accounts together. The analysis can be performed over the span of a year, a month, a week, or a day. Remember, too, that you must allow time for the unexpected. There will be gas shortages. There will be strikes. There will be missed flights. There will be customers who are unable to see you at the last minute. These unexpected events will add to the total time required and must be considered in your calculations.

Build your planning around this approach. Determine how much time you will need to reach your selling objectives. Focus your efforts. Look for ways to cut down on nonselling time or travel time. Improve your selling skills, research skills, prospecting skills, servicing skills, and interpersonal skills. Learn how to get better results in less time.

THE PAYOFF

What's the payoff? For most salesmen it is a better return on the time invested in their jobs. This return can also be calculated. To determine the return on time invested, use the following equation:

$$\frac{\text{Gross margin on potential value}}{\text{Cost of time invested}} = \text{Return on time invested}$$

Gross margin is the difference between sales and the cost of goods or services sold. Cost of time invested is determined by multiplying the total time units required to reach the sales figure by the direct cost of that time. Direct costs will include the salesman's salary, commission, bonus, travel expenses, and other expenses. If the return on time invested (ROTI) is greater than 1, you're doing well. The higher the ROTI above 1, the better. An ROTI lower than 1 indicates that you need to improve.

Try to equalize the return on time invested for all categories of accounts. In other words, the ROTI for A accounts should be equal to the ROTI for B accounts, C accounts, D accounts, and E accounts. You can do this by establishing a standard ROTI. Calculate the top 10 to 20 percent of your customers and use this as your standard. Then adjust all categories of accounts to get as close to the standard as possible. You can make adjustments by varying the number of calls, duration of calls, travel time, or nonselling time. As you balance the ROTI for all accounts, you will be spending time on each account in proportion to its potential value.

The ROTI calculation serves two important functions. It enables you to allocate your time to accounts on the basis of their relative value. It also enables you to determine the number of calls you should be making on any given account for maximum value.

Here is an example of how to bring the ROTI into balance. If the gross margin on potential value for an account is $20 and you reduce the number of calls on that account, the total sales may drop, reducing the gross margin to $18. However, the cost may drop from $17 to $11. This means that the ROTI, instead of being $20 divided by $17, will now be $18 divided by $11. The return on time invested has increased from 1.2 to 1.6. With this ROTI increase, you have gained additional time to produce still better results from other accounts.

Is it worth it to focus on selling time in this fashion? We think so. So does Stan, whom we met several years ago during a seminar. Stan was a hardworking, mediocre salesman. He never gave his boss much trouble. He usually came fairly close to his quota, and sometimes he actually made quota. He was too good to fire but not good enough to get excited about. His boss sent him to our seminar hoping for a miracle.

We started to work with Stan immediately. We showed him how to clarify his objectives—how to decide exactly what he was trying to accomplish with his time. We also showed him how to analyze his job—how to compare what he thought he was doing with what he ought to be doing, and with what he actually was doing. We encouraged him to keep a time log. We showed him how to plan his time every week and every day. We examined many of his time wasters and talked about how they could be eliminated or controlled. We finished off the seminar with a pep talk on conquering procrastination.

We didn't hear much from Stan for several months. Then one day we received a phone call. Stan said, "Look, the next time you're down this way, let's have lunch together. I want to tell you about all the wonderful things that have been happening to me." Well, Stan sounded excited so we made a special point of going down to see him.

He said he'd started keeping his time log just as he'd been taught—recording activities in 15-minute segments, assigning a priority value to each activity, examining why he was doing that particular task at that time. We'd told him to expect some surprises. He found them all right. But one thing puzzled him. He had discovered that most of his sales were closed before noon. At first, he thought he'd made a mistake in his time log. He worked regular hours, 9 to 5, just like most of the other salesmen. So he recorded two more weeks. The results were the same. Ninety percent of his sales closed before noon. Stan started thinking about that and searching for explanations. He found several. For example, although he had never noticed it before, many of his customers started the day much earlier than he did. They stopped earlier, too. Then he asked himself what would happen if he started work at 8 instead of 9. He tried it and sales went up. Stan got excited. He began starting at 7. Sales went up again. Wow! He started coming in at 6. It didn't work: no one was around to sell to.

Stan was now working 7 to 5 and he started thinking about afternoons. He wondered what would happen if he quit earlier. Twelve hours is a long day and Stan valued his personal time. So Stan began quitting at 4. Nothing happened. He quit at 3 and lost a sale. He quit at 2 and lost a few more. But the increase in the morning more than made up for the difference. He finally arranged things so he was working only from 7 to 12.

We said, "Stan, that's really fantastic!" He said, "Wait a minute, you haven't heard the best part yet. The shorter hours are OK, but now that I'm setting objectives and acting on the basis of priorities those shorter hours are producing better results. Here it is only September and I'm already selling at 137 percent of my quota! They have a picture of me on the wall in the office. I'm the leading salesman in this region. I'm 46 years old and this is the first time I've been on top. My sales manager thinks it's a miracle—and I haven't even told him I'm working only from 7 to 12! If he knew that, he'd probably make me work until 5 like everyone else."

Stan was beginning to feel like a winner for the first time in his life. He was getting more done and doing it in less time. He had more time for himself and more money to spend enjoying that personal time. Like most people, Stan had always wanted to do a lot of things. He now started doing them. He built a sailboat; he attended classes at the university; he began scouring antique shops in the area; he learned to refinish furniture.

Stan led his company in sales that year and the next year. He had more personal time and more money than ever before. His life took on a whole new dimension. Stan was clearly a winner in more ways than one.

No one can guarantee you the same kind of success that Stan found. But you can become more effective than you are now. Begin by analyzing how you currently spend your time and look for ways to spend it better. Clarify your objectives and determine your real priorities. Consistently plan your time weekly and daily. Tackle the time wasters in your life and eliminate them. Develop some new time habits, like learning to *do it now*. In short, plan for success through careful management of your time.

TIME TIPS FOR SALESMEN

Below are a number of time tips for salesmen. Many of these ideas may prove helpful to you in your efforts to achieve your goals.

1. *Respect your customer's time*. A customer will respect you more and therefore pay more attention to you if you are careful to make appointments and do not overstay your welcome. For your top-priority customers, determine meeting schedules, slack times, and times when deadlines may make people impatient.

2. *Use the telephone to make and verify all appointments*. A phone call can save you a useless trip when unexpected events force a change in your customer's plans.

3. *Cross the "drop-in visit" off your list of techniques—forever*. The drop-in visitor is the nemesis of busy executives. You do not need the ill will of your customer when you attempt to make a sale.

4. *Give your customer a fair estimate of how much time you will need to make your sales pitch*. Keep within your estimate. Plan your presentation carefully to ensure that you use your limited time wisely.

5. *Minimize the time that you will be wasting while your customer's time is being wasted*. Nothing is more frustrating than "cooling your heels" while your client is being delayed by an unexpected call, visit, or emergency. You can minimize these interruptions by following the guidelines above. You can also try to get the customer out of the office—where interruptions are less likely. If interruptions do occur, have standby activities ready so you can use the time productively. Background reading is a good activity during waiting time. You may also want to compose some short letters. If it appears that an interruption will take a great deal of time, you may want to reschedule your meeting.

6. *Know the decision makers in each company*. If possible, see the decision maker instead of his or her subordinate. If you talk directly to the decision maker, you will not have to wait until a third party gets around to conveying your message.

7. *Guard against the temptation to visit with customers who are your*

friends rather than those who can increase your profits. A few minutes with a new prospect may lead you to your goals faster than a relaxing, friendly chat with a close customer.

8. *Make good use of your travel time.* Salesmen spend a great deal of time in travel. This time should not be wasted. As noted in Chapter 13, there are many activities you can engage in while you travel in a car, train, or plane. Use dictating equipment for short memos. Listen to cassette tapes for useful training tips while on the road.

9. *Continue to read motivational materials.* Selling is always a matter of selling yourself. Motivational materials continually convince you that you are a useful product. These confidence builders are always a good investment of your time.

10. *Develop a successful selling habit.* Be timewise at all times. Write these four points on a card and carry it with you:

List objectives and priorities.
Prepare a daily action plan that includes daily priorities.
Work in order of priorities.
Do it now.

Success breeds success. As you begin to realize the benefits of successful time control, you will become more and more committed to implementing sound time management techniques. Why? Because they work! Once you begin living the rule that "time is money," you will never again be happy with a haphazard approach to life. Each moment will have value, both financially and nonfinancially. And you will gain a sense of satisfaction that comes only with achievement.

13
Travel Time

EFFECTIVE TIME MANAGEMENT has become one of the most popular topics of conversation in the business world today as more and more executives strive to make each day and each moment count. Successful executives know where their time goes, know how to plan their time, and know the value of careful scheduling. Their office time is organized, and they are happily on their way to accomplishing important goals. Then they go on a trip.

Business executives repeatedly complain that trips out of the office break down useful time management habits they have developed. Many report that they have to spend too much time getting ready, that the trip is an unpredictable mixture of joys and woes, and that they have too much work accompanied by an emotional letdown when they return.

Certainly, an out-of-town trip presents more of a challenge than the routine of office life. It can, however, become a stimulating diversion and a gift of time rather than an obstacle to effective time management.

BEFORE YOU LEAVE

The key to a successful business trip is to handle all the details of the trip before you leave. You want to eliminate as much uncertainty as possible so you can cut down on time-wasting hassles. Each trip should be a lesson on how you can eliminate unnecessary steps from an activity that usually takes a high toll on your time and stamina.

First of all, ask yourself, "Is this trip really necessary?" Must you be there in person? What purpose does your presence serve? Could you handle the business as well by mail or phone? Is there another person from your company who is in closer proximity than you? If not, is there someone else in your office who would profit from making the trip in your stead? Remember, you can delegate out-of-town tasks to your subordinates as well as in-house assignments.

If you make frequent trips to a particular location, perhaps you can cut down on the total number of trips. Is there a way you can do more on the trips you make so you won't have to travel to that location so often?

You might also consider asking your client to visit you. This approach will not always work, but the effort is well worth it. Your associate might just jump at the opportunity to get away for a while. For some people, particularly those who do not travel frequently, a trip is a welcome break.

When you must go yourself, be certain that you plan your trip carefully to make sure it is successful. Begin with a good travel agent. Try several agencies until you find one you like. Then stick with it. If you stay with the same travel agent, you will have someone who knows your needs, likes, and dislikes. The agent can make all the arrangements for your arrival and departure time, gather your tickets, arrange for ground transportation, and route you the way you prefer to travel. Also, if you stay with one agent, he or she will be more concerned with pleasing you than with making a sale.

Instead of automatically requesting a plane reservation each time you travel, consider other forms of transportation. Often it is simpler to drive a distance of less than 200 miles than to take a plane. When you drive, you do not have to worry about how you will get from the airport to your final destination. You avoid ticket lines, waiting rooms, flight delays, airline food, and baggage areas.

Remember, too, that driving time need not be wasted time. There are many things you can do while driving. Listening to tapes is an excellent activity. Many tapes on personal development, selling, languages, and time management are now available. If you get into the habit of driving, you might also consider having reports from subordinates put on tape for your review. Many of your people may even prefer this technique of reporting.

You can also make recordings while you drive. With today's portable dictating machines you can dictate correspondence, articles, and letters while you travel. You can also use these handy machines to record any important ideas that come to your mind as you drive—for your secretary to transcribe later.

When you drive, you are free to refresh yourself at your leisure. Numerous rest stops are inviting, and local restaurants provide a wider selection of foods than the airlines. You can engage in isometric exercises while driving—or pull off to the side for your daily jog if the spirit moves you.

You might also consider employing a driver on a part-time basis. College students are an excellent resource. They often need the extra money and enjoy a chance to get away from their routine. Employing your own chauffeur offers you convenience, privacy, and freedom.

A car is not the only alternative to air travel. Trains also offer certain advantages when time is not crucial. You are "chauffeured" as you travel—and you can get up and move about freely. A train is much less confining than a plane, and you can enjoy the scenery when you take a break from your labors.

Of course, the large majority of business executives will continue to travel by plane. The airlines are making a continued effort to improve air travel for their clientele. Here are some tips for making your plane trip more comfortable and pleasurable.

Try not to fly at peak traveling times. Holidays always bring on an extra number of tourists. More mix-ups, lost luggage, and ticketing inaccuracies take place as the volume of people increases. Fly at off-times whenever possible. Friday and Sunday nights are always busy. Commuter flights are also busy between 5:00 and 7:00 P.M. You will save a great deal of aggravation if you book less crowded flights.

Book your flight early. As soon as you know you will be taking a trip, have your travel agent make your reservation. If possible, take care of your other reservations as well—such as seat selection (when available), car rentals, hotel accommodations, prepaid tickets, diet or special foods, and any other requirements you wish. If you book early, you have a better chance of getting a more direct flight to your location. The fewer change points, the lower the chances of delays, mishaps, and lost luggage. Have your agent check for any recent changes in schedule a few days before your departure. Airline flights and departure times undergo thousands of changes every month. An alert travel agent can save you hours of grief.

Your secretary can also help you save time and energy while preparing for a trip. A few days before takeoff, she should verify all appointments you have made at your destination. Times and locations should be double-checked. Whenever possible, she should verify times for the various meetings you will attend so you and your associates can coordinate your schedules.

Your secretary should also make certain that your hotel reservations are confirmed. She should double-check any arrangements made by a travel agent or client. The room reservation is one of the most crucial concerns of any traveler. Nothing is worse than a hard day's travel followed by a "no vacancy" sign. Further reviews should also be made:

1. Do you have your tickets with your other materials? Are they correct? Will you be arriving early enough to get to your meetings?

2. Are all your materials ready to go? Do you need copies of handouts for distribution? A report to review? Are there background materials you should read? Could your secretary summarize them instead? If you need audiovisual equipment, will it be ready for you in the meeting room? Do you have note paper, calling cards, a detailed outline of your expected performance?

3. Do you have cash as well as credit cards? Credit cards are a boon to travelers, but there are still times when there is no substitute for cash. You should have enough for taxi fares, tips, and sundries as well as emergency cash—just in case.

4. Will you need any secretarial services at your out-of-town destination? Your secretary should arrange for such services beforehand so the help you need will be there to serve you.

5. How can you be reached? Does your secretary have a copy of your reservations as well as phone numbers and addresses where you can be reached in case of an emergency? Have you planned to check in with your home office at a regular time—at least once a day?

6. Who acts in your absence? Does your secretary know of all pending matters around the office which may require action? What action should she take in your place?

There will, of course, be certain tasks that only you can do. Review your schedule for appropriate clothes. Check the climate at your destination. Pack enough clothing, but guard against excess. Too many clothes are simply confusing. Shoes and clothing should be comfortable and should not distract from the business at hand. Your wardrobe should be coordinated around one or two compatible colors with interchangeable parts for travel, business, and daytime or evening occasions. Your hair should be styled simply so that it needs a minimum of attention as well as a minimum of appliances.

For a one- or two-night trip, one medium piece of luggage is generally sufficient. In some instances you can fit all your needs into a large attaché case. You can carry the case on the plane, thus avoiding the crowds and delays at the baggage claims area.

If your trip will take you across more than three time zones, make special provisions for jet lag. Whenever possible, allow an extra day at your destination so your body time can catch up with actual time. A good way to prevent jet lag is to go to sleep either a couple of hours earlier (when traveling east) or a couple of hours later (when traveling west) for a few nights before your trip. Most people experience more difficulty crossing time zones from west to east than from east to west. The greater the number of time zones crossed, the more severe the problem. Learn to recognize your limit and plan accordingly.

On departure day, collect your materials, your suitcase, your briefcase, and your tickets. Kiss your spouse and kids good-bye in time to get to the airport for a comfortable check-in. Relax a little before boarding the plane.

ON THE TRIP

A year or so ago we were waiting in one of the public lounges of the LA International Airport. Our curiosity was aroused by a distinguished gentleman carrying a large sack. As we watched with interest, the man sat down on a chair, put his briefcase and coat beside him, and emptied the sack on the next seat.

Right there in the middle of the LA International was a pile of mail. Magazines, letters, flyers, large manila envelopes—the works. He picked up the mail one piece at a time, glanced at it, made a note on some pieces and stuck them in his briefcase, and threw other pieces back in the sack. As our curiosity grew, we approached the man and asked him about what he was doing.

"I always save up my mail and take it with me on trips," he said. "I go through a whole month's worth at a time. It's my trip activity. It's a good idea; I don't have to bother with it at the office!"

We would hardly recommend that time-conscious travelers drag a month's worth of mail with them on a trip. We do have to give the man credit, though; he was certainly using his travel time! Many people waste valuable work time while they are traveling.

Travel time can be as productive as time in the office, if you plan for it. The secret is expectations—what you expect to accomplish while on the trip. Analyze the free time you will have on the trip and plan accordingly. This is a crucial activity if you hope to get something done while traveling. Many people who faithfully develop a daily to-do list at the office ignore this good habit when they are away. A to-do list is important in or out of the office. If you expect to get something accomplished when you travel, put your expectations in writing and take along the necessary materials.

The amount of work you want to accomplish on a trip is directly related to how much you travel. If you travel only once or twice a year, you will probably prefer to combine more pleasure than work with your business. An occasional trip away from the office is a welcome break from the routine, so go ahead and enjoy yourself! If you travel a great deal, though, travel soon loses its thrill. You grin weakly as others comment about your jet-set life and think to yourself, "If they only knew!" Lines are long, airport hallways are dirty, luggage areas are jammed, and airline food gets a little boring. In short, you really don't look forward to your next venture away from home.

The suggestions below are geared to those people who travel a great deal. Through careful planning, you can make the days you spend away from the office as productive as any day at home. Consider the tradeoffs: What do you have to lose if you work while traveling and what do you have to gain? You probably have very little to lose, because you've tried being a quasi-tourist before. And you have a great deal to gain, because you can accomplish many things away from your hectic office.

The secret to getting something done on a plane trip is to choose your seat carefully. The airlines now offer travelers a choice between smoking and nonsmoking sections, so both smokers and nonsmokers can be more comfortable. If you are particularly "antismoke," select a seat in the front of the plane—as far away from the smoking section as possible.

Fly first class as often as possible if you hope to get a lot of work accomplished. It is worth the additional cost to have more room, more peace and quiet, and fewer distractions. The flight attendant will be better able to accommodate your needs, since there are fewer passengers to serve.

The aisle seat is best for working, especially if you fly coach class. Your writing arm should be on the aisle side for comfort and maneuverability. The disadvantage to the aisle seat, of course, is that you have to get up to let the other passengers out.

Arrange your travel briefcase like a mini-office. With everything in its place, you can open the briefcase, get some work done, and close it again at dining or landing time.

What kinds of work are best done in the air? Background reading is an excellent activity. Many travelers enjoy writing reports or answering their correspondence while flying because of their total privacy in the air. Certainly there are hundreds of other people around, but they are not likely to interrupt you. The noise on the plane can easily be shut out. You are left with hours of "quiet time" for handling important projects.

With the newer-model calculators, you can also do mathematical calculations in the air. Portable dictating machines have made report and letter writing faster and easier than ever for travelers. With these small machines, you can also record various notes to yourself or to your secretary for review later. Once you learn how to use dictating equipment, you will find it far more convenient than writing your thoughts out in longhand.

Many dictating machines on the market are useful in the office, but they do not block out the heavy background noises travelers must contend with in planes and busy airports. How can you tell if you have a good machine? Give your selected model the Douglass Noise Test. Set up your machine on the plane. Wait until the pilot revs the engines, just before takeoff. The flight attendant will begin to announce safety instructions over the public address system. The level of excitement on the plane will rise as the passengers anticipate takeoff. Now is the time. Speak into your new recorder. If you can hear your dictation on the playback, you have a good machine. If you hear nothing but nonsensical noise, return the recorder to the store and get your money back. The machine is no good for travelling. Find a machine that works well under all circumstances.

IN THE HOTEL

You can perform the same types of work activities in the hotel that you perform on the plane. Indeed, a hotel room offers you a wider choice, since you can spread out your materials. Again, the important factor here is anticipation. Anticipate what you will accomplish during your stay, taking into consideration the appointments and other obligations of your trip.

Remember to pace your activities and consider a variety of things to do. If you can complete an A-1 project or at least make headway on it, you will feel a gratifying sense of accomplishment. But remember to break up your pace. Do other forms of work, background reading, or pleasure reading. Take walks or naps. The demands of travel can be heavy, particularly if you are making time zone changes. You should also take advantage of the hotel's exercise facilities. The swimming pool or sauna can be an excellent change of pace after a hard day at work.

Plan your diversions with care. Resist pressures to engage in night-time activities if you really aren't interested. Work or rest instead. Don't feel obliged to participate. If there is a purpose in the afterhours get-together, by all means attend. Carefully consider the purpose of any activity and act accordingly.

Resist the temptation to eat excessively during your stay. The abundant food on many business trips can make you sluggish and tired. After some unfortunate stomach reactions and a few too many "good times," many people have become older and wiser travelers. They eat less and eat more bland foods while traveling. This decision has helped make their trips more enjoyable.

Time-conscious travelers should also beware of the "cursed liquids." An amazing amount of alcohol can be consumed during a business trip. There are drinks at the airport, a couple of more drinks on the plane (before and after dinner), a drink following your arrival, a few more in the evening, and of course a nightcap. You must have an iron constitution to handle all this; most people can't take it. If they don't wind up absolutely drunk, they will at least be seriously debilitated—at a time when they may be called upon to make important decisions or perform at their peak.

You should also consider the pros and cons of extensive sight-seeing during your trip. If you will be staying in a city, you may find some tourist activity to your liking. Remember, though, that you pay a price if you try to do it all at once. Instead of trying to squeeze in all the sights while you conduct your business, investigate the special, though lesser-known attractions of the city. Plan a return visit for your next vacation and then do the town.

RETURNING HOME

Whether you are a frequent traveler or an infrequent traveler, there are a few activities you should always do on the trip home. While experiences are still fresh in your mind, write any follow-up letters or reports generated by your trip. A quiet plane trip is by far the best time to take care of these concerns. There will generally be new developments once you return to your office that will demand your instant attention. Complete your expense report for costs incurred during the trip. Have it ready for your secretary the moment you walk in the door so you won't have to bother with it later.

Your goal is to have the trip "over" as much as possible when you return. Leftover reports from a trip are difficult and boring once you are home and into other things.

REENTRY

Many people experience an emotional letdown when they return from a trip. This seems to be a problem for both the frequent and the occasional traveler. Even people who have excellent work habits in and out of the office find the transition period difficult. It is hard to psych yourself up for returning to the office routine. People do adjust but not that quickly, and the length of your absence from the office has a direct effect on how long it takes you to readjust. Trips that cross more than three time zones may require special recuperation efforts.

Depending on your body cycle, attitudes, and preferences, you can try one of the two approaches described below to get back into the swing of things. The first approach involves an earlier starting time and the second, oddly enough, involves a later starting time.

The Attack Approach

If travel letdown has you dragging, try an earlier starting time to move yourself back into the office routine. "Attack" the next day with a running start. Don't wait until you get to the office to begin work; start at home. Get up 15 minutes earlier than normal and do some wake-up exercises. If you're already into a morning exercise routine, try some new moves—to music. Put on a lively tape or a record from "your era"—whether it's Benny Goodman, Elvis, or the Bee Gees. Take a cold shower and sing a line or two of the melody you just heard. After a good breakfast, make a phone call before you head for your car and the office. Open that report you've been dreading and promise yourself you'll draft an outline before you finish your cup of coffee. Whoops! You've begun work without realizing it!

Arrive at the office a few minutes earlier than normal. Those extra minutes could be just what you need to be ready for action when your co-workers arrive. Some people find it useful to set appointments early on their first day back. These morning appointments force them to get it together faster.

Whatever you do, set significant objectives for early in the day. Don't chat about your trip, read the newspaper, or sort through that stack of mail. If you accomplish an important objective during the first hour back at your desk, you will find your travel letdown turning into energetic momentum.

The Retreat Approach

If the above scenario sends you reeling, try the reverse approach—a later starting time. If you've used your travel time well, you needn't feel guilty.

Ease back into your routine. If possible, take the morning off to gather your wits. Play a round of golf, watch Phil Donahue, or do a little unhurried shopping. Many travelers find suitcases, airports, and taxis tiring and stressful. If you need to unwind, try several of the relaxation techniques described in Chapter 15. View them as a vital part of your work cycle—a needed transition period.

The more you travel, the more you should view airports, planes, and taxis as an extension of your office. When you master this attitude, you will no longer feel that you've been away from the routine, and reentry will be less of a problem. As you settle into your trip, learn to open your briefcase, shut out extraneous noises, and concentrate on the project at hand. You may find yourself looking forward to uninterrupted travel time so you can get something accomplished.

Travel need not ruin your time management discipline. If travel is a part of your job, treat it as such and apply the same time management principles to your trips that you use at home. Once you honestly decide that you can control your travel time, you will find many new opportunities to use it better. Learn to make travel time work for you instead of against you.

14
Conquering Procrastination

PROCRASTINATION PLAGUES ALL of us. More plans go astray, more dreams go unfulfilled, and more time is wasted by procrastination than by any other single factor. Procrastination is a major stumbling block for almost everyone seeking to improve his or her use of time. For many people, procrastination becomes an insidious habit that can ruin their careers, destroy their happiness, and even shorten their lives.

Procrastination is doing low-priority activities or tasks rather than high-priority activities or tasks. It's all a matter of priorities. Avery Schreiber, the comedian, once identified the problem in a humorous song with a serious message:

> Priorities, think of what you're doing
> Priorities, you may soon be bluing
> Priorities, you'll drive yourself to ruin
> If you pick the wrong priorities.

Procrastination is straightening your desk when you should be working on that report, watching TV when you should be exercising, having a martini when you should be getting back to the office, calling on the friendly customer who buys very little when you should be preparing a sales presentation for that tough prospect who would buy much more. Procrastination is avoiding co-workers rather than telling them bad news, staying away from the office so you do not have to discipline a subordinate. It is postponing activities with your children because you have more urgent things to do—until one day the children are grown and it's too late to do all the things you talked about doing together.

Procrastination prevents success. Success comes from doing the really important things that lead to results. Yet these important things are usually the very focus of our procrastination. We seldom put off unimportant things. If we could only learn to shift our procrastination from important things to unimportant things, our problem would disappear. One reason we postpone important things is that we tend to confuse them with merely urgent things. We constantly respond to the urgent. Our days are filled with demands and pressures from all quarters. Important things seldom exert this kind of pressure until they reach the crisis state. By responding to the urgent and postponing the important, we guarantee a continual number of crises in our lives.

To conquer procrastination, we must understand that it is a habit. Procrastination breeds procrastination. Much of what we do, the way we approach things, even the way we think, is based on habit. For most of us, one day looks very much like another. Our lives are full of routines and patterns. To overcome procrastination we will undoubtedly have to change our habits.

From physics we learn that a body at rest tends to remain at rest. It takes greater force to start movement than to sustain movement. To conquer procrastination, we must overcome our inertia—our tendency to resist taking action. Once action is begun, it is much more likely to continue. It's the beginning that is difficult. Most of the techniques discussed in this chapter are designed to help people begin.

Procrastination can be traced to three major causes. We tend to put off things that are unpleasant, things that are difficult, and things that involve tough decisions. Yet these are the very things that contribute most to our success.

A variety of techniques can be used to conquer procrastination. Not all these techniques will apply to your situation. To make good use of the concepts presented here, you will need to find the best combination of techniques for your purposes. If a technique works, you're on your way. If it doesn't, try another technique or a different combination of techniques until you find the ones that work for you.

UNPLEASANT TASKS

Let's first tackle procrastination caused by unpleasant tasks. For most people, this is the greatest single cause of procrastination.

When you postpone an unpleasant task, you are attempting to make life easier for yourself—to avoid the distasteful. Ironically, though, putting off the task only increases the unpleasantness, since the task will seldom disappear.

Often, the best way to handle unpleasant tasks is to do them first. Try scheduling your most unpleasant tasks, the ones you tend to put off most often, at the beginning of your day. Do the distasteful first and get it behind you rather than dreading it and continually putting it off. Take a lesson from the little boy who eats his spinach first, to get it out of the way, so he can enjoy the rest of the meal.

Putting off the unpleasant can be costly. If a task must eventually be done, the work may expand with delay. If you wait until the last possible minute, you will have to work under increased pressure. The longer you wait, the greater the number of things that can go wrong. You've put off that report until the last minute and suddenly your secretary comes down with the flu. You have another crisis on your hands. And the crisis may spread to others. Tempers flare, unkind words are exchanged. Anxiety increases. You become depressed and frustrated with the whole thing. No one works well under these conditions. The quality of your actions is bound to suffer. You dislike yourself.

Other costs of delay are not as immediate, but they can be far more serious. For example:

1. Delay answering an inquiry and you may lose a customer.
2. Delay servicing a machine and you may have a costly breakdown.
3. Delay developing new products and your competitors will have them first.
4. Delay going to the dentist and you may have to live with false teeth.
5. Delay exercising and you may shorten your life.
6. Delay making a will and your heirs will struggle with red tape for years.
7. Delay doing the things that are really important to you and you will lose out on the richness of life.

Considering the costs of delay may help you get moving. When you are tempted to procrastinate, stop and think for a moment. What problems are you likely to create for yourself? If you don't want to live with those problems, don't procrastinate. Analyze your unpleasant task. Exactly what is it that makes the task unpleasant?

Learn to confront the unpleasantness and deal with it directly. Many people challenge themselves to do at least one thing they dread every month. If you do this, you will add a new dimension to your life. You will gain new confidence and respect for yourself as you begin to master some of your fears.

Sometimes it helps to tackle unpleasant tasks in small pieces. You can endure anything for a few minutes at a time. Try tackling an unpleasant task for five or ten minutes. You may find that it's not so unpleasant after all once you get moving. And even if you stop after five minutes, you're still gaining on the task. You've been planning to start that new exercise program that the doctor says you need, but the thought of all that work is too much. Don't focus on an hour at a time. Begin with five minutes. Still putting off washing all 39 windows in your house? In five minutes you can wash one window.

Setting a deadline for the task helps some people get started. The pressure of a deadline, even a self-imposed one, can be sufficient to create action. Make sure your deadline is realistic and put it in writing. Post the written deadline on the wall, set it on your desk, or put it wherever you will see it frequently.

To strengthen your resolve, let other people know about your deadline. We frequently break commitments we make to ourselves, but we are not so likely to break a commitment we make to others. It's painful and embarrassing to admit we haven't done it. So make a commitment to your spouse, or secretary, or boss, or friend, or whomever you like. Schedule appointments with others to discuss results, set deadlines, and promise action. See if you don't find it much harder to fall behind at the risk of losing face.

Another way to get yourself started and keep going is to promise yourself a reward for completing the task. You might reward yourself with a special lunch for finishing that project you've been putting off, a weekend vacation for painting the house, or a Friday afternoon off for finishing all your assignments by noon. A reward can be anything that appeals to you—large or small. There are two main points to remember here: If you don't earn the reward, don't give it to yourself, and if you do earn it, be sure to take it. Occasional rewards can make life more interesting and at the same time can help you conquer your procrastination.

Sometimes unpleasant tasks will get done much more quickly if you can find someone else to do them. You might consider buying a reprieve. For instance, you won't have to continue dreading the thought of painting the living room if you hire a painter to do it. Often the cost of hiring someone makes good sense economically as well as psychologically. How many of your unpleasant tasks could be done by someone else?

Occasionally, you will come across a task that is so unpleasant that nothing seems to get you moving. When this happens, try thinking of the task in a larger context—in terms of the ultimate benefit to you. This may not reduce the unpleasantness, but it may make the task more palatable. You can do the task grudgingly and feel miserable, or you resign yourself to it and do it cheerfully. Why make things any worse than they are? Begin to generate some enthusiasm to counterbalance the unpleasantness.

DIFFICULT TASKS

Procrastination caused by difficult tasks usually calls for a different approach. Quite often we avoid difficult tasks because we simply don't know where to start. The task may be so complex that it overwhelms us. We need to find some way to reduce the apparent complexity so the task no longer appears difficult.

Quite often it's the difficult, perplexing tasks that give us some of our greatest opportunities. Paul Tournier, in *The Adventure of Living,* describes them in terms of adventures:

> There is an astonishing contrast between the heavy perplexity that inhibits before the adventure has begun and the excitement that grips us the moment it begins. . . . As soon as a man makes up his mind to take the plunge into adventure, he is aware of a new strength he did not think he had, which rescues him from all his perplexities.*

One excellent way to begin your adventure is to break the task down into smaller parts. Keep breaking down the parts until you can see the first step. Essentially this is a matter of working backward. You start with the desired result, the finished task. Then keep asking yourself what you have to do to achieve this result. Once you have broken the task down, focus on only one part at a time.

For example, you've been putting off doing a feasibility study for a new process that might help your company. No one has ever applied this process in your industry. There are no guidelines to follow. How do you break it down to smaller parts? Start by outlining the finished report. What should the key topics be? Then look at each topic and determine what you need to discuss. What steps must you take to

* New York: Harper & Row, 1965.

obtain the information you need? Who should you talk with? Continue in this fashion until you've broken the task down into a number of subunits. The subunits never look as difficult as the entire task.

Another approach is to break a task down into "minijobs" that can be accomplished in less than ten minutes. Assume that you need to prepare a forecast of sales for next year. You estimate that it will take you 30 hours to complete the project. Not only is the task difficult, but you have no idea where you will find the 30 hours you need. So you keep putting if off. How can you break the project down into minijobs? Within a few minutes, you might be able to get a copy of last year's forecast, locate the file you will need, determine what information will be required, decide whom you must contact, arrange appointments with other people, request additional information, or assign parts of the project to others. As you begin to think about it, you will come up with many minijobs that can be done in less than ten minutes.

An added benefit to this approach is that you can do the minijobs during odd moments of the day that would otherwise be wasted. At the same time, performing the tasks will lead you to your goal. To make the approach work best, prepare a list of all the short tasks you will need to do to complete the project. Then you won't have to think them up again each time you find a few odd moments. Establish priorities so you can start on the most important tasks first. After you have finished several of the short tasks, you may discover that the project is not as overwhelming or as difficult as you thought. You may come up with a few shortcuts. You may find it easier to schedule large blocks of time to finish it. The main point is that the short tasks will get you started. The more you get done, the easier it is to keep going.

Another technique to help you get started is to find a leading task. Again, consider that report you've been putting off. One obvious way to begin is to make notes on the points you need to cover. If even this seems too much to tackle, try sharpening your pencil. A leading task should be extremely easy and quick and should not require planning. It should entail very little conscious effort on your part. Rolling a sheet of paper into the typewriter can lead to typing that letter. Picking up the telephone can lead to calling on new customers. Buying a paint brush can lead to resuming your art lessons. You certainly can't finish until you start.

Sometimes the difficult task you keep postponing calls for creative thought. You keep saying that you're waiting for inspiration or for the right moment to strike. Someone once said that inspiration is 90 percent perspiration. If you wait for inspiration, it seldom appears. A little physical action is what you need. One author we know waited three years for the inspiration to begin writing his book. A friend finally convinced him to set aside 30 minutes each day for writing. He could write whatever he wanted, as long as he wrote for the entire 30 minutes. For the first two weeks the author wrote nonsense phrases, paragraphs about the weather, poetry, notes to himself, and other nonproductive pieces. Gradually, though, his writing began to become more serious. He began outlining ideas for his novel—short descriptions of characters, various ideas for plots. Before long, he was writing his novel. Don't wait for inspiration. Take action now.

"Not feeling in the mood" is another common excuse for putting things off. The trick is to take advantage of your moods rather than have your moods take advantage of you. Occasionally, it may be best to wait until your mood is right before starting a task. However, there is usually some aspect of the task that will fit your current mood. You may not feel like papering the kitchen today, but you might at least be willing to select the wallpaper. When you find yourself procrastinating because your mood is wrong, ask yourself, "Is there anything, no matter how small, that I am willing to do?" Once you find something you're willing to do—and do it—you're on the way to making your moods work for you instead of against you.

Often when you say you're not in the right mood you're busy feeling sorry for yourself. A general lack of motivation or feeling of depression has set in. What you need is a pep talk. Find a corner to stand in and talk to yourself—out loud. Really lay it on the line! Build yourself up. You can't do anything until you believe you can. A little positive thinking may be what you need. A pep talk is one good way to get yourself going in the right direction again.

Things often seem difficult because people don't know enough about them. Nonfamiliarity can lead to lack of interest. The more you know about something, the more you want to know. The more you know, the more likely you are to get involved and excited. So get more information. Read a book, attend a lecture, talk with people who know. A short course in auto mechanics may prompt you to make those needed repairs on your automobile. Finding a photo of your great-grandmother may get you started on developing your family tree. Learning about linear programming may make you excited about solving that inventory control problem in your office.

INDECISION

Indecision is the third major cause of procrastination. Indecision usually stems from a strong desire to be right, a strong desire to avoid being wrong, or a desire for perfection.

There is a time to deliberate and a time to act. The time to decide is when further information will add very little to the quality of the decision. Delay beyond that point seldom improves the decision. No one is right all the time. Often there simply is no right or wrong involved. Make a sincere effort to obtain the best information possible within the time you have available. Then make the decision and move on. Above all, don't keep fretting and fussing over the decision, and don't keep rehashing it.

Perfectionism is often at the heart of indecision. Budding authors who keep rewriting Chapter 1, striving for the perfect phrase, seldom publish books. Managers who keep pushing their subordinates for perfect results seldom achieve them. Perfectionism leads to anxiety and tension, strains relationships between people, and accomplishes little. Learn to do your best the first time around and call it good.

When you are tempted to reach for perfection, recall Pareto's Principle, or the 80–20 rule: "80 percent of the value comes from 20 percent of the items, while the remaining 20 percent of the value comes from 80 percent of the items." Some people have called this the concept of the important few and the trivial many. Learn to recognize your few critical activities and focus your attention on doing those things first.

Indecisiveness can often be traced to vague worries and fears that something will go wrong. Everyone encounters obstacles at one time or another. But you should not borrow trouble or procrastinate because of vague worries. Instead, focus on what you want to accomplish. Write down all the obstacles or problems that might prevent you from achieving your goal. Review the problems and think of various ways you might solve them. Write down all the possible solutions and pick the ones most likely to work for you. You now have a basis for positive planning that will take you beyond your procrastination.

Another way to overcome your vague worries and fears is to develop a worry list. Write down all the things you worry about, all the things you think might go wrong, all the horrible things you think might happen. From time to time, read over the list and note what has actually happened. You will probably find that most of the things you worry about never happen. A worry list can help you worry less.

PREVENTIVE ACTION

Changing your do-it-later urge into a do-it-now habit will require positive action. Things don't just happen. Things happen because people make them happen. Do things differently. Answer your mail as soon as you open it. Don't set it aside for later. Whenever you say to yourself, "I've got to do something about that," do something about it now, not later. Schedule things and live by your schedule. Learn to check those impulses to do unscheduled things—impulses that often hide your procrastination. Learn to do the most important things first.

Procrastination is a psychological problem, and a victory over procrastination is essentially a psychological victory. You may have to play games with yourself in order to overcome your inertia and change the habits that hamper your progress.

One woman who tended to put off unpleasant household chores used the game approach. She wrote notes to herself about various tasks and then taped the notes to the walls of her home. For instance, the note by the bookcase reminded her to dust the books, and the note in the bathroom told her to clean the tiles. This kind of game is a variation of setting deadlines for yourself. However, it soon takes on the power of a commitment to others. When this woman posted her notes, she did not think about the friends who frequently stopped by for coffee and conversation. When they asked about the notes around the house, she realized that she would have to get the tasks done quickly to avoid embarrassing comments. This led her to reschedule her days and do at least one unpleasant task each morning. Within a few days she had learned the secret of conquering procrastination. She gained new confidence in herself and new respect from her friends. Her game helped her achieve her goal.

Take some time to analyze your procrastination habits. Begin by answering the following questions:

1. What things do you tend to put off, or delay, most often?
2. What things are you currently putting off?
3. How do you know when you're procrastinating? Do you have a set of favorite replacement activities?
4. How do you feel about your procrastination?

5. What happens when you procrastinate? Are the results positive or negative?
6. What do you think causes your procrastination? Try to link a specific cause to each procrastinated task.
7. What can you do to overcome your procrastination? List specific steps you can take to get started and set deadlines on them.

The easiest way to overcome procrastination is to never let it happen in the first place. There are two things you can do. First, clarify your objectives. Setting objectives is the best way to cope with daily problems and pressures. Make sure you are pursuing the right things for you. Often what you think you want to do is not what you really want to do. So you put things off. Your procrastination is a subconscious message that your priorities are out of focus. If you continually think through your objectives and priorities and focus your efforts on what's most important, you will seldom be bothered by procrastination.

Second, develop the habit of planning every day. Ask yourself what you want to accomplish with each day. Write out a list of things to do and then follow your plan. Do the most important things first. If you develop the habit of making a list of things to do each day, and then doing them, you will find that procrastination is something that happens to other people.

Procrastination is a habit—a very bad habit. The more you procrastinate, the more likely you are to continue to procrastinate in the future. The more you resist the temptation to put things off, the easier it is to continue resisting. Do everything you can to develop a do-it-now habit.

The most valuable thing you can do when you are procrastinating is to admit it. As long as you continue to deny or rationalize your procrastination you are not in a position to overcome it. Once you admit that you are indeed procrastinating, examine your situation and determine why. Then find a technique for conquering your procrastination. In the end procrastination, like any problem, can be solved only by positive action.

15
Stress and
Personal Performance

As NOTED IN Chapter 3, our relationship to time is very personal. Our age, attitudes, values, and body cycles affect how we use our time. Another factor also plays a critical role in shaping our perceptions of time and our ability to use time well. This factor is well known to all of us. We call it stress.

Most of us fear stress. We don't understand it. We try to escape or avoid it. But stress is unavoidable and a certain amount of stress is even necessary for good performance. The trick, of course, is to maintain a proper balance.

WHAT IS STRESS?

Stress is defined as any action or situation that places special physical or psychological demands upon a person. Anything abnormal can throw us into a state of disequilibrium. We react by attempting to bring the body back into equilibrium. It is this reaction that creates most of the stress symptoms we know so well. Since stress is associated with disequilibrium, it is also frequently associated with change. Change creates new situations. With new situations, we must establish new patterns of living that will bring us back to a state of equilibrium. Positive change can have just as much stressful impact as negative change.

Most people think of stress as something to be avoided, but some stress is necessary to perform effectively. Too little stress can be harmful. Figure 22 shows the relationship between stress and performance. Note that as stress increases, so does performance—up to

Figure 22. Stress and performance.

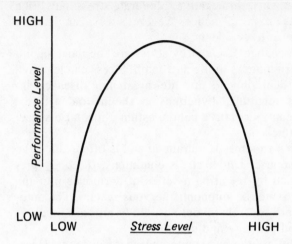

a point. Beyond that point, stress hampers performance. Some stress is good, but too much stress is bad.

This curve explains why many people seem to do better under the pressure of a close deadline. The approaching deadline creates a stress reaction that stimulates performance. However, if a person is already close to the top of the curve, the stress from the approaching deadline could be enough to put the person over the top, with a decrease in performance.

How much stress is too much? This varies from person to person. Researchers have discovered that there are basically two types of people: racehorses and turtles. Racehorses thrive on high stress levels. They are happy with vigorous, fast-paced lifestyles. Turtles are happier in peaceful, quiet environments. Either type, if placed in the opposite environment, will function poorly. A big danger, of course, lies in mistaking your type. If you incorrectly believe you are a racehorse, you will push beyond your normal stress endurance. If you wrongly believe you are a turtle, you will live a life of frustration.

EFFECTS OF STRESS

Stress affects people in three ways: emotionally, behaviorally, and physiologically. The emotional changes are the ones many people commonly associate with stress. These range from feelings of mild annoyance to blustering rage; from slight anxiety to overpowering fear; from amusement to ecstasy. The behavioral changes brought on by stress can be positive or negative. Moderate stress may bring about improvements in performance. Severe stress can lead to greater errors and even to accidents.

The physiological changes created by stress are the most significant, for they concern matters of life and death. Stress can lead to a wide variety of physical ailments and life-threatening diseases, including peptic ulcers, migraines, hypertension, rheumatoid arthritis, backaches, emphysema, ulcerative colitis, asthma, mental disease, cancer, and heart attack.

The body's reaction to stress is automatic and is often called the "fight or flight" response. Under stress conditions, the body prepares for either action by releasing a series of hormones into the bloodstream that activate the autonomic nervous system. The autonomic nervous system controls involuntary body muscles, such as those that alter blood pressure and digestion.

Under stress conditions, the body undergoes many changes. Hearing and smelling become more acute. Pupils dilate to admit extra light. Breathing is deeper and faster. Mucous membranes in the nose and throat shrink to make wider passages for the increased air flow. The heart pumps extra blood, sending more food and oxygen to the brain, lungs, and muscles for greater strength and energy. Blood clots more quickly, helping to prevent loss of blood in case of injury. Increased perspiration flushes wastes and cools the overactive body system. The body conserves its energy for top-priority functions by shutting down lower-priority activities.

These physiological reactions to stress prepare the body to fight or flee. When either route is taken, the system naturally restores itself. The problem today is that very few of the situations that create stress allow for either flight or fight. Most stress situations are psychological rather than physical. This is one of the penalties of modern civilization.

Because the body neither fights nor runs, stress reactions tend to accumulate and become prolonged. This is where ailments and disease enter the picture. Under chronic stress, people are ripe for an organic crisis. Thomas Holmes and Richard Rahe, psychiatrists at the University of Washington Medical School, have pioneered in relating stress to disease. They developed a yardstick for evaluating personal stress called the Life Events Scale (or Social Readjustment Rating Scale). The scale in Figure 23 can help you evaluate your potential stress problems.

According to Holmes and Rahe, some life events create more stress than others. A life crisis is defined as the accumulation of at

Figure 23. The Social Readjustment Rating Scale.*

Life Event	Mean Value	Life Event	Mean Value
1. Death of spouse	100	23. Son or daughter leaving home	29
2. Divorce	73	24. Trouble with in-laws	29
3. Marital separation	65	25. Outstanding personal achievement	28
4. Jail term	63		
5. Death of close family member	63	26. Wife begins or stops work	26
6. Personal injury or illness	53	27. Begin or end school	26
7. Marriage	50	28. Change in living conditions	25
8. Fired at work	47		
9. Marital reconciliation	45	29. Revision of personal habits	24
10. Retirement	45	30. Trouble with boss	23
11. Change in health of family member	44	31. Change in work hours or conditions	20
12. Pregnancy	40	32. Change in residence	20
13. Sex difficulties	39	33. Change in schools	20
14. Gain of new family member	39	34. Change in recreation	19
15. Business readjustment	39	35. Change in church activities	19
16. Change in financial state	38	36. Change in social activities	18
17. Death of close friend	37	37. Mortgage or loan less than $10,000	17
18. Change to different line of work	36	38. Change in sleeping habits	16
19. Change in number of arguments with spouse	35	39. Change in number of family get-togethers	15
20. Mortgage over $10,000	31	40. Change in eating habits	15
21. Foreclosure of mortgage or loan	30	41. Vacation	13
		42. Christmas	12
22. Change in responsibilities at work	29	43. Minor violations of the law	11

* See T. H. Holmes and R. H. Rahe, "The Social Readjustment Rating Scale," *Journal of Psychosomatic Research* (November 1967), pp. 213–218, for complete wording of the items.

least 150 points in a 12-month period. The body is "at risk" for the next 24 months following a life crisis. The risk factors for moderate, medium, and severe life crises are shown below:

Life Crisis		Probability of Health Change
Moderate	(150–199 points)	.37
Medium	(200–299 points)	.51
Severe	(300 or more points)	.79

The Holmes–Rahe theory linking stress and disease is not a perfect fit, but it is certainly cause for reflection. The accumulation of 300 or more points in a single year indicates an almost 80 percent chance of a health change! Given this fact, it would seem advisable to stretch significant changes over long periods if possible. In this way, the danger of facing a life crisis could be reduced. As Alvin Toffler pointed out in *Future Shock,* the rate of change can be even more devastating than change itself.

Each of us responds to stress with a particular set of symptoms. Our specific response is determined by our genetic heritage, our training, our outlook on life, and other variables. Whatever our response to stress, we should keep in mind that dysfunctional stress symptoms signal a breakdown in the most vulnerable parts of the body. Dr. Hans Selye, an expert on stress, has identified the common signs of dysfunctional stress—or what Dr. Selye terms "distress." These include:

General irritability
Increased heart rate
Dryness of throat or mouth
Impulsive behavior
Emotional instability
Tendency to vacillate in making decisions
Inability to concentrate
Accident proneness
Tendency to overemphasize trifles
Tendency to misjudge people
Feelings of persecution
Forgetfulness
Decrease in sex drive
Fatigue
Vague feelings of dissatisfaction
Insomnia
Excessive sweating
Frequent need to urinate
Migraine headaches
Loss of appetite or excessive appetite
Missed menstrual cycles
Premenstrual tension
Pain in lower back or neck
Trembling or nervous tics
Increased smoking

Increased use of alcohol
Increased use of prescribed drugs, such as tranquilizers
Procrastination
Inability to get organized
Confusion about duties
Uncertainty about whom to trust
Stuttering and other speech difficulties

Learn to be a good judge of your own stress symptoms. You don't need a complex scientific test. You can develop an instinctive feel for when you're running at too high or too low a stress level. When you know you've had enough, it's time to quit.

ALLEVIATING STRESS

If stress is unavoidable, what can you do to decrease it? There are several ways to alleviate the problem. None of these techniques will prevent or eliminate stress, but they can dissipate the stress reaction and help you function better.

1. *Develop a different attitude.* By changing your attitude, you can convert negative stress into positive stress. Although the reason is not yet known, positive stress takes far less of a toll on the human body. So work on your attitude. Try to enjoy your work. Forget about harboring grudges. Learn to look at things positively. Follow the advice of the proberb: "Imitate the sundial's way, and count only the pleasant days."

2. *Get a checkup.* If you suffer from chronic stress, a physician can be your best friend. Let your physician know all the things that are happening in your life. Follow good medical advice. Don't undertake radical changes that might impair your health without consulting your physician. Avoid self-medication. A variety of pills mask stress symptoms, but they may ultimately do tremendous damage. Stress symptoms are a message that your system has had enough. Covering up the symptoms is not coping; it is running away.

3. *Get adequate rest.* When you're tired, you're in even worse shape to cope with stress. And since high stress often results in insomnia, you may find it harder than ever to get the proper sleep. Try rearranging your work and sleep schedule. For many people, short naps of 15 to 20 minutes are refreshing and help alleviate tension and anxiety.

4. *Watch your diet.* Stress can deplete your body's store of water-soluble vitamins. When this happens, your body is less able to

counter infections and function well. Under stress, many people change their eating habits for the worse. Often, they also drink more alcohol, which complicates the problem. Adequate nutrition is especially important when you are under stress. If you are concerned about your diet, you might consider taking vitamins or other nutritional supplements.

5. *Exercise*. Regular, noncompetitive exercise is excellent for dissipating stress. Before you embark on strenuous activity, consult your physician for advice on a program suited to your needs and abilities. Pick an exercise you enjoy. Whatever you do, set aside a regular time for exercise and make it part of your schedule.

Exercise offers a double advantage. In addition to releasing stress, it can help develop the cardiovascular system. Any exercise that demands intense effort for 20 to 30 minutes will probably accomplish both. Jogging, running, tennis, racquetball, basketball, swimming, cycling, squash, and cross-country skiing are excellent. Even walking can do wonders. Many people who have begun vigorous exercise programs report fewer stress symptoms, increased physical and mental stamina, greater work capacity, and a trimmer body.

6. *Do relaxation exercises*. The value of relaxation exercises designed to trigger the release of the autonomic nervous system has long been recognized. The exercises consist of tensing particular muscle groups, holding the tense position for several seconds, and then relaxing the muscles. The exercises can be done in about 15 minutes. Here's how they work. Assume a comfortable body position. Concentrate on tensing and then relaxing different muscle groups one at a time. Start with your toes and progress upward to your legs, trunks, and arms, and finally your head. Eventually, your entire body will feel relaxed. Several cassette tapes are available to guide you through these exercises.

7. *Meditate*. Many people find meditation a valuable technique for coping with stress. It is easy and can be done almost anywhere. Pick a spot where you won't be disturbed for 15 to 20 minutes. Make yourself comfortable, relax, close your eyes, and concentrate on your breathing. Say the word "one" to yourself silently each time you exhale. Do not think of anything. Repeating "one" will help you keep your mind blank.

Try meditating twice a day. Do not try meditation close to bedtime, though, because it often acts like a mental "high" and can keep you awake. Midmorning and midafternoon are ideal times. Take a meditation break instead of a coffeebreak.

8. *Change your reaction patterns*. Learn to desensitize yourself to

tension-producing situations. Try this approach. First relax, then imagine yourself getting tense. Stop, relax, and then visualize the situation again. Imagine yourself handling the situation calmly. Gradually, you will be able to go through the entire scene without feeling tense. Practice your new calm behavior in real situations.

9. *Adapt to your environment realistically.* Learning to control your environment can go a long way toward reducing stress-causing events. For example, many of the time wasters that contribute to stress can be eliminated or controlled. This book is devoted to helping you control your time and minimize wasted effort. Remember, though, that not everything can be controlled. Some things are simply beyond your influence. It helps to keep in mind the poet's prayer:

> God, grant me the courage to change
>   the things I can,
> The patience to accept the things
>   I cannot change,
> And the wisdom to know the difference.

10. *Listen to music.* Music stimulates an emotional response. Try listening to relaxing, soothing music. Let yourself float with the melody. Imagine yourself in a serene environment. Let the music relax your muscles.

11. *Take a break.* When you feel yourself tensing up, leave the situation. Take a walk around the block. Go shopping. Do anything to break the pattern and give yourself a release.

12. *Express your anger.* Much stress is associated with unexpressed anger and hostility. Look for acceptable ways to express your anger. Physical activity is an excellent outlet. Use a punching bag to vent your feelings. Or run around the house.

13. *Take a vacation.* Vacations provide a break in the pattern. But don't make your vacations as hectic or competitive as your daily routine. You'll only be trading one stress situation for another.

14. *Talk it out.* Stress can often be reduced by talking things over with someone else. Many cities now have organizations that provide "listeners" for just this purpose. A listener doesn't even have to respond. He or she can simply serve as a sounding board and help guide your conversation. You can talk things out with a family member, friend, minister, counselor, psychologist, or anyone who is a good listener.

15. *Slow down.* Stress often makes people feel rushed, but rushing only increases the pressure. Practice going slower. Eat with slower

movements. Slow your walking pace. Don't speak so rapidly. Repeat what others have said before you respond. You'll understand them better and learn patience as well. Don't try to do everything at once. Don't make too many changes at the same time. String things out a bit. Pace your life a bit better.

16. *Do something for others.* Sometimes stress causes people to focus on themselves too much. This often leads to self-doubt or self-pity. Instead of focusing on yourself, try helping others. In addition to taking your mind off your problems, you will render a valuable contribution and you may even make new friends.

STRESS AND TIME MANAGEMENT

All time management concepts are aimed at helping people make sense out of the turmoil of modern life. If you consciously sit down and evaluate how you presently use your time, identify your top priorities, plan and schedule your days, weeks, and months to reflect the priorities you have established, and follow your plan, your level of stress will decrease. It's guaranteed! And even a small reduction in your stress level can improve your attitude and performance. If you have planned carefully, you can feel confident that you are handling the situation to the best of your ability. This knowledge alone should relieve you of some of the pressure, because you simply can do no more than your time and abilities permit.

Learning to cope with stress has countless rewards. The alternative is to risk poor health, poor performance, wasted time, and a wasted life. Chronic stress is a killer. Resolve today to seek new ways to lead a more relaxed life, get more accomplished through managing your time, and experience greater pleasure by reducing your stress and anxieties.

16
Time for You

HARD AS IT is for some people to believe, there is more to life than work. One of the prime reasons many of us become concerned about time management is so that we can reduce our workweek and gain more personal time. Time management is a basic consideration in every aspect of our lives. Just as we should be concerned with the best use of our work time, so we should be concerned with the best use of our personal time. Work time is measured in terms of work-related objectives; personal time is measured in terms of satisfaction, emotional gain, quality of relationships, fulfillment, or service to others.

Many of us live our lives as though we were in training for the future. Unlike a game, life has no time-outs, no instant replays, no practice sessions. All time is real time; every day counts. We often postpone living. There are so many things we want to do—someday. Someday is a myth. It never arrives because it was here all the time. To enrich our lives we must act now. We should ask ourselves this question: "If I were to die today, would I be pleased with the way I have spent my time?" Few of us could answer yes truthfully.

CLARIFYING PERSONAL GOALS

If we can't do anything about the past, we can certainly do something about the future. We can start by clarifying our personal goals. Clarifying personal goals is more a matter of finding a direction than of defining specific end points. Life is found in the running, not in the arrival. When we know the things that are really important to us, we

253

will be amazed at the number of opportunities we have for obtaining them. But if we never clarify our objectives, our opportunities remain hidden.

Certainly our time is not entirely our own, to do with as we please. Our boss, spouse, children, friends, and others make legitimate demands on our time. Yet most of us resist having our time and our lives defined for us. We seek more autonomy, more freedom to decide how to spend our time.

The paradox of time applies to our personal lives as well as to our work lives: We never have enough time to do everything we'd like to do, yet we have all the time there is. Furthermore, there is always enough time to do what is most important to us. The difficult part is defining what is important. We must know ourselves extremely well before we can answer that question.

Even when we realize that we can do almost anything we want, we usually prefer to spend our time in the same way other people spend their time. The question remains: What do we really want to do? If we cannot answer this question, our lives will be aimless. We will come to believe that whatever it is we really want to do we cannot do because of circumstances, human nature, or the fear of what others might think. Finally, we will say there just isn't enough time.

Most of us operate with an intermediate personal time horizon. We think in terms of days or weeks and occasionally months. We rarely think in terms of minutes and in fact never even consider our idle minutes as a waste of time. Nor do we think in terms of years or lifetimes—in terms of how the present is related to the future. So we start over each day. As a result, we lead a random, unfocused existence. We have the vague realization that we are going nowhere, but we do not know why.

What do you wish was happening in your life? What do you wish you had time for? The concepts outlined in this book for solving work time problems also apply to personal time problems. There are personal activity traps, just as there are work activity traps. People become so engrossed in personal activities that they cease to ask themselves about the purpose and value of those activities.

The way you spend your time defines who you are. Thinking about the best way to spend your time means asking yourself what kind of life you want to lead, what kind of person you want to be. You can't plan for the present without also planning for the future. Tomorrow is connected to today just as today was connected to yesterday. You cannot afford to leave those connections to chance.

Changing the way you use your time requires that you set some goals—goals about what you want to be and do. Uncertainty breeds inactivity. Psychologists tell us that goals are the key to successful living. The reason more people are not successful is that they do not pursue specific goals. They simply shift from one activity to another without any focus or purpose, naively assuming that things will take care of themselves or will be taken care of by others.

PERSONAL TIME ANALYSIS

Before you can set objectives for spending your time differently, you must analyze how you spend your time now. Exactly where does your day go? Surveys and observations of several thousand people suggest that the average day is divided into six major segments, as shown in Figure 24. Generally speaking, people have about two hours each day to do the various personal things that make life worth living. That's not much, but it gets worse. By their own account, most people waste at least two hours every day! It's

Figure 24. Where your day goes.

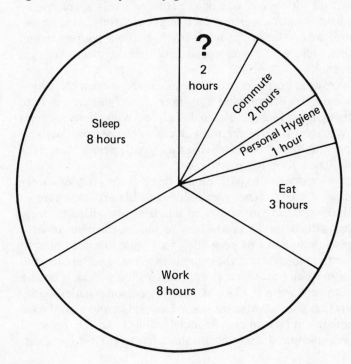

no wonder that so many people feel depressed or dissatisfied with life in general.

Most people work only five days a week. Theoretically, then, they should have an additional 20 hours on the weekend for enriching their lives. However, many people work more than 40 hours each week. Managers, for instance, work an average of almost 60 hours weekly. Some regularly work 70 to 80 hours a week, and even more. Not surprisingly, for many managers weekends are lost. An evening off is a luxury. Sleep time gets cut dangerously short; meals are eaten too fast; tension and stress build to high levels. What better reason for learning to manage your time better? It's your life we're talking about!

As noted in Chapter 2, it is important to know exactly how you spend your time. Although you may think you know how you spend your time, you probably do not. Countless studies show that most people can't remember exactly what they did only yesterday or the day before. For the next week or two try keeping track of your personal time and what you do with it. Be honest with yourself. At the end of the week, summarize your activities. Examine what percentage of your time is devoted to each activity. How much of your time is spent on "have to" activities? How much is spent on the things you want to do? Question each activity closely. Is it necessary? Does it add value to your life? What would happen if you didn't do it at all? Could you spend less time at it and still get acceptable results?

The answers may surprise you. You may discover that the "total you" is a lot different from what you think. If so, you are ready to consider changing. Most people find their personal time analysis extremely valuable. It helps them break out of the personal activity traps that prevent them from achieving their goals. Seeing their lives on paper is often a sobering experience.

When you examine your goals, do not think exclusively of career goals or financial goals. Other aspects of your life are important as well—family, social activities, and so on. If you want to be truly effective and satisfied with yourself, you must determine how to balance the various parts of your life. You must discover how to allocate your time to cover all those areas that are important to you. Realize that the balance which is appropriate for you may not be appropriate for anyone else. This is purely a personal undertaking.

The things that people value most can be divided into eight broad areas: career, family, social life, financial stability, health, personal development, spiritual development, and leisure. How do you distribute your time across these different areas? We are not suggesting here that you should divide your time equally across the eight areas; no one's life is so evenly divided. However, most people emphasize only two or three of these areas—without realizing it. A careful time analysis will help you get a clearer picture of where your time is actually spent.

Before you undertake your time analysis, think about what you expect to find. Draw a circle and divide it into "pie" segments according to how you think you distribute your time in the eight different areas. How much time each day do you spend on your career, your personal development, and so on?

After you make your time analysis, draw another circle to indicate how you actually distribute your time. Now think about how you would *like* to spend your time. What are your most important goals? Considering the eight areas discussed, what do you wish your life looked like? Draw an "ideal" circle for how you would like to spend your time.

Most people think very little about their goals. They respond or react to pressures from other people or things. But if you want to control your own time and life, you must decide what your goals are. No one can do this for you. And since you are likely to find what you are looking for, it is important that you pursue appropriate personal goals.

SETTING "GOOD" GOALS

Goals are far more than dreams, yet many people use the two words interchangeably. They think of goals in the abstract—in terms of happiness, wealth, or fame. But goals mean something more. To have a goal is to have a concrete objective, a well-clarified purpose. It is to have something specific you wish to achieve. If you can determine what you want, you can probably find a way to obtain it.

For example, instead of deciding that your goal is to "be rich," think about how much money would make you feel "rich" today. Is it $50,000, $500,000, or $50 million? If your goal is to be a good family person, what exactly do you mean? Do you plan to spend ten hours a week playing with your kids? Do you need to go out on the town with your spouse two evenings a week? If your goal is personal development, can you achieve it by attending four adult education classes a year? Exactly—specifically—what does your goal mean to you?

Goals should not only be specific and concrete; they should also be realistic. Finishing the Boston Marathon may be a realistic goal; winning it may not. Goals should make you stretch, but they should be attainable. They should also be measurable. Above all, they should be set in writing, with a time schedule for their completion. It is not easy to define a goal that meets all these criteria, but the effort is well worth it. The result is a goal that stimulates you, a goal that motivates you to begin pursuing it right away.

Try the following exercise to sharpen your goal-setting skills. Lay out eight sheets of paper. On each sheet list one of the eight major aspects of life discussed earlier.

Now write down everything you can think of that you would like to accomplish in each area during your lifetime. Don't evaluate anything, just write down your thoughts. Try to fill each sheet of paper. Write quickly, but take as much time as you like. Reach back into your memory. Try to remember all the things you ever wanted to accomplish. The more ideas you write down, the better.

When you have listed everything you can think of, review all the items you have noted. Some of them are more important to you than others. Since you are after the best use of your time and since you will not be able to do everything, you need to set priorities.

Some people are frightened by the idea of setting priorities in their personal life. They needn't be. Here is a simple but effective approach to establishing priorities. As you read over the eight lists of objectives you have prepared, rate them with an ABC system. Put an A beside those items that are very important to you. Put a B beside those that are moderately important, and put a C beside those that are not important at all. You now have a simple priority system. If you were to spend your personal time most effectively, you would concentrate on doing the A activities first and the B activities next, and you would forget about the C activities.

Like most people, you probably have several A items on each list. If you do, rank-order them. Go through each sheet and indicate them A-1, A-2, A-3, and so forth, until all your A activities are ranked.

Now look to see what item you have ranked A-1 on each sheet. You might list all the A-1 items on a separate sheet of paper and then rank-order them relative to one another. In other words, the various aspects of your life are not equally important. Determine which ones are more important to you than others. In this way, you can be sure of focusing on the most important objectives first.

Do any of your objectives conflict? Many people find, for example, that they are torn between family and career. No matter how much they protest, their children always seem to come out second.

It's hard to take your son to the ballgame when you could be earning a bonus if you devoted the day to work. And, if you decide to work, you rationalize that the bonus enables your son to have advantages you didn't have. But your relationship with your son probably depends more on the quantity and quality of the time you spend with him than on his material well-being. There are no easy answers, just hard questions.

Review your time analysis again. How many of the things you do actually relate to your A objectives? Are you spending time in a way that is consistent with achieving your A objectives, or do your activities lead somewhere else? You should devote some time to your A objectives each day—even if it is only a few minutes. Spend some time doing the things that are really important to you. Personal activity traps occur when your daily routine does not lead to your A objectives. For example, if your objective is learning to play the piano, don't fall into the activity trap of spending so much time dusting it that you never have time to play. Stop dusting and start playing.

Resolve to give up the C items in your life forever. Is TV really worth that much time? Are you sure you have to do all that housework? Why can't you play golf instead of cutting the grass? Did you really want to join the bowling league, or were you just unable to say no? Cutting out the C items and replacing them with A items can change your life. You're likely to become excited about living. The most interesting people to be around are those who are achieving things that are important to them. When you're focusing on your A objectives, it's impossible to have an apathetic, humdrum life.

People often get trapped into thinking that the C activities have to be done. This is not always the case. Remember Pareto's Principle, or the 80–20 rule. The 20 percent of the items accounting for 80 percent of the value in your life are probably related to your A objectives. The remaining 80 percent of the items accounting for 20 percent of the value in your life probably relate to the C activities you have deluded yourself into doing each day. If you want to be more satisfied with your personal life, learn to concentrate on the 20 percent of the items with high value. If you don't have time to work on your A objectives, it's because you are doing all those C activities, not because there isn't enough time.

If you are married, you and your spouse should undertake the lifetime objectives exercise separately. Each of you should determine the objectives that are important to you individually. When you each have your own list of A objectives, compare the items on both lists. There will probably be some conflict, so be prepared to negotiate and compromise. If you have children, let them participate in the process too.

The members of your family have a legitimate claim on some of your time. Many of your A objectives are likely to relate to family activities. When more than one person is involved, compromise is inevitable. Your challenge is to find a balance that will allow each family member to attain as many A objectives as possible.

A PLAN FOR ACTION

Setting objectives is only the first step toward a more satisfying and fulfilling life. Your next task is to prepare an action plan for achieving your objectives. For example, if your goal is to improve your physical condition and you have decided that you need to jog 12 miles a week to achieve this goal, you must schedule a time to do your jogging—or it won't happen. Write it down and stick to your schedule.

Scheduling is the best way to eliminate those vague, random activities that waste your time and lead you nowhere. If you want something to happen, you must make a place for it. You must carve out the time and space that your goal demands. Nothing happens unless you make it happen.

If you really want to control your time, you cannot rely on luck. You must plan. Failing to plan often means planning to fail. Plans for accomplishing lifetime objectives are usually long range. Plans for accomplishing daily objectives are short range. Over time, however, all those short-range daily goals should lead to your long-range goals. So whether you are planning for tomorrow or for the rest of your life, the system is essentially the same: Identify your objectives and priorities and decide on your plan of action.

Since lifetime goals are usually complex and since it will probably take some time to achieve them, it is helpful to break each goal down into subgoals. This will make your goals more believable and will motivate you to take the first step. Set a realistic target date for achieving each subgoal. Write down what you will gain by achieving that subgoal. Then move toward your larger goals by working on subgoals one step at a time. As you achieve your subgoals, you will gain a great deal of self-confidence and satisfaction. And all the while you will be gaining on your important lifetime goals.

Do not be concerned if you do not have much time each day to devote to your goals. Even 15 minutes a day can make a tremendous difference in your life. In 15 minutes a day, you can learn a foreign language, trace your family history, learn to play a musical instrument, or read a good book. Fifteen minutes a day adds up to over 90 hours each year. That's the equivalent of two full workweeks. Minutes do count. If you use them wisely, they can make a big difference in the quality of your life. Realize, of course, that as your situation changes your goals may change. Different things may become more or less important to you. Your goals will change to reflect changes in your values, experiences, and aspirations.

Take time to review your long-range personal goals periodically. Your birthday is a good time to do this. Once a year reflect on who you are and who you want to be, what you'd like to accomplish in your life and what things you find valuable. Share your thoughts with those who are important to you. Encourage them to improve the quality of their lives too.

CONTROLLING YOUR TIME—AND YOUR LIFE

You can control your time and your life. In doing so, you will accomplish more, gain more satisfaction from the things you do, and feel more fulfilled. As your feelings of achievement, satisfaction, and fulfillment increase, the quality of your life increases. Your time is your life. As you become more effective in managing your time, you create a better life.

Satisfaction lies in accomplishing the things that are really important. This is one of the secrets of success, as a time-conscious young friend of ours named Chuck found out. Chuck was an extremely gifted person, always eager to learn and involve himself in a new venture. He spent several years in the Air Force and traveled around the world. His inquisitive mind led him to investigate the wonders of mathematics and science, while his love of beauty called him to art and music. As he grew older, his mechanical abilities merged with his artistic soul and he found his vocation as a photographer.

But Chuck was no ordinary picture taker. True to his character, he approached his career with no holds barred. He was going to be the best photographer in the area, perhaps even in the state or the country. He advertised. He slaved. He ran to weddings. He raced to graduations. He took portraits of anyone who could find his number in the telephone book. He was consumed by his job. His photos were signed "By Charles." He had arrived.

One day, almost by accident, "Charles" found his way into a course of time management while he was taking pictures for a yearbook. As he snapped away at the various participants, he listened to the discussion of time. The discussion aroused his attention and he asked the instructor if he might have one of the workbooks.

"Charles" took the workbook home. One day when a scheduled wedding was canceled, he decided to read it. He was fascinated by the content, stimulated by the idea of applying the concepts to his own life, and horrified when he did a time analysis and saw what he had become. He was a workaholic! His wife, Cheryl, and his two children were nearly strangers. He had no associates or friends outside the photography business; he had not given his church a minute's time in five years; his former interests in math, music, science, and art had become nothing but a memory.

He vowed to change. He announced to his wife that things would be different from now on. Her reply? "Yea, sure."

But, today, Cheryl is amazed and happy. "Charles" has turned back into the Chuck she married, and he is even more fascinating than before. By applying time management principles to his work, Chuck has made his photography studio more successful than ever. Equally important to Chuck and his family, his private life is also a success. He knows his goals and priorities. He also lives them. He spends hours each day deeply involved with the family he loves very much. He plans for tomorrow, but lives for today—in the ways that are important to him.

Like Chuck, you should demand as much return on your personal time as you do on your business time. If you don't like the return on your personal time investment, change the way you spend your time. Quality of life is a function of what you do, when you do it, who you do it with, and what you accomplish in the process. Through proper application of time management techniques, you can be more productive on the job than ever before—and you can gain more personal time in the process. By applying the same techniques to your personal life, you can begin to achieve many of your dreams.

If your life has been too hectic, if you have been totally absorbed in your work to the neglect of other aspects of your life, it's time to take a new look at your priorities. Consider the following questions:

1. The last time you spent a quiet evening at home (do you remember it?), did your spouse and children look at you suspiciously? Did they know what to do with you? If they didn't, did they care? Have you been gone so much of the time that your family has learned to live nicely "around" your presence?

2. Have you been promising yourself that you're going to "get in shape" soon? Do you continually say that someday you'll start run-

ning, swimming, or playing tennis? Did you forget to have a medical or dental checkup last year? Some doctors claim it's all downhill after age 26!

3. When was the last time you spent the evening with friends? Do you continue to see people here and there but never get beyond saying, "We'll have to have you over sometime"? When you do have people over, are you too tired to enjoy the evening? Are you still thinking about your work?

4. Are you honestly in control of your life? If you could write the script of the life you'd like to lead, what would it look like? What choices do you have to make *now* to live the life you desire?

A number of years ago, an elderly man wrote to *Guidepost* magazine expressing his regrets. He said, "If I had my life to live over, I would relax more. I wouldn't take so many things as seriously. I would take more chances. I would climb more mountains and swim more rivers. I'd ride more merry-go-rounds. I'd pick more daisies."

"Merry-go-rounds" and "daisies" mean different things to different people. One point we've tried to emphasize throughout this book is that good time management is a highly subjective process. You know what a "daisy" is to you. If you don't know, find out. The world is waiting for you when you do. It is pointless to attack life in a desperate frenzy. You'll never get out alive! Relax your way through. Try to make the world just a little bit better because you were there. Your time will be well spent if you do.

17
Commitment and Success

EVERYONE WANTS TO be successful. Success is a powerful word, with strong positive connotations. Promise to make people successful and they will line up to hear you.

Why should people be concerned about using their time more effectively? To be more successful. Success means different things to different people. For some, success is the additional money they are likely to obtain with a better job. For others, success means the opportunity to expand the programs of their organization. For many, success means more personal time for playing golf, camping, or puttering around the house. For still others, success means the increase in prestige or fame that comes with building a reputation for always getting results.

Regardless of what motivates people to develop better time habits, the end result is always the same: Using time better leads to greater success, however success is defined. Success is not something that happens by accident. People who have become successful have usually earned their success. But not everyone who wants to be successful will actually do so.

SECRETS OF SUCCESS

Exactly what is success? The dictionary defines success as "accomplishing what is attempted; a person or thing that prospers." Success may be measured by position, wealth, family relationships, or dozens of other personal and professional variables. But regardless of how we define it, success means something rather specific to each of us.

Hard work alone will not make us successful. The willingness to work hard may be a big part of our success, but it is not the only factor. Many people work hard and never succeed. Some of the most obviously qualified fail, and some with tremendous handicaps succeed. Clearly, something besides hard work accounts for the difference between success and failure.

Earl Nightingale, in his speech "The Common Denominator of Success," points out that the secret of success lies in forming the habit of doing the things that failures don't like to do. Success, he said, is achieved by only a minority of people. Success, therefore, is "unnatural"; we cannot achieve it by following our natural instincts, habits, or preferences.*

What are some of the things failures don't like to do that successful people are willing to do? According to Nightingale, they are the things no one likes to do. In working with time problems, for example, most people don't like to clarify objectives, record and analyze their time, or plan their week.

If no one likes to do these things, why do some people do them while others don't? Successful people don't like to do them, but they know that doing these things will help them achieve their goals. In other words, unsuccessful people are motivated by pleasing methods and will accept whatever results they can obtain from doing only what they like to do.

All of us go into a slump from time to time when the things we do not like to do seem to become more important than our reasons for doing them. We find it easier to adjust to the hardships of poor results than to face the hardships of improving results. Just think of all the things we're willing to do without in order to avoid doing the things we don't like!

Since success is not a natural state, we will have to change to be successful. We must set our sights higher. The *Christopher's Bulletin†* recently printed an American Indian legend about a brave who found an eagle's egg and put it into the nest of a prairie chicken. The eaglet hatched with a bunch of chicks and grew up with them. All his life, this changeling eagle—thinking he was a prairie chicken—did what

---

* Cassette-tape version of speech (Chicago: Nightingale-Conant Corp., 1978).
† "Christopher News Notes" (October 1977).

the prairie chickens did. He scratched in the dirt for seeds and insects to eat. He clucked and cackled. And he flew in a brief flurry of wings and feathers no more than a few feet off the ground. After all, that's how a prairie chicken was supposed to fly.

Years passed. The changeling eagle grew old. One day he saw a magnificent bird far above him in the cloudless sky. Hanging with graceful majesty on powerful wind currents, the bird soared with scarcely a beat of its strong golden wings.

"What a beautiful bird!" said the changeling eagle to his neighbor. "What is it?"

"That's an eagle, the chief of the birds," the neighbor clucked. "But don't give it a second thought. You could never be like him."

So the changeling eagle never gave it another thought. And he died thinking he was a prairie chicken.

It is all too easy to go through life thinking you're a prairie chicken when you might really be an eagle. By doing so you shortchange yourself and everyone else. Be what you are. But be all that you can be. Don't settle for failure when you can have success. How you view yourself plays a vital role in how you choose to spend your time—and your life. Don't sell yourself short when you don't have to.

TIME HABITS AND SUCCESS

Habits are important to success. People form habits, but habits form futures. If you don't form your habits consciously, you will form them unconsciously. Unconsciously formed habits are seldom as good as conscious ones. To find better ways to use your time, you must change your habits.

Time use is a habit. To improve, you must discover your present habits and change the ones that need changing. You must clarify your goals. You must continue to ask yourself, "What is the intended result of my action?" You must learn to plan your time every day, every week, every year. You must resolve to use time in better ways. Of course, any resolution you make will not be worth much unless you keep it. You must stick to your resolution day in and day out until it becomes a habit—until one day you become a different person in a different world, until you have become the master of your likes and dislikes, until you have formed the habit of success.

Success requires commitment. Start where you are. Evaluate your potential. Then expose yourself to the risks and rewards of developing it. If you don't make a start, you can't possibly get anywhere.

Underachievers are not born, they are made. Psychologists have spent years evaluating people's achievements in relation to their potential. They have observed that a lot of people never come close to realizing their potential. Out of this has come the notion that there is hope for underachievers.

If you have been an underachiever most of your life, realize that it is possible to reverse the tide of affairs. Find a goal, a purpose in which you have a sincere interest and to which you can devote yourself wholeheartedly. You will be amazed at what you can achieve. Without a goal—and a sincere commitment to it—you will continue to modify your expectations, shifting them to even lower levels of anticipated achievement.

CHANGING FOR THE BETTER

You can change. You can be better. Begin right where you are, whenever you choose. Start with simple activities. For example:

1. Do something you don't want to do.
2. Do something you want to do.
3. Spend a few minutes every day in meditation or quiet thought.
4. Be of benefit to someone else every day.
5. Make a list of things you like to do, things you want to do, and things you have done successfully in the past. Compare it with a list of things you don't want to do and things you have not done successfully in the past.
6. Set a goal for yourself—something that seems possible at this point in your life: You can afford it; you have the time; your family is behind you; it will not conflict with any of your current responsibilities.
7. Turn off the TV and read a good book.
8. Break a habit, any habit.
9. Do something constructive to make yourself a better person. Make the first phone call. Write the first letter. Do whatever it takes to get started. Take a concrete step toward achieving whatever goal you choose.

People who know what they want suddenly find their life filled with opportunities. A compelling purpose makes it easier to develop the discipline required to build good habits. And good habits will propel you toward achieving your goal.

The primary objective of this book has been to give you the concepts, techniques, and motivation you need to improve the way you use your time. Commit yourself to action now. But don't expect miracles. Don't expect a dramatic turnaround. The habits that control how you currently use your time were not developed overnight. Change is not likely to occur overnight either. Only steady, persistent effort brings about change.

Furthermore, realize that you will never be able to control 100 percent of your time. There are some parts of the day which you simply will never be able to control. If you can consistently control even 25 to 50 percent of your day, you can achieve a significant increase in results. Controlling 25 percent of the day may mean finding no more than one additional hour to devote to really important tasks. Most people waste at least an hour or two each day. Recovering this time would be well worth the effort.

What might you do with an extra hour each day for the really important things? An hour a day might get you through that work you normally carry home each evening. An hour a day may be all the time you need to launch that project you have not yet implemented. An hour a day may give you an opportunity to develop your staff. An hour a day could add another 15 to 30 percent to your personal income. As one executive put it, "The difference between success and failure is probably no more than one or two hours each day."

MONITORING YOUR PROGRESS

One good way to ensure your progress is to monitor your improvement efforts regularly. Make sure that your evaluations focus on positive accomplishments. For instance, you would undoubtedly like to become much better at using your time. You try several time management techniques, some of which work and some of which do not. In the process, you don't make a huge gain, but you make several small gains. Are you satisfied and encouraged to continue? Possibly not. People often become discouraged when they fail to make huge gains. As long as you continue to focus on what you did not accomplish instead of on the positive progress you have made, you will feel disappointed and will be less likely to continue.

To keep yourself on track, retake the quiz at the end of Chapter 1 periodically to see whether your score improves. If it does, your use of time has probably improved—and improved time management should lead you to better results.

Some people keep a daily record in diary or journal form of their successes and their use of time. They make notes about the approaches they've tried—which ones seem to work and which ones do not. This type of record can be a valuable source of information on your progress.

Another way to monitor your progress is to use graphs or charts. For instance, if you are seeking to reduce the time you spend in meetings, you might chart the average amount of time you currently spend in meetings each week. This is your baseline. Then set a target objective—the amount of time you believe you should spend in meetings. Each week ask your secretary to keep a record of all the time you spend in meetings and post this number to the graph. Eventually, the line on the graph should go downward. Each week may not show a decrease over the week before, but if your attempts to improve meetings are successful, the line should move downward over a period of weeks.

You can also use this approach to track your progress in reducing the number of drop-in visitors in your office. Many drop-in visitors are, of course, unnecessary. To establish a baseline, keep a record of the average number of drop-in visitors you receive each week. If your improvement efforts are successful, the graph should show a decreasing number of drop-in visitors arriving in your office.

If you truly are successful in using your time better, you should notice a number of changes. An analysis of job results should indicate improvement. There should be a significant decrease in the number of recurring crises in your office. Operations should be running more smoothly. You should be getting more positive feedback in performance reviews with superiors. There should be fewer things on your list of undone items. You should be able to leave the office earlier and spend more time with your family or in other pursuits. You should feel more on top of situations, more in control of your job.

Whatever methods you use to evaluate your progress, the important thing is to evaluate it regularly. Any step in the right direction should be a source of encouragement. You should feel good about the progress you make, no matter how small that progress is. Consistent, small improvements will lead you to the long-term results you desire.

Another important step in your improvement effort is developing a time management action plan. Clarify your objectives, the ways in which you hope to improve your use of time. Then decide on the actions necessary to accomplish those objectives. Put both the objectives and the actions in writing. Give a copy of your written plan to someone who is important to you. Promise improvement by a certain date. Tackle your improvement effort in progressive steps.

When you begin drafting your action plan, be sure to think about possible obstacles. Obstacles tend to be of two types. The first are those that come from within, your own shortcomings. The second are those created by your environment. Both types of obstacles can prevent you from reaching your time management objective.

As you uncover potential obstacles or problems, consider ways to overcome them. Some solutions can be implemented immediately. Others will require outside help. Make a note of what other people can help you with and ask them for assistance in a very positive manner. Do not worry about imposing on them. Most people are more than willing to help anyone who sincerely wants to improve. Everyone likes to participate in success.

Ultimately, to be successful—in managing your time or in anything else—you must act. You must know what to do, and you must do it.

Commit yourself to success. Start where you are. Stop dreaming about tomorrow and start living today. If you can't find big time chunks, start with little time chunks. Act on the things you fear. Behave like the kind of person you would like to be, and you'll become that kind of person.

Remember that your success in managing time relates to your purpose in life and your commitment to that purpose. Examine your goals and make them as large as you can. Big goals make big people. Remember, too, that you can never succeed beyond the purpose to which you are willing to surrender. And that surrender is never complete until you have formed the habit of doing things that failures don't like to do. Success is up to you.

18
Twenty Steps to Successful Time Management

1. Clarify your objectives. Put them in writing. Then set your priorities. Make sure you're getting what you really want out of life.

2. Focus on objectives, not on activities. Your most important activities are those that help you accomplish your objectives.

3. Set at least one major objective each day and achieve it.

4. Record a time log periodically to analyze how you use your time, and keep bad time habits out of your life.

5. Analyze everything you do in terms of your objectives. Find out what you do, when you do it, why you do it. Ask yourself what would happen if you didn't do it. If the answer is nothing, then stop doing it.

6. Eliminate at least one time waster from your life each week.

7. Plan your time. Write out a plan for each week. Ask yourself what you hope to accomplish by the end of the week and what you will need to do to achieve those results.

8. Make a to-do list every day. Be sure it includes your daily objectives, priorities, and time estimates, not just random activities.

9. Schedule your time every day to make sure you accomplish the most important things first. Be sure to leave room for the unexpected and for interruptions. But remember that things that are scheduled have a better chance of working out than things that are unscheduled.

10. Make sure that the first hour of your workday is productive.

11. Set time limits for every task you undertake.

12. Take the time to do it right the first time. You won't have to waste time doing it over.

13. Eliminate recurring crises from your life. Find out why things keep going wrong. Learn to proact instead of react.

14. Institute a quiet hour in your day—a block of uninterrupted time for your most important tasks.

15. Develop the habit of finishing what you start. Don't jump from one thing to another, leaving a string of unfinished tasks behind you.

16. Conquer procrastination. Learn to do it now.

17. Make better time management a daily habit. Set your objectives, clarify your priorities, and plan and schedule your time. Do first things first. Resist your impulses to do unscheduled tasks. Review your activities.

18. Never spend time on less important things when you could be spending it on more important things.

19. Take time for yourself—time to dream, time to relax, time to live.

20. Develop a personal philosophy of time—what time means to you and how time relates to your life.

Index

AMACOM Paperbacks

John Fenton	The A to Z of Sales Management	$ 7.95	07580
Hank Seiden	Advertising Pure and Simple	$ 7.95	07510
Alice G. Sargent	The Androgynous Manager	$ 8.95	07601
John D. Arnold	The Art of Decision Making	$ 8.95	07537
Curtis W. Symonds	Basic Financial Management	$ 8.95	07563
William R. Osgood	Basics of Successful Business Planning	$ 7.95	07579
Dickens & Dickens	The Black Manager	$10.95	07564
Ken Cooper	Bodybusiness	$ 5.95	07545
Laura Brill	Business Writing Quick & Easy	$ 5.95	07598
Rinella & Robbins	Career Power	$ 7.95	07586
Andrew H. Souerwine	Career Strategies	$ 7.95	07535
Beverly A. Potter	Changing Performance on the Job	$ 9.95	07613
Donna N. Douglass	Choice and Compromise	$ 8.95	07604
Philip R. Lund	Compelling Selling	$ 8.95	07506
Joseph M. Vles	Computer Basics	$ 6.95	07599
John D. Drake	Effective Interviewing	$ 8.95	07600
Louis V. Imundo	The Effective Supervisor's Handbook	$ 8.95	07621
William A. Cohen	The Executive's Guide to Finding a Superior Job	$11.95	07607
Kristy & Diamond	Finance Without Fear	$ 9.95	07605
Edward N. Rausch	Financial Management for Small Business	$ 7.95	07585
Loren B. Belker	The First-Time Manager	$ 6.95	07588
Whitsett & Yorks	From Management Theory to Business Sense	$17.95	07610
Ronald D. Brown	From Selling to Managing	$ 7.95	07500
Craig S. Rice	Getting Good People and Keeping Them	$ 8.95	07614
Charles Hughes	Goal Setting	$ 4.95	07520
Richard E. Byrd	A Guide to Personal Risk Taking	$ 7.95	07505
Brooks Fenno	Helping Your Business Grow	$ 8.95	07622
Charles Margerison	How to Assess Your Managerial Style	$ 6.95	07584
S. H. Simmons	How to Be the Life of the Podium	$ 8.95	07565
German & German	How to Find a Job When Jobs Are Hard to Find	$ 7.95	07592
W. H. Krause	How to Get Started As a Manufacturers' Representative	$ 8.95	07574
Sal T. Massimino	How to Master the Art of Closing Sales	$ 5.95	07593
William A. Delaney	How to Run a Growing Company	$ 6.95	07590
Vella & McGonagle	Incorporating	$15.95	07608
H. Lee Rust	Jobsearch	$12.95	07557
James Cribbin	Leadership	$ 9.95	07619

Marc J. Lane	Legal Handbook for Small Business	$ 7.95	07612
Robert L. Montgomery	Listening Made Easy	$ 7.95	07625
George T. Vardaman	Making Successful Presentations	$10.95	07616
John Stewart Jr.	Managing a Successful Business Turnaround	$14.95	07609
William P. Anthony	Managing Your Boss	$10.95	07597
Elam & Paley	Marketing for the Non-Marketing Executive	$ 5.95	07562
Edward S. McKay	The Marketing Mystique	$ 7.95	07522
William M. Luther	The Marketing Plan	$10.95	07623
Donald E. Miller	The Meaningful Interpretation of Financial Statements	$ 6.95	07513
Robert L. Montgomery	Memory Made Easy	$ 5.95	07548
Donald P. Kenney	Minicomputers	$ 7.95	07560
Frederick D. Buggie	New Product Development Strategies	$ 8.95	07602
Dale D. McConkey	No-Nonsense Delegation	$ 4.95	07517
Donald P. Kenney	Personal Computers in Business	$15.95	07627
Ellis & Pekar	Planning Basics for Managers	$ 6.95	07591
Alfred R. Oxenfeldt	Pricing Strategies	$10.95	07572
Blake & Mouton	Productivity: The Human Side	$ 5.95	07583
Daniels & Barron	The Professional Secretary	$ 7.95	07576
Herman R. Holtz	Profit from Your Moneymaking Ideas	$ 8.95	07553
Joseph F. Engelberger	Robotics in Practice	$24.95	07587
Webster Kuswa	The Sales Rep's Letter Book	$12.95	07618
James F. Evered	Shirt-Sleeves Management	$ 7.95	07626
Don Sheehan	Shut Up and Sell!	$ 7.95	07615
Bolton & Bolton	Social Style/Management Style	$ 9.95	07617
Hanan & Berrian & Cribbin & Donis	Success Strategies for the New Sales Manager	$ 8.95	07566
Paula I. Robbins	Successful Midlife Career Change	$ 7.95	07536
Leon Wortman	Successful Small Business Management	$ 8.95	07503
Terry A. Mort	Systematic Selling	$ 6.95	07541
George A. Brakeley Jr.	Tested Ways to Successful Fund Raising	$ 8.95	07568
Charles H. Ford	Think Smart, Move Fast	$ 9.95	07624
Joe D. Batten	Tough-Minded Management	$ 9.95	07620
William A. Delaney	Tricks of the Manager's Trade	$ 6.95	07603
Alec Benn	The 27 Most Common Mistakes in Advertising	$ 8.95	07554
James Gray Jr.	The Winning Image	$ 6.95	07611
John Applegath	Working Free	$ 6.95	07582
Richard J. Dunsing	You & I Have Simply Got to Stop Meeting This Way	$ 5.95	07558
C. Colburn Hardy	Your Money & Your Life	$ 9.95	07577